AMERICA

FLYING HIGH

WHITE STAR PUBLISHERS

FLYING HIGH AMERICA

TEXTS AND PHOTOGRAPHS

Jim Wark

graphic design
PAOLA PIACCO
PATRIZIA BALOCCO LOVISETTI

© 2004 WHITE STAR S.R.L.
Via Candido Sassone, 22-24
13100 Vercelli - Italy
WWW.WHITESTAR.IT

ISBN 88-544-0003-3

REPRINTS:
1 2 3 4 5 6 08 07 06 05 04

Printed in Singapore - Color separation: Chiaroscuro, Turin, Italy

1
Snow covers the Monument Valley, Utah.

2-3
New York City, Lower Manhattan skyline is seen here looking northwest from over the East River.

FLYING HIGH AMERICA

Contents

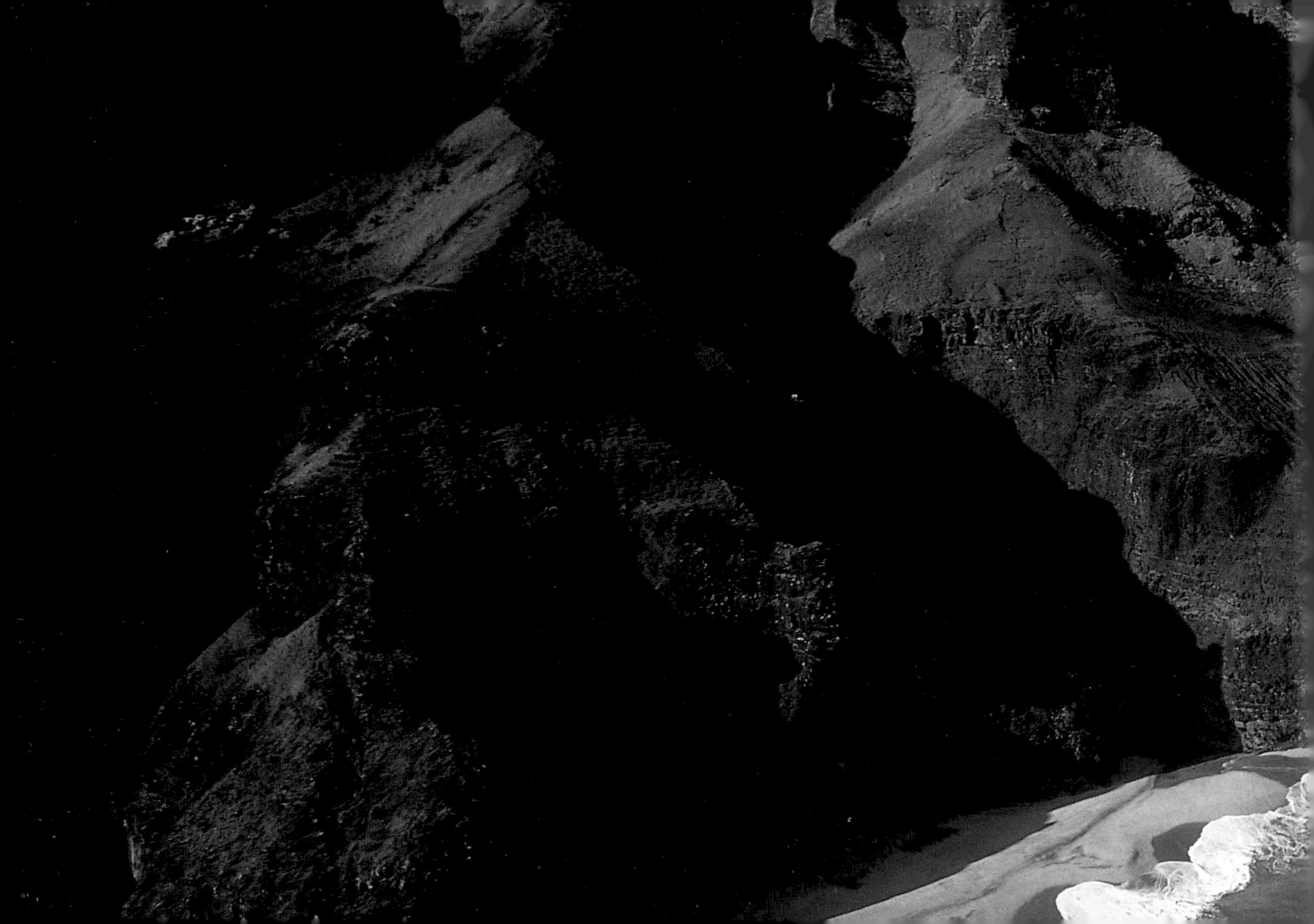

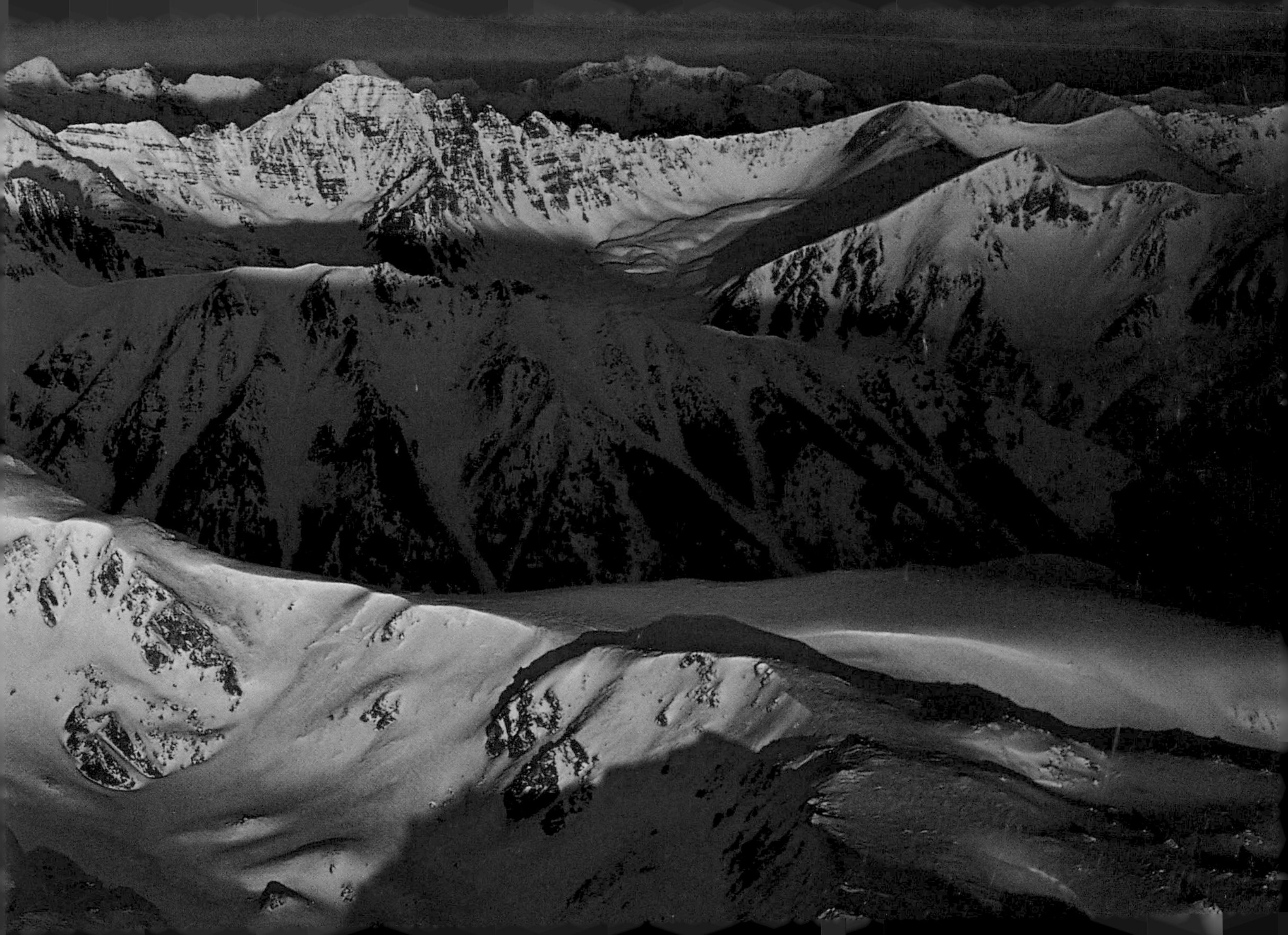

The author

JIM WARK IS AN AERIAL PHOTOGRAPHER WHO SPECIALIZES IN CAPTURING UNUSUAL LANDSCAPE AND CULTURAL IMAGES THROUGHOUT NORTH AND CENTRAL AMERICA. DRAWING FROM HIS EXPERIENCE AS A NAVAL AVIATOR AND AIRSHOW PILOT – PAIRED WITH HIS REVERENCE FOR THE EARTH'S GEOGRAPHY GAINED DURING A CAREER IN MINING AND GEOLOGY – HE SET OUT AFTER RETIREMENT IN 1990 TO DOCUMENT HIS VISION OF AMERICA FROM ON HIGH.

"IN DOING THIS WORK, THE AIRPLANE, CAMERA AND PHOTOGRAPHER ARE A UNIT," SAYS WARK. "I LOVE THE FREEDOM, MOBILITY AND ADVENTURE THAT THE CANDID AERIAL CAMERA GIVES ME TO WORK WITH THE SEASONS, THE WEATHER, AND THE LIGHT, AND THE ABILITY TO SEEK OUT HIDDEN OR INACCESSIBLE PLACES AND SERENDIPITOUS VIEWS. IT IS A CONSTANT AND COMPELLING CHALLENGE TO WORK THESE FACTORS INTO UNIQUE AND EXCITING PHOTOGRAPHS THAT CAN BE SHARED."

WARK UTILIZES A HIGH-WING BUSH TYPE PLANE WITH A LARGE SIDE OPENING FOR UNOBSTRUCTED CAMERA WORK. HIS CHRISTEN HUSKY AIRCRAFT HAS THE CAPACITY TO OPERATE IN ROUGH AREAS, ALLOWING REMOTE SITES TO BE USED AS OPERATING BASES.

16
Jim Wark allows himself a lunch break at the dirty Devil Canyon, Wayne County, Utah.

Introduction

I AM AN AVIATOR, A MINING ENGINEER AND A PHOTOGRAPHER, IN THAT ORDER. OR MAYBE IT'S THE OTHER WAY AROUND. MY LIFE'S WORK HAS BEEN IN AVIATION AND EARTH SCIENCES, AND COMBINING THESE INTERESTS WITH AN INHERITED INSTINCT FOR PHOTOGRAPHY HAS FULFILLED MY DEEPEST AMBITION. THE OPPORTUNITY TO SHARE MY AERIAL PHOTOGRAPHS WITH OTHERS TAKES A STEP BEYOND THAT FULFILLMENT. OVER THE LAST FOURTEEN YEARS, MY CHRISTEN HUSKY AIRPLANE HAS PROWLED NORTH AND CENTRAL AMERICA, FROM THE ARCTIC SHORES OF ALASKA TO THE TROPICAL JUNGLES OF COSTA RICA, AND FROM THE REMOTE AND HARSH UNGAVA PENINSULA OF LABRADOR TO THE BALMY ISLAND OF GRENADA. MY SINGLE-ENGINE AIRPLANE IS LOADED WITH A

18
A small airplane prowls a cliff of the Superstition Mountains,
Pinal County, Arizona.

Introduction

LARGE COLLECTION OF CAMERAS, LENSES, CAMPING EQUIPMENT AND PROVISIONS CAPABLE OF SUSTAINING AN ADVENTURE OF SEVERAL WEEKS. THE ONLY REPLENISHMENTS NEEDED ARE AVIATION FUEL AND FRESH WATER. NIGHTS ARE SPENT SLEEPING UNDER THE WING — OR SOMETIMES ON THE WELL-WORN COUCH OF A FRIENDLY SMALL-AIRPORT MANAGER. A NORMAL WORKING DAY IS EIGHT HOURS OF FLYING, RESULTING IN 300 TO 400 PHOTOS. THERE ARE TIMES WHEN FAIR WEATHER PREVAILS FOR WEEKS AT A TIME. AT OTHER TIMES, LOW CLOUDS AND STORMS HAVE KEPT ME GROUNDED FOR SEVERAL DAYS AT ONE CAMP.

MOST PILOTS HAVE HEARD THE SAYING, "FLYING IS HOURS OF BOREDOM PUNCTUATED WITH MOMENTS OF TERROR." PERHAPS THAT WAS TRUE OF LONG, HIGH-ALTITUDE WWII BOMBING MISSIONS, BUT IT BEARS NO RESEMBLANCE TO THE EXPERIENCE OF FLYING ALONE – LOW AND SLOW – OVER THE INCREDIBLE, CHANGING TEXTURE OF THE EARTH BELOW. IT IS

Introduction

A VIEW NOT SEEN FROM 6 MILES HIGH IN AN AIRLINER, OR EVEN FROM ONE MILE UP IN A SMALL PLANE. IT IS TOUCHING THE FACE OF THE LAND AND SENSING ITS TEXTURE, HABITATIONS AND GEOLOGY. IT IS A CLOSE ENCOUNTER WITH WEATHER AND TERRAIN AS A SINGLE ELEMENT. WHEN THE DAY'S WORK IS DONE, THERE IS A CLOSER ENCOUNTER WITH THE LAND ITSELF, SOMETIMES WITH A FRIENDLY COMRADE, FREQUENTLY WITH SWARMS OF BITING INSECTS, OFTEN WITH CHALLENGING WEATHER AND RARELY WITH A MENACING ANIMAL. I HAVE SEEN A WOLF APPEAR, SEEMINGLY OUT OF THIN AIR, THEN DISAPPEAR JUST AS MYSTERIOUSLY. A BEAR HAS CIRCLED MY TENT FOR AN ARCTIC TWILIGHT HOUR, OBLIVIOUS TO SHOUTS AND BANGINGS, BUT FLEEING AT THE SIGHT OF ANOTHER ANIMAL — ME — EMERGING FROM THE TENT FOR A SHOWDOWN. IF YOU ARE A COMMERCIAL AIR TRAVELER, WHAT ARE YOU SEEING? NOT MUCH, EXCEPT AN OCCASIONAL MAGNIFICENT CLOUD TOP. FROM A

Introduction

SMALL AIRPLANE FLYING A QUARTER MILE ABOVE THE GROUND, THE SCENE CAN VARY FROM THE INTIMACY OF A LAUNDRY LINE IN AN URBAN BACKYARD TO THE GEOMETRIC BEAUTY OF LINES AND PATTERNS OF RURAL FIELDS AND ROADS; FROM THE HYPERACTIVITY OF BIG-CITY HIGHWAYS AND HEAVY INDUSTRY TO THE MEASURED PACE OF SHIPPING AND SMALL CRAFT ON RIVERS, LAKES AND HARBORS.

THERE ARE COUNTLESS CIRCUMSTANCES TO CREATE CAPTIVATING AERIAL PHOTOGRAPHS OF HUMAN ACTIVITY AND ACHIEVEMENT, BUT THE BIGGEST RUSH COMES FROM NATURE. THE OPPORTUNITIES AND VARIETIES ARE INFINITE: A SPECIAL LIGHT, A DRAMATIC CLOUD, AN UNUSUAL EXPRESSION OF GEOLOGY, A CRAGGY PEAK, A REFLECTING LAKE, A SPLENDID PALATE OF TEXTURE AND COLOR. A JUXTAPOSITION OF ANY OF THESE THINGS, INCLUDING HUMAN ACTIVITY, IS WHAT MAKES AERIAL PHOTOGRAPHY A UNIQUE EXPERIENCE FOR THE PHOTOGRAPHER AND FOR THOSE WHO VIEW IT.

Introduction

THIS BOOK IS A STUDY OF AMERICA FROM ABOVE. THERE ARE MANY COUNTRIES WITH MAGNIFICENT SCENES TO PHOTOGRAPHED, BUT NONE WITH THE DIVERSITY OF AMERICA — FROM THE ROCK-BOUND COASTS OF MAINE, TO THE STORM BATTERED MID-ATLANTIC OUTER BANKS, TO THE SUNNY BEACHES OF FLORIDA; FROM THE INDUSTRIAL, STAID AND ETHNIC CITIES OF THE NORTHEAST, TO THE BOOMING HYPERACTIVE, MELTING-POT CITIES OF THF SOUTHWEST; FROM THE RUGGED, HOSTILE PEAKS AND GLACIERS OF ALASKA, TO THE COMFORTABLE MAGNIFI-CENCE OF THE GRAND CANYON; FROM THE ISLAND PARADISE OF HAWAII TO THE DESOLATION OF DEATH VALLEY; FROM THE MIGHTY MISSISSIPPI TO THE ROARING COLUMBIA RIVER; FROM LEWIS AND CLARK TO THE BIOSPHERE. WHERE ELSE IN ONE COUNTRY CAN THIS COMPLETE ARRAY OF HUMAN ACTIVITY AND NATURAL BEAUTY BE FOUND? AND ONLY IN AMERICA DOES THE FREEDOM EXIST FOR A SKY-BUM TO ROAM UNFET-

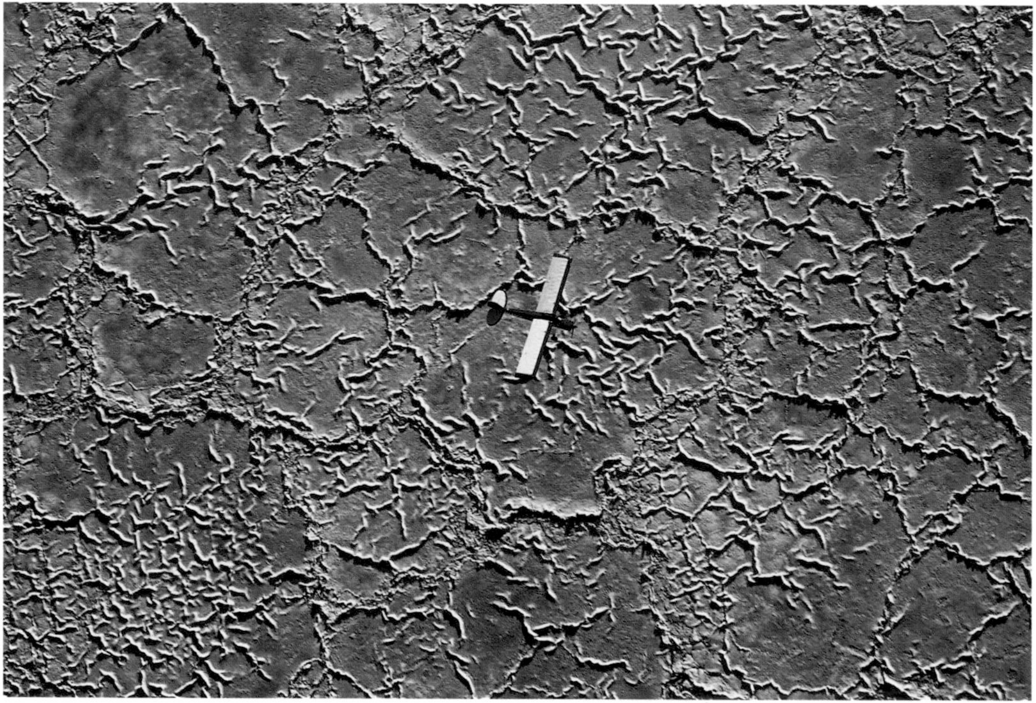

24
Flying over Soda Lake, San Luis Obispo County, California.

26-27
Small stream and blueberry barrens, Washington County, Maine.

TERED WITHOUT A PLAN, EITHER FILED ON AN OFFICIAL FORM OR OUTLINED IN HIS MIND. THE PILOT-PHOTOGRAPHER, SO INCLINED, CAN STILL GO WHERE THE PICTURES AND THE WEATHER BECKON.

"UNIQUE," WHICH IS DEFINED AS SOMETHING ONE-OF-A-KIND, WITHOUT EQUAL, IS PERHAPS THE MOST IMPROPERLY USED WORD IN THE ENGLISH LANGUAGE. THE LANDSCAPE OF AMERICA IS INDEED UNIQUE, AND THE FREEDOM OF FLIGHT IN AMERICA IS EQUALLY SO. NOW THAT WE HAVE THIS IN SOME PERSPECTIVE, I INVITE YOU TO JOIN ME IN "FLYING HIGH AMERICA"!

28-29
Canola fields glow at the foot of Palouse Hills, Washington State.

30-31
The red color of this iron mine tailings pond is from the non-hazardous iron oxide mineral hemitite. Ishpeming, Michigan.

CITIES AND METROPOLISES

FLYING HIGH

33
Lower Manhattan encloses Battery Park to the north, New York City, NY (left); Illinois Lakefront and Downtown Chicago open on Lake Michigan (right).

Genesis 28:9 *And they called the name of the place Beth-el: but the name of that city was called LUZ at first.* This may be the first recorded use of the word "city." Who decides if it's a city, a town, or just a place? The dictionary definition is not much help; *An inhabited place larger than a town.* New York City has a population of over 8,000,000, Atlantic City, New Jersey is 40.000 and Atlantic City, Wyoming is 67 by one count, 70 by another. They are all in the end habitations — the places we choose to live. And if we choose we can call them all cities.

How do these places of habitation come to be located where they are? Being on a major body of water is certainly the biggest factor. Access to transportation is also important. Being close to a major job source can trump everything — until the jobs source goes away as it often does in mining or major construction projects. When this happens if the other factors were not part of the equation we get what is called in America a ghost town. Thriving mining towns that once boasted populations on the order of 25,000 have virtually disappeared in just a few years. Climate seems to play a very minor role in city and town location.

Damascus, Syria; Jericho, Israel and probably others claim the title as the World's oldest city. These places are thought to date from 11,000 to 8,000 BC. America's cities are infants by these standards, or even those of European civilizations. For some reason the concepts of the great native cities of South and Central America did not extend to what we are here calling America. The ancient Native Americans

34
The suspension cables of the Golden Gate Bridge frame Downtown San Francisco, California.

Cities and metropolises

had some small places of permanent habitation such as Chaco Canyon, New Mexico, and Mesa Verde, Colorado, but these have long ago passed into ruins. Only a few Indian pueblos in New Mexico remain from the more recent Native American population centers. San Juan, Puerto Rico, could claim the title of the oldest city in America. Juan Ponce de León first settled San Juan. In 1508, just sixteen years after Christopher Columbus "discovered America". In 1513 Ponce de Leon set foot in the area of St. Augustine, Florida, however the city is officially considered to have been founded by a Spanish military expedition in 1565. St. Augustine if usually counted as America's oldest city.

When we think of American cities certainly New York is the first to come to mind; then Los Angeles, San Francisco, Chicago, and perhaps Honolulu in somewhat that order. Each of these cities has a unique place in American history and current culture. Henry Hudson, working for the Dutch East India Tea Company, settled New York City in 1614 as New Amsterdam. New York is now the financial center of America and has the highest population density of any American city with 26,000 people per square mile. Felipe de Neve first established Los Angeles as a Mexican city in 1781. The city was first named El Pueblo de Nuestra (Village of our Lady, the Queen of Angels), and was the capital of the Mexican province of Alta, California. With its semi-tropical ambience it shook off an early attempt to become an oil industry center to become the entertainment capital of America. Los Angeles is the sprawl capital of America as well. With less than one-half the population (3,700,000) its 470 square mile area is twice the size of New York City. San Francisco is the New York City of West Coast America. Spanish troops and missionaries first settled here in 1776. Later the city passed into Mexican hands, and then to the United States government in 1848. After 1848 it soon became the headquarters for the mining, financial, timber and shipping industries that were just beginning to build the American West. In 1906 San Fran-

Cities and metropolises

cisco was virtually destroyed by earthquake and fire, but like many of the World's great cities to endure such disasters it soon emerged a more beautiful and vibrant community. In many ways Chicago seems to be the typical American city, bustling, industrious, cosmopolitan and beautiful. The city is considered to have been established by John Kinzie in 1796, and is now the No. 3 U.S. city with a population of 2,900.000. Much of the city was destroyed be the Great Fire of 1871, but like San Francisco it soon rose from the ashes to resume its role as the financial and industrial capital of America's heartland.

The most atypical American city is no doubt, Honolulu, Hawaii. Polynesian Islanders may have first set foot here more than 2000 years ago, however, oral histories and archaeological studies set a date of around 1100 AD as the first settlement in the area. American missionaries first came here in 1820, and the Territory of Hawaii was annexed to the United States from Spain in 1898. In 1959 the Territory of Hawaii became the 50th state of America. Honolulu and adjacent Pearl Harbor are indelibly entered into the American consciousness as the place where America entered World War II. Since that time Honolulu and Hawaii have become one of the world's most sought after tourist destinations.

America's towns — defining that as places of population of fewer than 100,000 — probably bespeak more of the traditional character of the country than do its large melting-pot cities. Let us look at a sampling of America's towns. In May 1607 a group of 104 men and boys from the Virginia Company of London landed near what is now Jamestown, Virginia. They came to establish the first permanent English colony in America. Castine, Maine was established as a French trading post in 1613. After brief occupancies by the Dutch and English it came permanently under the American flag in 1813. Nineteenth-century Castine saw a period of whaling and shipbuilding, which in the twentieth century gave way to a place of tourism and wealthy vacation homes.

Sunset shines on Manhattan's Upper East Side and Central Park, New York City, NY.

Houghton, Michigan was founded in 1848 to serve the commercial and shipping interests of Upper Michigan's fabulously rich new copper mining industry. That industry has been gone for fifty years, but the mining college it fostered in 1885 remains today as one of America's leading engineering schools.

In America's West Cripple Creek, Colorado had a booming beginning in 1891 with the chance discovery of gold by cowboy Bob Womack. By the end of that year a mountain cow pasture had a population of 25,000 with 91 lawyers, 88 doctors, 14 newspapers and 70 saloons. Today's Cripple Creek has a permanent population of about 1200. The principal industry of Cripple Creek has become casino gambling. But against great odds and historic trends it is still the proud home of a major gold mining operation. The area around Seaside, Oregon on the Pacific Ocean Coast near the mouth of the Columbia River had been occupied by Native American Clatsop Indians for centuries before it was discovered by English ship captain Robert Gray in 1792. In November 1805 the Lewis and Clark expedition established a winter camp nearby and used the Seaside beach for a salt-making operation. In 1846 the Seaside area first came officially under the American flag in accord with the Oregon treaty with Great Britain. Seaside became a town around 1871, and by the turn of the century it had become a thriving seashore resort, which it continues to be more than 100 years later. The city of Nome, Alaska was formed in 1901. Prior to that Eskimo tribes had historically occupied the area. That changed in 1898 with a series of fabulously rich gold discoveries. Nome is too far from major population centers to have a significant tourist industry. It does however serve as a regional air-transportation hub, and it still has some placer gold mining activity.

By 1900 almost all the present cities and towns of America had been well established. New names after that were mostly suburbs of existing places, and that is likely the way it will remain.

Washington

40

Looking east from the Lincoln Memorial, the view is dominated by the Washington Monument, Washington, DC.

41

This view looks over the U. S. Capitol to the Washington Monument and beyond to the Lincoln Memorial.

42
Thomas Jefferson Memorial, Washington, DC., reflects the tastes of the third President of the Unisted States, obviously ispired by classical Rome.

43
The White House, Washington, DC is the official residence of the President of the United States.

44

Looking northwest to the Potomac River, Washington, DC, a cobweb-like layout of streets is centered on Dupont Circle.

45

The construction of Washington Monument, a marble obelisk 550 ft. high, was begun in 1848 and completed in 1884.

46

The statuary group *Mars on a Horse with Valor* stands at the entrance of Arlington Memorial Bridge, Washington, DC.

47

This aerial view of Washington looks over the Pentagon (lower left) across the Potomac River to the Lincoln Memorial and the Washington Monument. The White House is slightly beyond and left of the Washington Monument.

IN HONOR AND MEMORY
OF THE MEN OF THE
UNITED STATES MARINE CORPS
WHO HAVE GIVEN
THEIR LIVES TO THEIR COUNTRY
SINCE 10 NOVEMBER 1775

48

The United States Marine Corps War Memorial in Washington DC is by sculptor Felix W. de Weldon and is patterned from a Joe Rosenthal photograph of Marines raising the U.S. flag in Mt. Suribachai, Iwo Jíma.

49

Arlington National Cemetery, Washington, DC., is a resting-place of America's heroes and leaders.

New York

50-51
Sun is setting on Midtown Manhattan. The Chrysler Building is the slender spire at left center. The Empire State Building stands tall at right center. New York City, NY.

52
Lower Manhattan is seen here, looking west from above the East River.

53
In this view of Lower Manhattan Battery Park is at the lower left.

54
Sunset sheds its red-gold light on Lower Manhattan and Castle Clinton, to the center right of the photo.

55
With its green "pyramid" on the top, this building reached the height of 927 ft in 1929, thus becoming for a while the world's tallest skyscraper.

56
Woolworth Building's the Neogothics spires earned the building the attribute of "Cathedral of Commerce" in 1913, the year of its completion.

57
In this view of New York City's East River, Brooklyn Bridge is in the shadows, Manhattan bridge above it, north.

New York

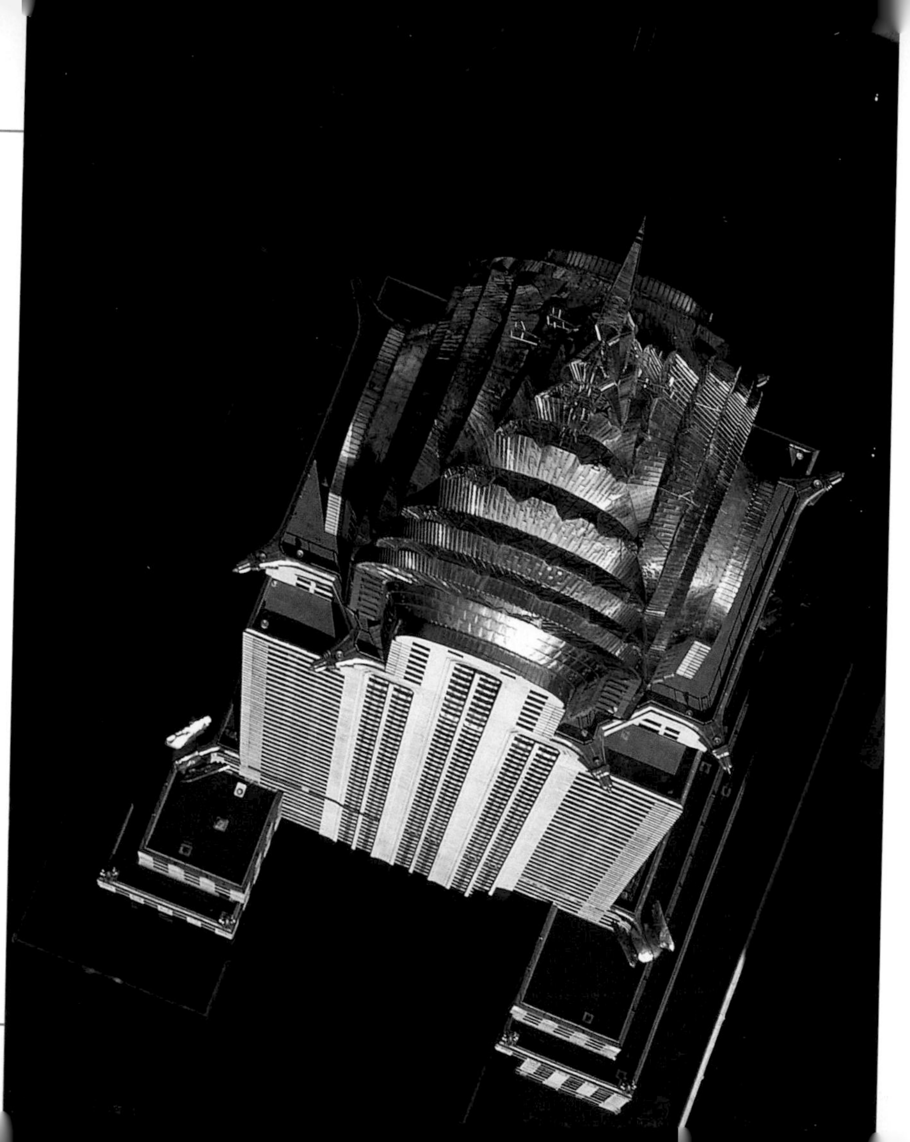

58

The Chrysler Building, with its Art Deco crown, is considered one of America's architectural gems.

59

The Empire State building, at 1472 feet, was the world's tallest building until 1972. It was begun at the height of the America's depression years and completed in just 14 months at a cost of $ 41 million.

60-61
Manhattan's concrete-and-steel forest encircles Central Park at sunset. Manhattan Upper East Side, New York City, NY.

62
The Statue of Liberty was a gift of France to America in 1884. The statue itself is 152 feet in height, is constructed of 350 individual pieces, and contains 225 tons of copper and steel.

63
From 1892 to 1954 when it closed Ellis Island processed more than 12 million immigrants, mostly from Europe. New York and New Jersey Bay.

64
Holding her flaming torch high over the dark waters of Upper New York Bay, the Statue of Liberty Enlightening the World looks east toward Europe.

66
Boston, Massachusetts: North End and Inner Harbor are viewed looking southwest.

67
Boston Financial District: Northern Avenue Bridge is at left, Charles River in distance, New England Aquarium at lower right.

68

Cambridge, Massachusetts: B.U. (Boston University) Bridge is at left. The view looks northeast.

69

An elegant Neoclassic dome tops Maclaurin Building at Massachusetts Institute of Technology, Cambridge, Massachusetts.

70

Despite the austere appearance of University's buildings, Cambridge, Massachusetts is a unique community with a strong mix of social diversity and intellectual vitality.

71

The ranks of typical storied residences at Back Bay Boston stand in what once was a marshy creek, drained in 19th century.

ladelphia

72

Philadelphia, Pennsylvania: this view looks southeast on the Schuylkill River from the vicinity of the Fairmont Park.

73

Glass-and-steel buildings seem to flung at the observer from the invisible streets of Downtown Philadelphia.

Pittsburgh

74
The Allegheny River is on the left, the Monongahela on the right in this view of Downtown Pittsburgh, Pennsylvania.

75
Downtown Pittsburgh: the Golden Triangle marks the point where the Allegheny meets the Monongahela to form the Ohio River.

Detroit

76

The Ambassador Bridge linking Detroit, Michigan with Windsor, Ontario was opened in 1929. At the time it was the world's longest suspension span.

77

The Renaissance area in Downtown Detroit includes a 73-story cylindric tower, surrounded by four 39-story buildings.

Chicago

78

The Sears Tower, world's tallest building until 1996, totals 110 stories and a quarter of mile in height over Downtown Chicago, Illinois

79

Two antennas and a truncated pyramid shape mark the unmistakable Hancock Building (1126 feet). The view looks southeast across Lake Michigan.

80 and 81
In Downtown Chicago, the Chicago Sanitary and Ship Canal, 30 miles long, was completed in 1900 to prevent the pollution of Lake Michigan by Chicago's sewage.

82
Futuristic skyscrapers overlooking Lakeshore Drive, Downtown Chicago, are the works of famed architects from "Chicago Schools."

83
Home of the Bears, New Soldier Field is growing fast in Downtown Chicago. The seats dismantled from the old stadium have been sold to nostalgic fans.

84

Reaching straight into Lake Michigan from Chicago Lakefront, Navy Pier, a Chicago landmark since 1916, was originally was designed as a shipping and recreational facility.

85

Though it fell into disuse at the end of 20th century, thanks to its unique setting and history Chicago Navy Pier has been redesigned as a premier family entertainment center with exhibition facilities, restaurants and shops.

86 and 87

Modern sculpture is a valued sight in Windy City plazas like Federal Center, where the titanic *Flamingo* by Calder graces the milieu with its bolted steel structure.

Chicago

88-89
Sunset over Belmont Harbor and the Chicago Yacht Club.

Cincinnati

90-91
The new Bengal's football stadium is at left center of this view of Cincinnati waterfront on the Ohio River. The old Riverfront Stadium, Cincinnati Red's baseball field, is at lower right. A new Red's stadium is being constructed just to the right of that.

St. Louis

92

At Downtown St. Louis, Missouri, the Gateway Arch on the Mississippi Rive is at the lower right. Busch Memoria Stadium, home of the Cardinals base ball team is on the left.

93

The Gateway Arch was erected in 1964 1966. It stands 640 feet tall with a base span of 640 feet. The arch frames the Old St. Louis Courthouse.

94

The Gateway Arch was constructed entirely of stainless steel and has an elevator to an observation point at the top.

95

The Jefferson Barracks Bridge crosses the Mississippi River south of St. Louis, Missouri.

FLY DELTA
SPORTS TOWN
Coca-Cola
Bud
BUD LIGHT
Just wait'll we get our Hanes on the Games.

96

The Atlanta skyline and Turner Fields: the Atlanta-Fulton County Stadium, in the foreground, is home of the Atlanta Braves baseball team since 1965.

97

The skyscrapers in downtown Atlanta skyline reflect the unprecedented growth of the city during the past three decades. Today metro Atlanta's population totals more than million people.

Atlanta

98 and 99
Futuristic skyscapers in downtown Atlanta (the photos show to Sun Trust Plaza, left, and Peachtree Plaza) and capture the ever-changing attitude of this modern city, constantly reshaped by luminaries in modern architecture and engineering.

Miami

100 and 101
Born in 1913 as a small agriculture venture, Miami Beach, Florida soon became one of the world's most renowned seaside communities, developing particularly during the late 1980s.

102

In South Pointe Park and Lummus State Park, at the southern end of the Miami Beach area, trendy restaurants, boutiques and venues are steps away from white-sand beaches and palms.

103

Downtown Miami grew greatly during the past century, and specially between the 1960s and 90s, when thousands of Cubans fled to the city to start new lives. Miami is now the leading gateway for international arrivals in the States.

104
Geometric ornamentations grace the pre-war modernist buildings in Miami Beach's Art Deco District, built primarily in the 1930's.

105
Colorful hotels and buildings accent Downtown Miami.

106-107
In this view Miami Beach, once called the "billion dollar sandbar," is seen with Biscayne Bay in distance.

108

Disney World (lower left) and Epcot Center (upper right) opened 20 miles southwest of Orlando, Florida respectively in 1971 and 1982.

109

Pleasant climate, lakes, lush landscaping and public spaces characterize downtown Orlando, Florida, a growing city of 200,000 persons.

110

Up-close animal interactions, world-class shows and stirring rides attract millions visitors to Sea World, Orlando, Florida, world's premier marine adventure park.

111

Showing visitors the world of future, Epcot Center, Orlando, Florida is dominated by the geosphere called "Spaceship Earth.

MAGIC KINGDOM

112 and 113

-d, Orlando, Florida clus-
- world of fancy: 27,400
far from the city to
om the intrusion of
ment.

1.

New Orleans

114

Downtown New Orleans, Louisiana is the very core of a growing city with a population of 500,000 persons.

115

Once named Place d'Armes and used as a drill field by the French, Jackson Square, in the French Quarter of New Orleans, is now a public park.

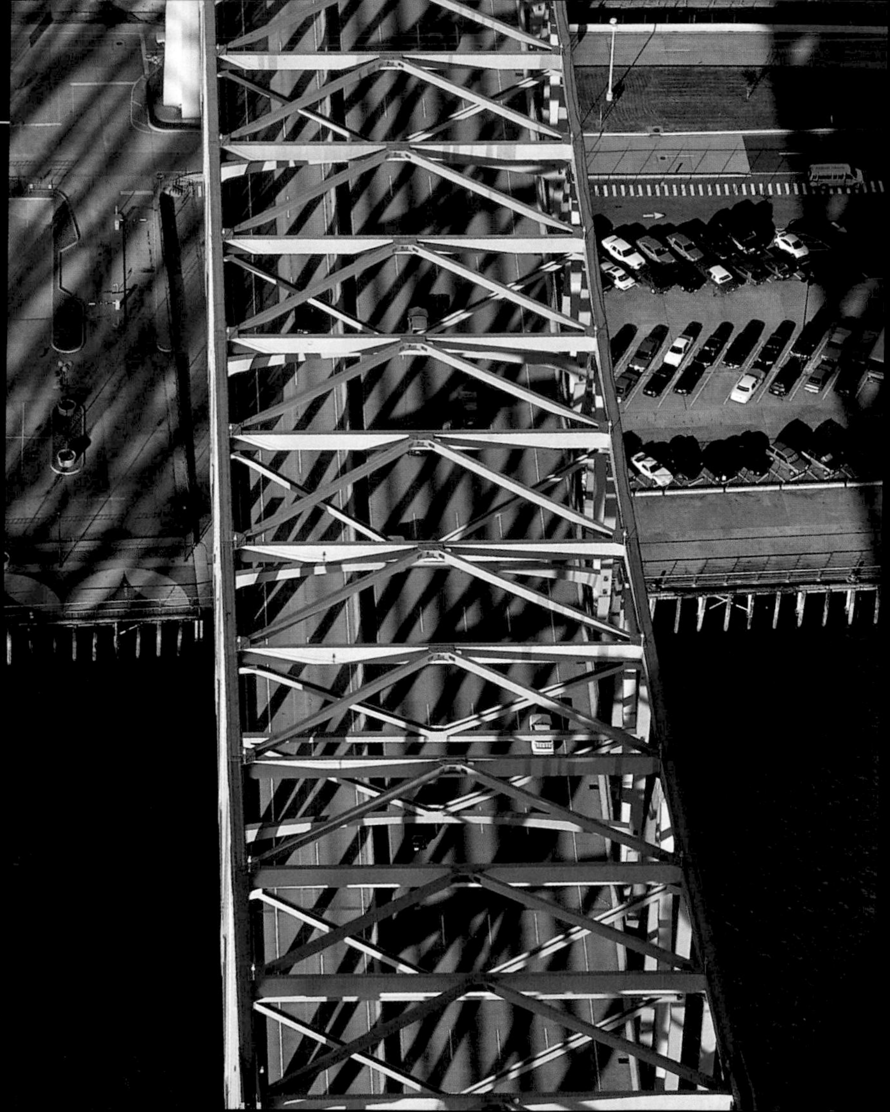

116

With a vertical clearance of 150 feet, the Greater New Orleans Bridge No. 2 crosses the Mississippi River with a main span of 1,595 feet.

117

Ultramodern towers soar over downtown New Orleans, a place where ther past and the future co-exist in enticing ways.

New Orleans

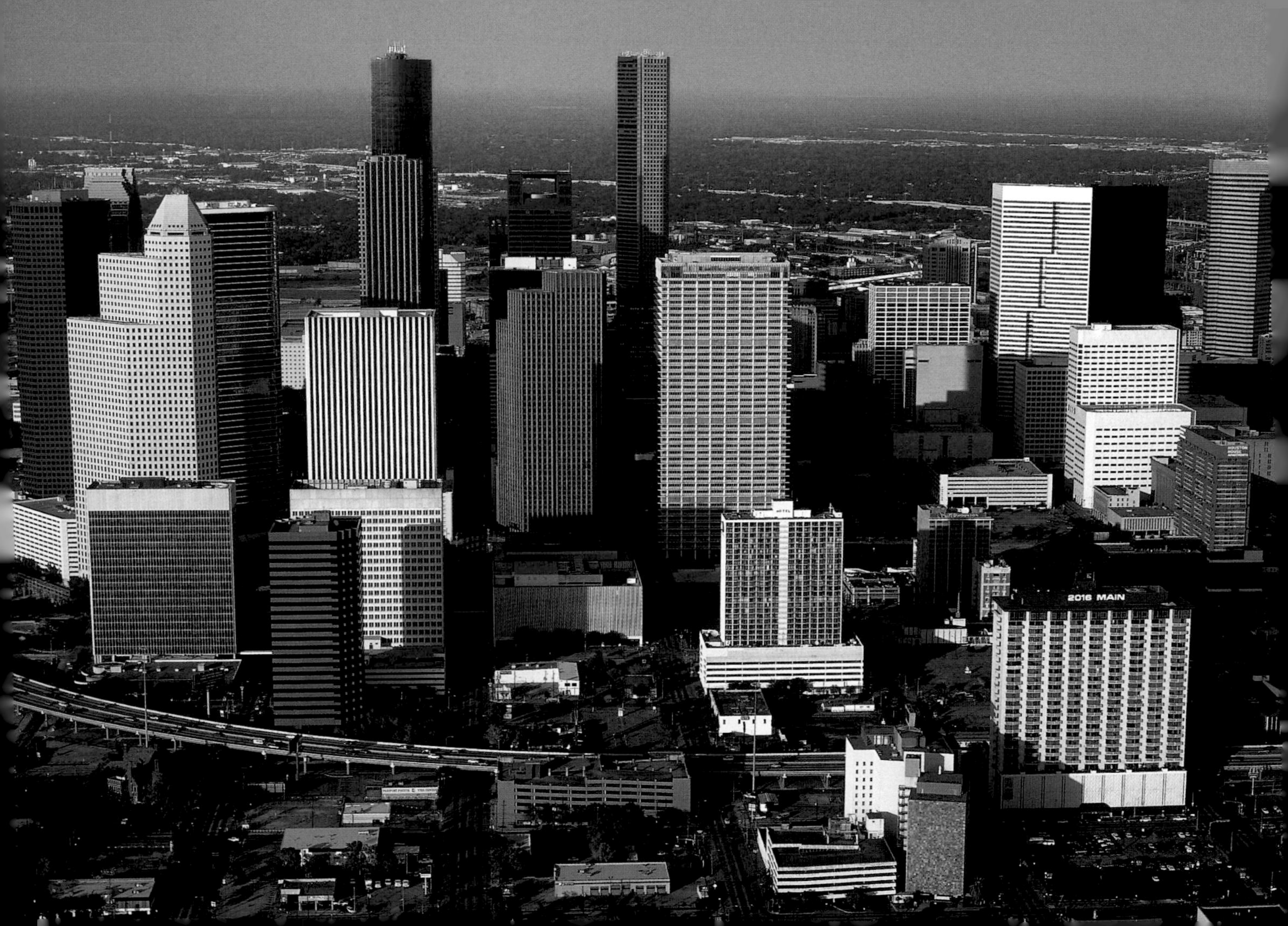
2016 MAIN

Houston

118
The central business district in downtown Houston, Texas is an important hub of the nation's petroleum industry.

119
The suspension structure of the Baytown Bridge crosses the Houston Ship Canal.

Dallas

120
Glass-and-aluminum notched corners give the Bank of America Plaza skyscraper a somewhat modern Art Deco styling.

121
The most recognizable landmark in downtown Dallas is the Bank of America Plaza skyscraper, 72 stories clad in reflective glass.

Denver

122

Downtown Denver, Colorado, is seen here looking northwest from over the Colorado State Capitol Building.

123

Some 20 highrises have dominated downtown Denver since the 1980s construction boom office. In the following decade the city became home to computer, telecommunications, and high-tech firms.

COLORADO
COORS FIELD

124

Denver, Colorado. The stands are crowded during a baseball game at Coors Field: Colorado Rockies vs Atlanta Braves.

125

Private houses cluster around a concentric drive at Cul de Sac, a Denver suburb.

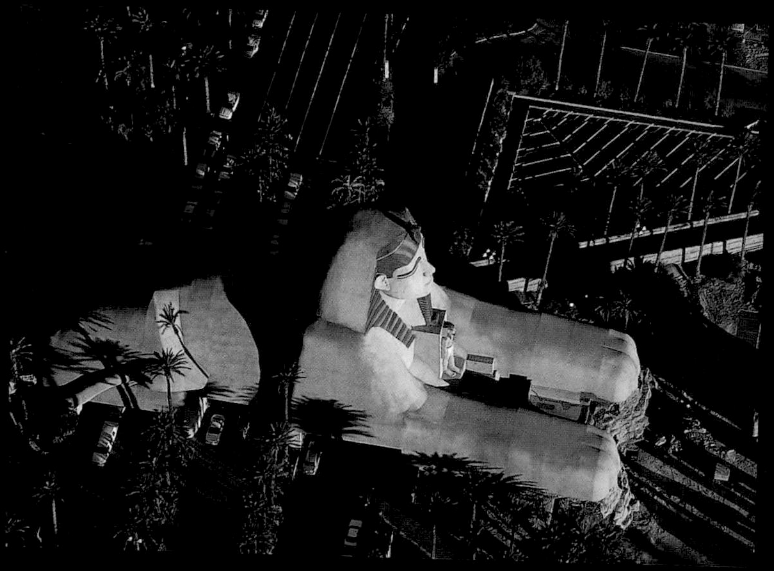

126
A modern Sphinx crouches in front of the Hotel Luxor, Las Vegas, Nevada.

127
The most ambitious resort project in Las Vegas, MGM Grand, is introduced by a huge lion, the world famous symbol of the film company.

Las Vegas

BALLY'S
ALADDIN

128

Paris Las Vegas Hotel, with its replica of the Tour Eiffel in Paris, France dominates this view of the Strip.

129

At 1149 feet of height, the Stratosphere Tower Hotel and Casino offers the best views on Las Vegas and the surrounding desert. This is USA's tallest building west of Mississippi.

130 and 131

Manhattan in Las Vegas: New York New York resort and amusement park highlights some of the most famous buildings and landmarks the "Big Apple" has to offer, including a Coney Island Rollercoaster behind the Statue of Liberty.

132

Las Vegas' Excalibur Hotel, with its round towers and dawbridge, imitates an European medieval castle, complete with a medieval shopping village.

133

Las Vegas by night glows like a galaxy in the outer space; around the city stretches only the desert.

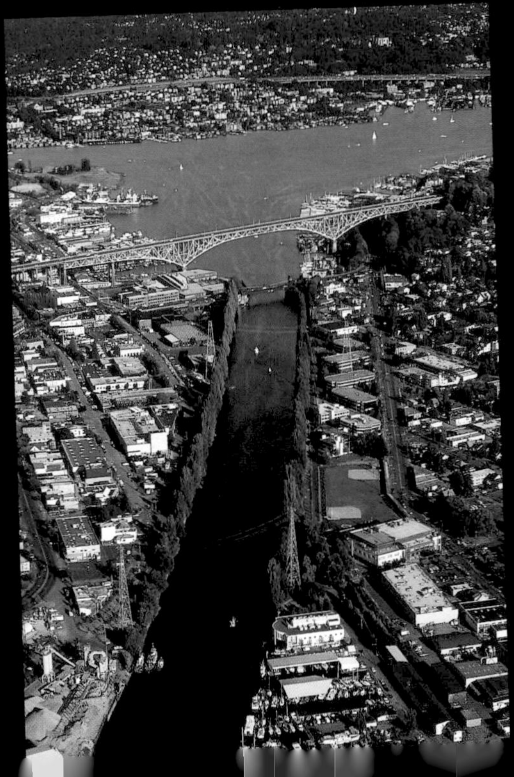

Seattle

134
Looking northeast, this view of Seattle, Washington, Fremont District, shows Salmon Bay leading into Lake Union. Washington Memorial Bridge is in the foreground.

135
Nicknamed by its residents the "Emerald City," Seattle is situated in a landscape of greenery, surrounded by lakes and rivers.

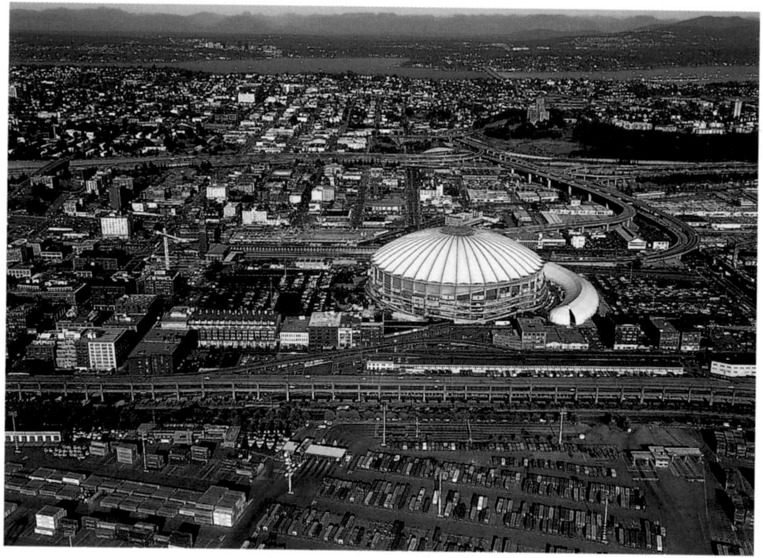

136 and 137
A dome-like covering marks the Seattle Seahawks Stadium, a facility with a 67,000 seat capacity. In the view looking south (right) the Stadium is upper right, with downtown Seattle in the foreground.

138-139
High-rise in downtown Seattle, here at sunset, show the wealthiness of this city, whose economic backbone is represented by tech firms.

San Francisco

140-141
Dakland Bay Bridge and Treasure sland, in the background, frame downtown San Francisco and its andmarks, like the Transamerica Pyramid, to the left in this view ooking northeast.

142
Somewhat more vertiginous than other aerial views, this one shows downtown San Francisco looking across the Art Deco north tower of the Golden Gate Bridge.

143
The Golden Gate Bridge opened in 1937 after four years in construction and at a cost of $ 35 million in 1930s dollars.

145
Golden Gate Bridge casts its striking shadow on the waters of San Francisco Bay in this bird's eye view.

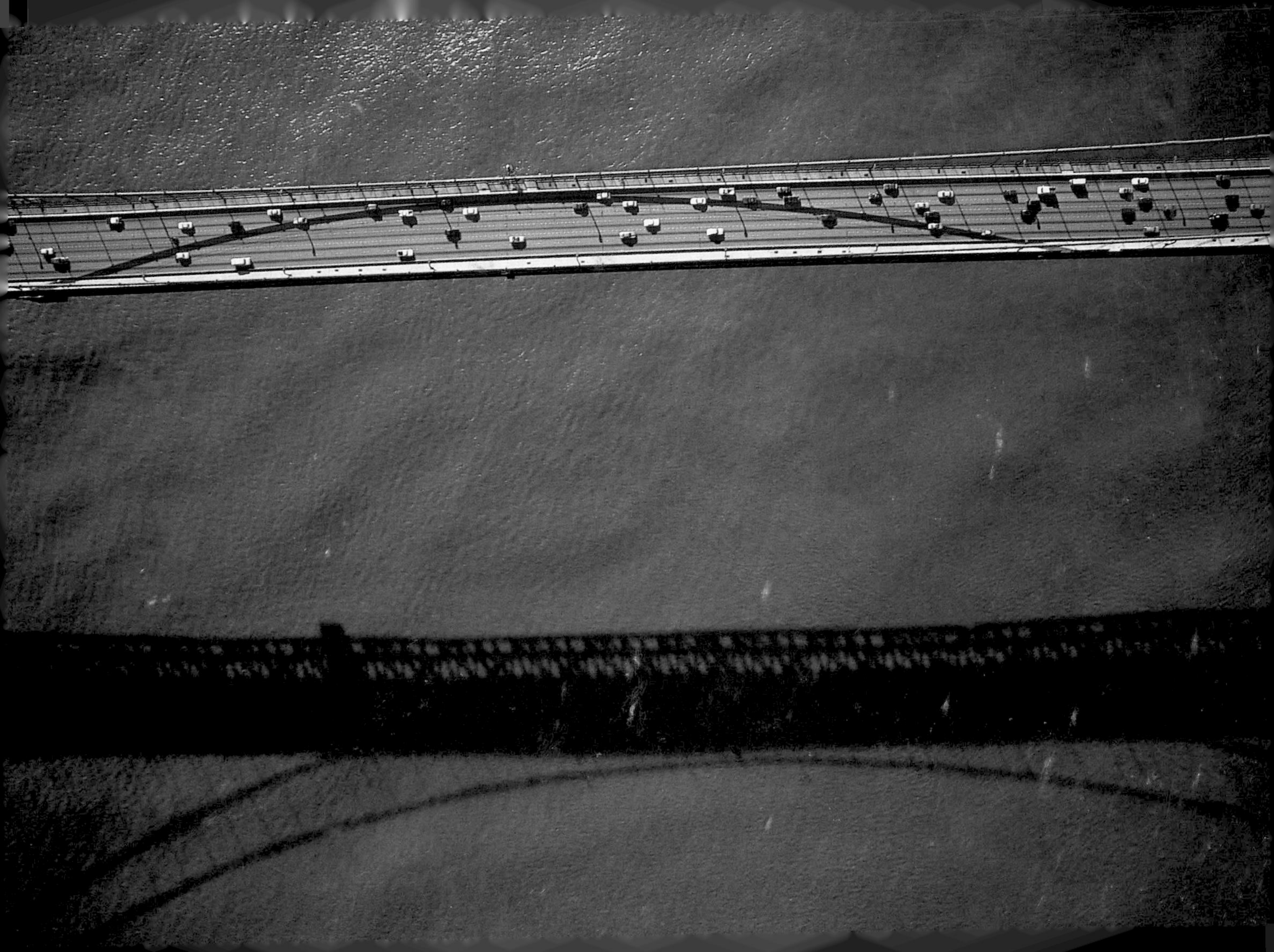

146

Coit Tower stands on Telegrah Hill with a view of Alcatraz and San Francisco Bay.

147

Formerly home of one of the world's most notorious prison, Alcatraz Island in San Francisco Bay derives its name from a quite "peaceful" word: *alcatraces*, Spanish word for "pelican" or "strange birds."

San Francisco

148

The centerpiece of the Montgomery street Financial District soars in downtown San Francisco.

149

Transamerica Pyramid is a trade building in itself, but its mere presence acts as a powerful tourism-promoting imagine.

BRANDY HO'S
GOOD FORT
STAURANT

150 and 151
San Francisco, a city most protective of its history, takes pride in its Eclectic and Beaux-Arts-style architectures, and colorful row houses.

HOLLYWOOD

Los Angeles

152-153
The famous Hollywood sign was erected in 1923 as a real estate promotion. It has been recon-structed several times and is now maintained by a voluntee trust. The original sign was sup-posed to last two years.

154

Downtown Los Angeles rises in this view looking northwest toward Santa Monica.

155

Los Angeles Freeways: in the photo center is Interstate 10 leading west to Santa Monica and the Pacific Ocean. Across the photo bottom is the Harbor Freeway.

Los Angeles

156 and 157
Downtown Los Angeles reflects the massive development of the city during the past century. LA's population, in fact, grew from fewer than 3,000 to more than 15 millions residents in 150 years.

158

The stylish Beverly Hills City Hall, with its dome reminiscent of Hispanic and Italian religious architecture, was designed in 1932 by William J. Gage.

159

Los Angeles - Beverly Hills: the intersection of Rodeo Drive and Wilshire Boulevard is the heart of upscale L.A. fashion shopping.

VALENTINO

160-161

Venice Beach, Los Angeles, considers itself to be America's funk culture capitol. In 1914 this was the site of the first official airport in California, Ince Field. In 1923 shops replaced the airfield.

162 and 163
Walt Disney's dream came true at Anaheim, California (right): Disney Adventure (left) and Disneyland are places where children and parents can have fun together.

San Diego

164 and 165
The attractive, elegant lines of modern architectures in downtown San Diego, California, grace the center of what has been the first european settlement in California, where Spanish settled in 1769.

166 left and 167

Coronado Peninsula stretches across the bay from downtown San Diego to Tijuana. The centerpiece of the peninsula is Coronado Hotel (right), built in 1888.

166 right

Downtown waterfront, San Diego, in its 27-miles stretch gathers parks, restaurants, hotels, marinas, shopping centers and cultural activities.

168
Looking northwest across Diamond Head and Diamond Crater, downtown Honolulu appears under a typical Hawaiian overcast sky.

169
Downtown Honolulu, Ala Moana Beach Park: Magic Island is at right center.

Honolulu

170 and 171

Every kind of entertainment, recreational and cultural activity is found in Waikiki Beach, Honolulu District, one of the world's most famous places.

Honolulu

172-173
Perpetually battered by ocean's waves, the sinuous coastline west of Diamond Head shows one of the most exciting views of the planet: Waikiki and Honolulu (at far left) nestled in the lush Hawaiian greenery.

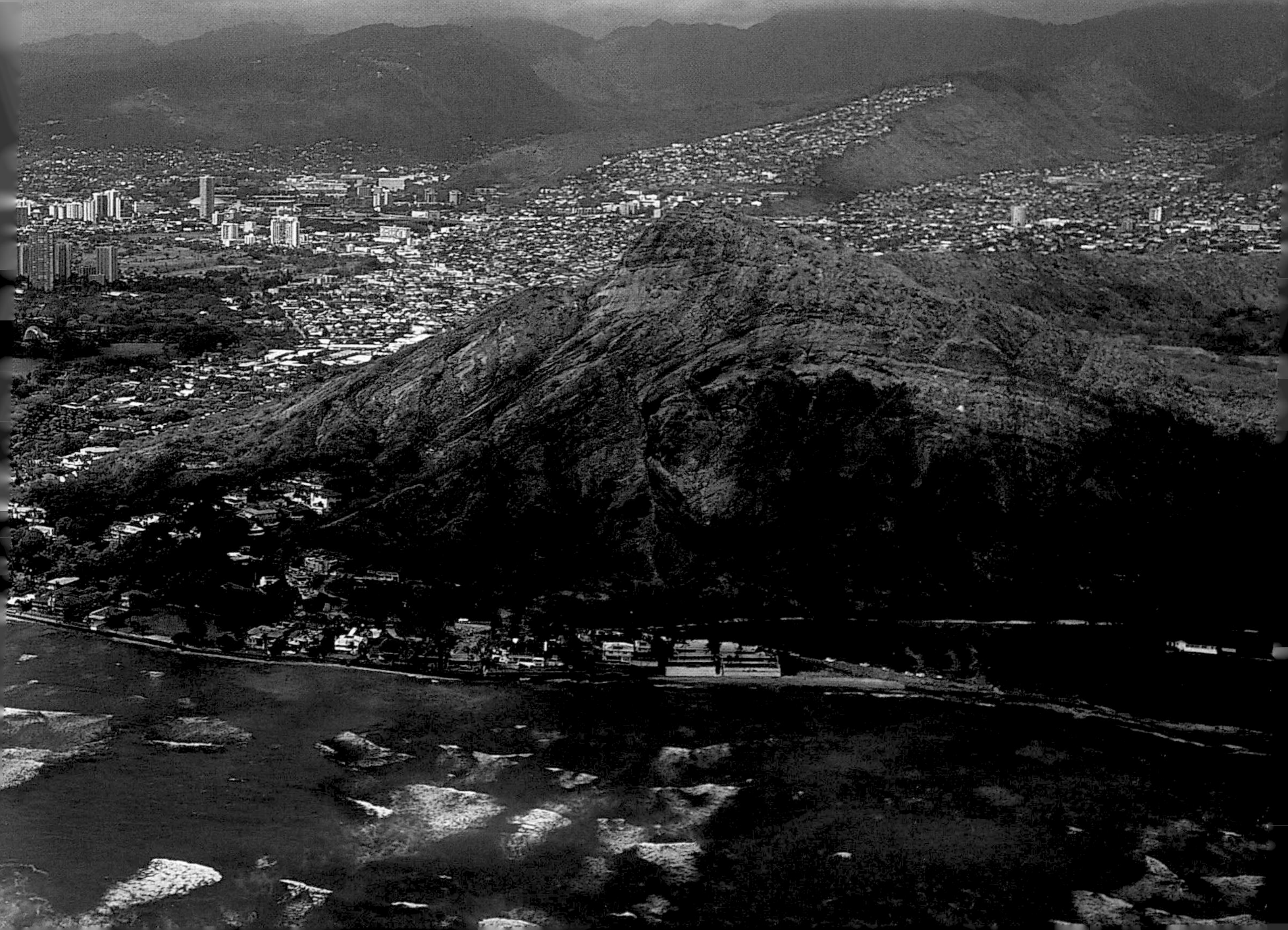

SCULPTED LANDS

FLYING HIGH

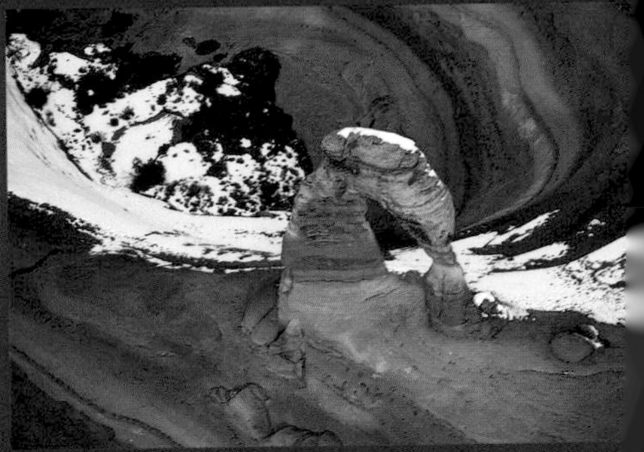

175
Tables of the Sun, San Juan County, Southeast Utah (left);
Delicate Arch, Arches National Park, Grand County, Utah (right).

The Sculpted Lands in this book is mostly confined to the Colorado Plateau Geologic Province of Colorado and Utah. In this region, along the Arizona/Utah border a geologic structure known as the Monument Uplift, or Monument Anticline, had a hand in forming some of the American West's best known parks and monuments. A remarkable geographic feature known as Comb ridge defines the eastern edge of the Monument Uplift. This ridge stands like a 70-mile long saw-toothed fence extending from northeastern Arizona into southeastern Utah.

Monument Valley Tribal Park lies close to the axis (high point) of the Monument Uplift. When an uplift forms it creates vertical stress fractures in the overlying rock strata which can extend for many miles. With these planes of weakness in place the relentless process of erosion by water and temperature-change gains an easy foothold. Rainwater hydraulically washes away rock particles. When the rain stops the residual water begins dissolving the cements that bind the rock grains. In winter, freezing water wedges the rock fissures wider. First produced from this process are the large flat-topped landforms we call mesas. These are then worn down to smaller versions called buttes, and finally to slender rock spires and "Michelin Man" shaped hoodoos. Once the cliff faces of the mesas emerge, erosion from wind-blown sand becomes a factor. This simplified explanation of how the rock structures of Monument Valley were formed applies to the formation of all the features of the Stone World.

Monument Valley would be a national park were it not

176
Kaibab Plateau and Colorado River, Arizona.

179
Shiprock in fog. Navajo Reservation, New Mexico.

Sculpted lands

wholly owned by the Navajo Indian Tribe. It is a place known to Americans as the Wild West of John Wayne movies, and the place where automobiles magically appear on the top of precipitous 1000-feet tall tall rocks in new car ads. Pre-historic people may have visited Monument Valley as long ago as 10,000 BC. The Anasazis were in the area from about the time of Christ until about AD 1300. The Monument Valley area first shows up in European records on a 1776 Spanish map. In the mid-1800s American silver and gold seekers, led by mountain man Kit Carson, forced the Navajos from the land with government sanction. In the late 1860s the Navajos returned, also with government sanction, to reclaim their land. Today many tourists visit the area and can be escorted by Navajo guides to the valley's most secret and compelling places.

The southern end of 530-square mile Canyonlands National Park begins about 60 miles north of Monument Valley. The Green and Colorado Rivers divide this park into three sections. The crotch of the "Y" formed by the confluence of the two rivers is called Island in the Sky. It is predominantly a flat-topped mesa that is easily accessible and offers stunning views of the canyons of both rivers. Its one major geologic feature is Upheaval Dome and crater, thought by some geologists to have been formed by forces within the earth. Others think it is an artifact of a meteor impact. On the east side of the "Y" is the Needles District, which is fairly accessible with many wonderful arches and a few Anasazi cliff dwellings. To the west of the "Y" is the Maze District, a barely accessible and wholly inhospitable maze of canyons and fins.

Much smaller Arches National Park lies just twenty miles northeast from Canyonlands. The Colorado River forms a small portion of its southern boundary but there are no major drainages within it. Nevertheless, it boasts more than 2000 natural arches. The most famous arch is the marvelous, amazing, freestanding Delicate Arch whose creation and endurance seem to defy both logic and imagination.

Bryce Canyon and Zion National Parks are the most visited of Utah's parks. For me, Bryce is best seen

180

Pueblo Bonito, Chaco Canyon, New Mexico.

from the air, Zion from the ground. Bryce canyon is actually a misnomer, as it is not a canyon, but is the highly eroded rim of a large mesa. The incredible spires, hoodoos and box canyon labyrinths of Bryce form a fairyland of nature. Before the area was established, first as a monument in 1923, then as a park in 1928, a rancher who ran cattle here described it as "A bad place to loose a cow." The nature of the park began forming in the Cretaceous period of great plants and dinosaurs. Some 100 million years ago marine sediments were deposited in a great inland seaway that extended to the Gulf of Mexico. These rock formations were much softer than those of the other parks in the region, and thus once the uplifting began they were rapidly eroded to their present shapes. In geologic time they will not long endure. Zion Park is dominated by the narrow, steep gorges of the Virgin River. To really appreciate this park one needs to hike the gorge from its upland beginnings twenty miles to the park headquarters. At the end you will be wet, cold and awestruck. The awestruck will be with you forever. Though the ancients of the Colorado Plateau no doubt visited Bryce, Zion, and Monument Valley they left little record of their presence.

No discussion of the Colorado Plateau is complete without fair mention of the Anasazi. These people were in the area from at least 1 to AD 1300. In the later of these centuries their culture flourished and many centers of activity were constructed: Mesa Verde, a center of population; Chaco Canyon, a center of science and religion; Canyon de Chelly, a center of agriculture. They also left a gallery of incredible artwork on the rock walls of the area. It is speculated that persistent drought drove the Anasazis farther east where they assimilated with other cultures. There is no habitation today at Mesa Verde and Chaco except for park visitors, but Canyon de Chelly (pronounced de-shay) is still an area of Navajo farming. The magnificent rocks and cliffs of the area seemed to draw these native people to them – just as millions of visitors are drawn there each year today.

183 and 184-185
Storm clouds roll in during a beautiful sunset over the Grand Canyon, in Grand Canyon National Park, Arizona.

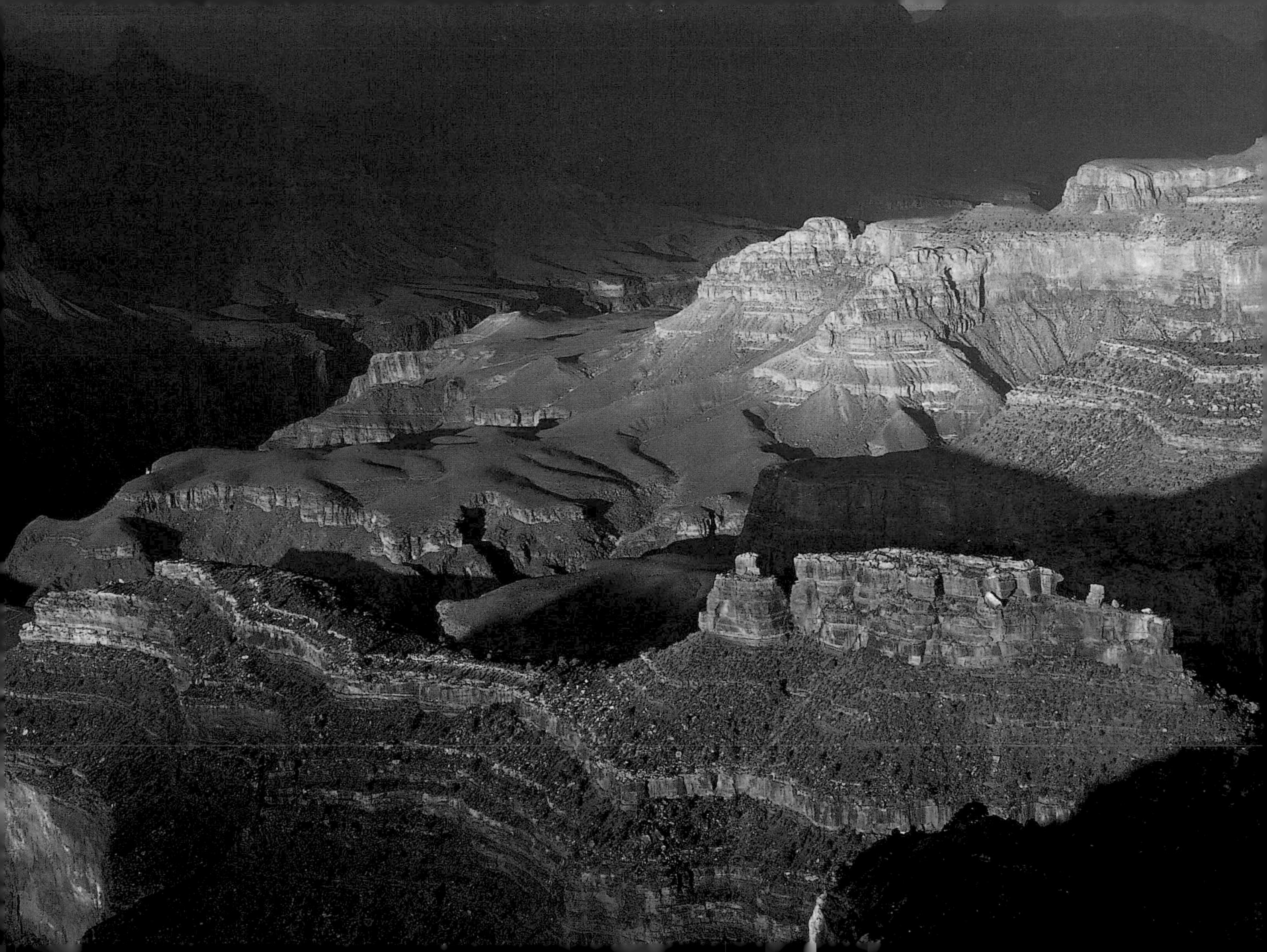

186-187
Vulcan's Throne (lower left) overlooks the Colorado River in Grand Canyon National Park, Arizona.

188

The fog extends to the rim of the Grand Canyon, Grand Canyon National Park, Arizona.

189

Fog creeps over an eastern rim of the Grand Canyon.

Monument Valley

190
Castle Butte formation towers over the Monument Valley, in the Navajo Indian Reservation, San Juan County, Utah.

191
North Mitten is a typical Monument Valley structure with a capping of resistant conglomerate, a core of hard sandstone and a base of soft easily eroded shale.

192

The line of rock spires of the Yei Bi Chai formation, in Monument Valley, is thought to resemble a line of the healing dancers of the same name.

193

The totem pole is in the foreground in this view of the Yei Bi Chai formation in winter.

194
Sunset highlights the strong orange hue of Castle Butte, in Monument Valley.

195
Early winter light strikes Castle Butte, one of the most scenic in Monument Valley.

197

Rock swirls add to the bizarre rock formations in Western Monument Valley, San Juan County, Utah.

198-199

In this winter view, Castle Butte is on the left, Natani Tso (Big Leader) in the center, Brigham's Tomb on the right, Eagle Rock Mesa behind. Monument Valley lies at the approximate crest of the Monument Uplift. Erosional forces begin the sculpting by first producing mesas, which then further erode into buttes and spires.

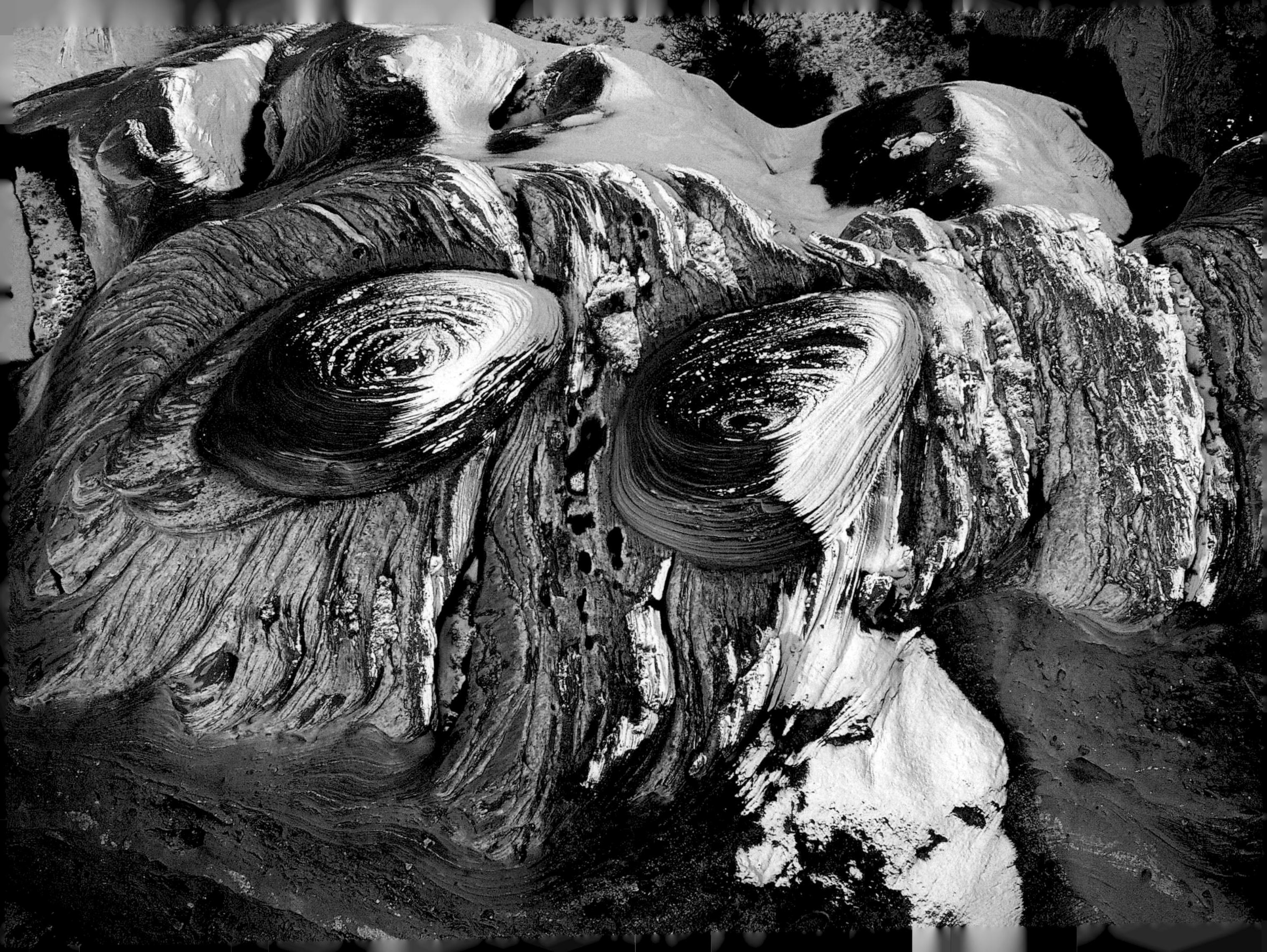

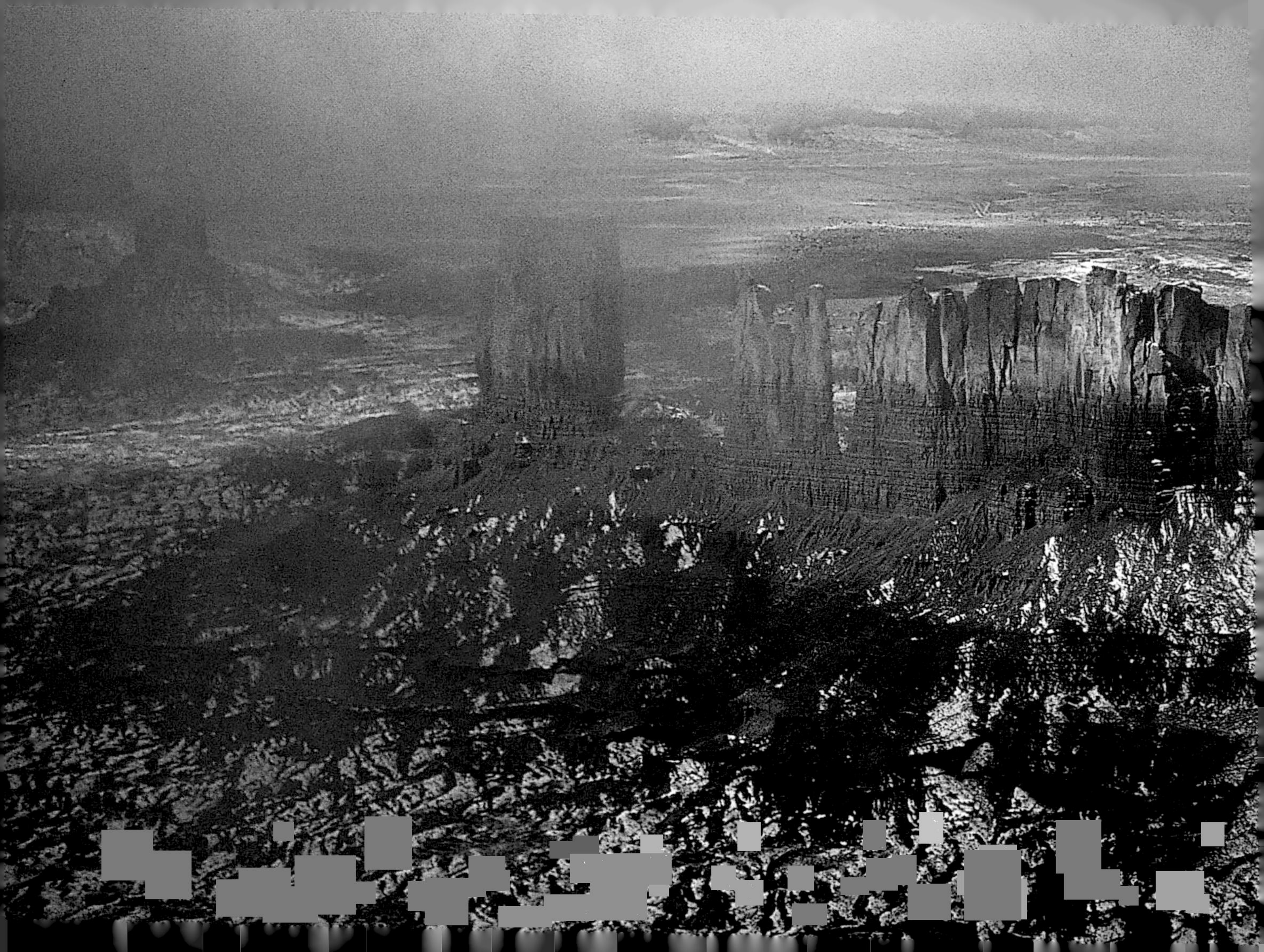

200-201
Winter fog creates an eerie archipelago over the bottom of Monument Valley. Left to right in the foreground are Castle Butte, Natani Tso, Brigham's Tomb.

202 and 203
Snow lingers on the sharp ridge of Castle Butte, Monument Valley.

Canyonlands

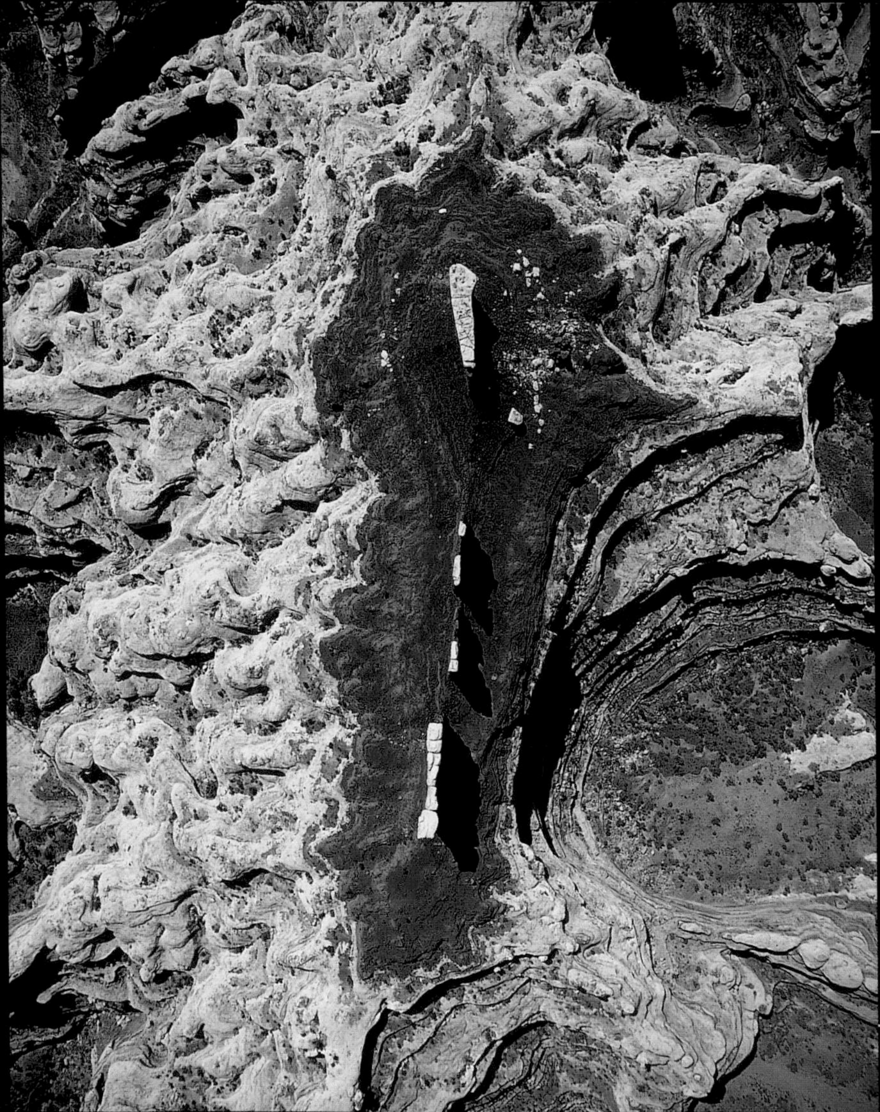

204
The meandering landscape of Needles District strikes the eye in Canyonlands National Park, San Juan County, Utah.

205
Bird's eye view of the Chocolate Drops, where a soft brown shale has been protected from erosion by the hard white sandstone capping. Maze District, Canyonlands National Park, Wayne County, Utah.

206 left
Severely eroded sedimentary sandstone forms mesas, buttes, and gorges in the Canyonlands National Park, Utah.

206 right and 207
Recalling objects of everyday life, the weird rock formations in Needles District bear names like Wedding Ring Arch (left) and Paul Bunyan's Potty (right).

208

A potty hole draws a perfect circle on the sandstone layer in Needles District, Canyonlands National Park, San Juan County, Utah.

209

The elongated Kirk Arch spans in Needles Ditrict, Canyonlands National Park..

210
Arches National Park's rock formations, in Grand County, Utah, are readable like pages of a gigantic book on geological history of our world.

211
Fiery Furnace Area, in Arches National Park', is a maze of meandering canyons: it's quite easy getting lost there.

Arches National Park

212

Rainbow Bridge National Monument is reached by a 14-mile foot/horse trail or a 50-mile trip on Lake Powell. Navajo Indian Reservation, Lake Powell, Utah.

213

Rainbow Bridge is the world's largest natural bridge with a span and height both of about 290 feet. Rainbow Bridge began forming several million years ago.

Zion Park

214-215
Snowcapped buttes and sheer red cliffs tower in the Kolob region of Zion National Park, Washington County, Utah.

216 and 217

First Light strikes the buttes of the southern district of Zion National Park, Utah.

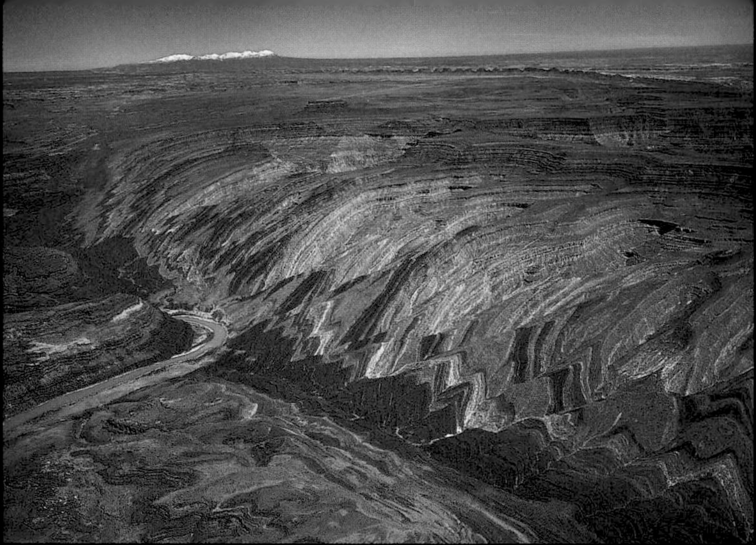

218

Chinle Shale cuestas run along San Juan River near Bluff, Utah.

219

Comb Ridge overlooks Chinle Creek, near Bluff, San Juan County Utah..

220-221

Layered "rock waves" form the slopes of Chinle Shale Cuestas. Monument Upwarp, Navajo Indian Reservation, San Juan County, Utah.

San Juan County

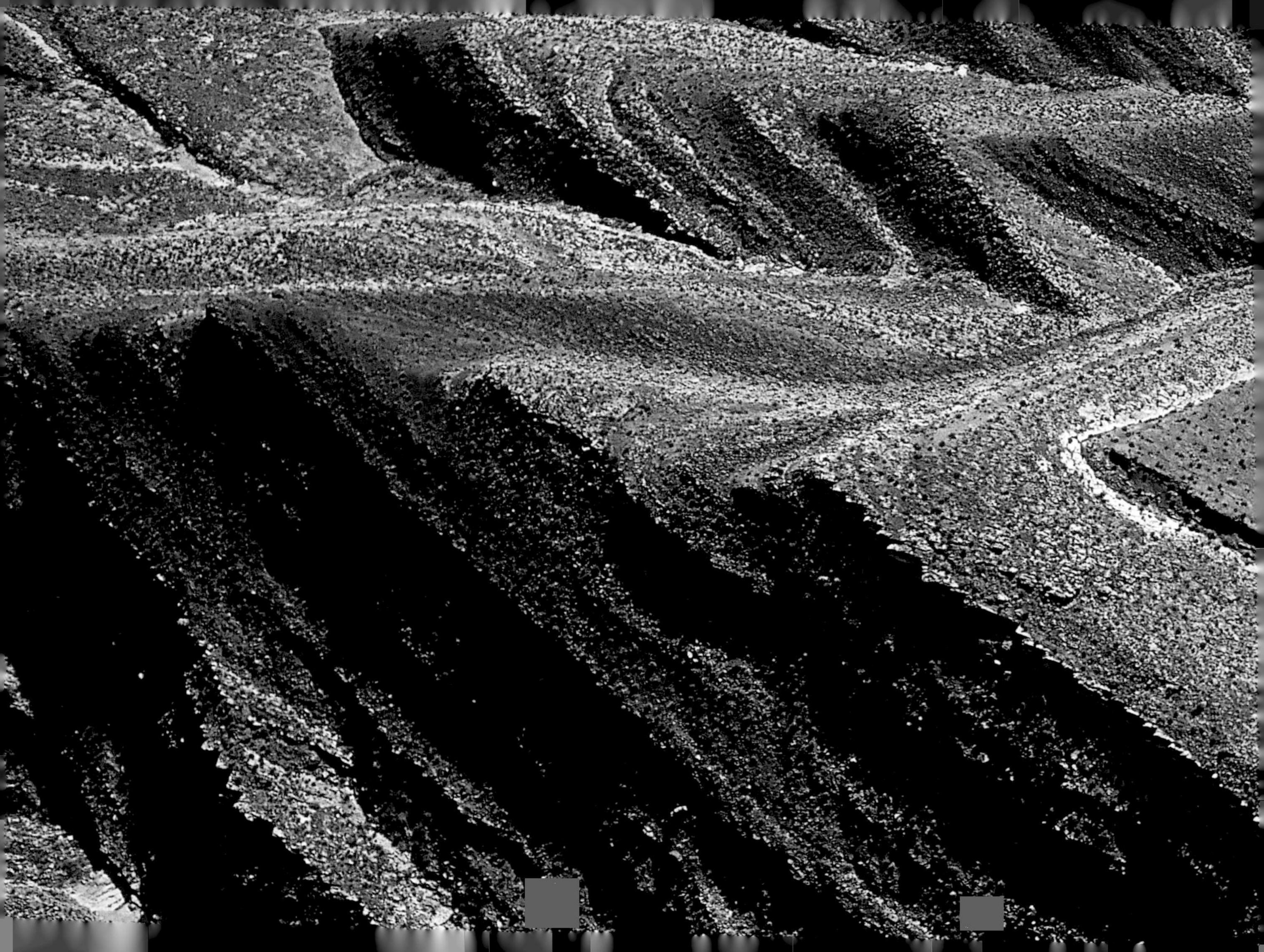

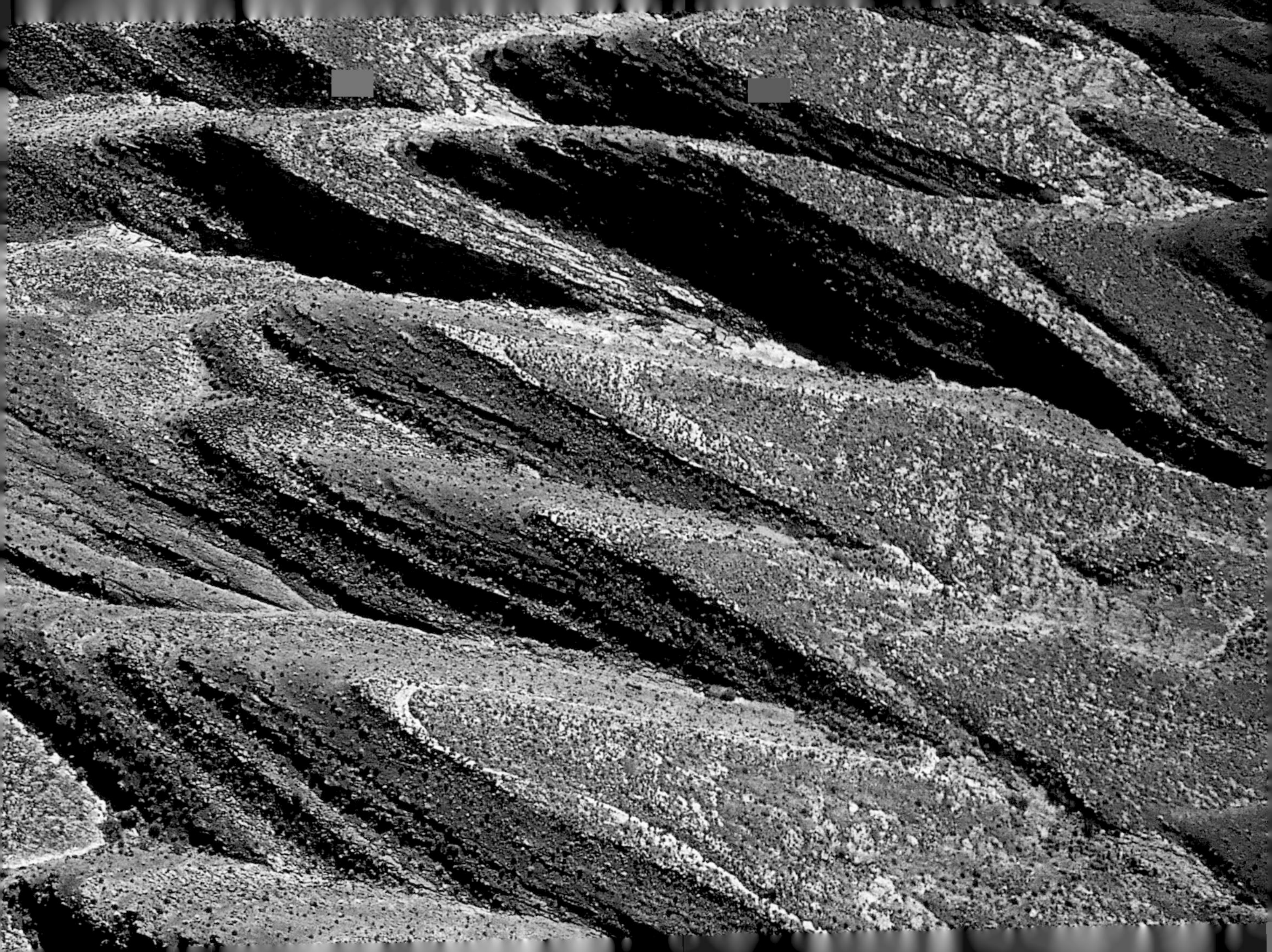

Grand Escalante

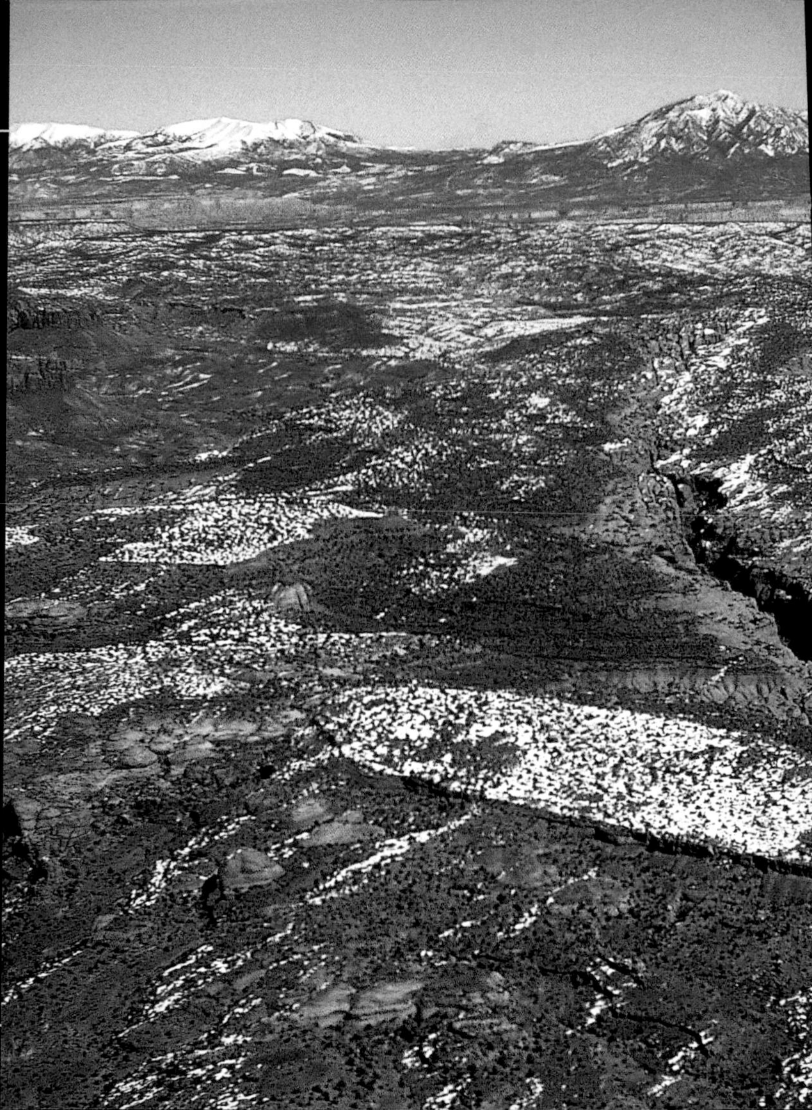

222-223
This view of the canyons in the Grand Staircase–Escalante National Monument looks northwest to the mountains of the Sevier Plateau. Kane County, Utah.

Bryce Canyon

224, 225 and 226-227

The slopes of the Bryce Canyon Amphitheater are steep and the rock of the 60-million-year-old claron formation is very soft, leading to rapid erosion. Bryce Canyon National Park. Garfield County, Utah.

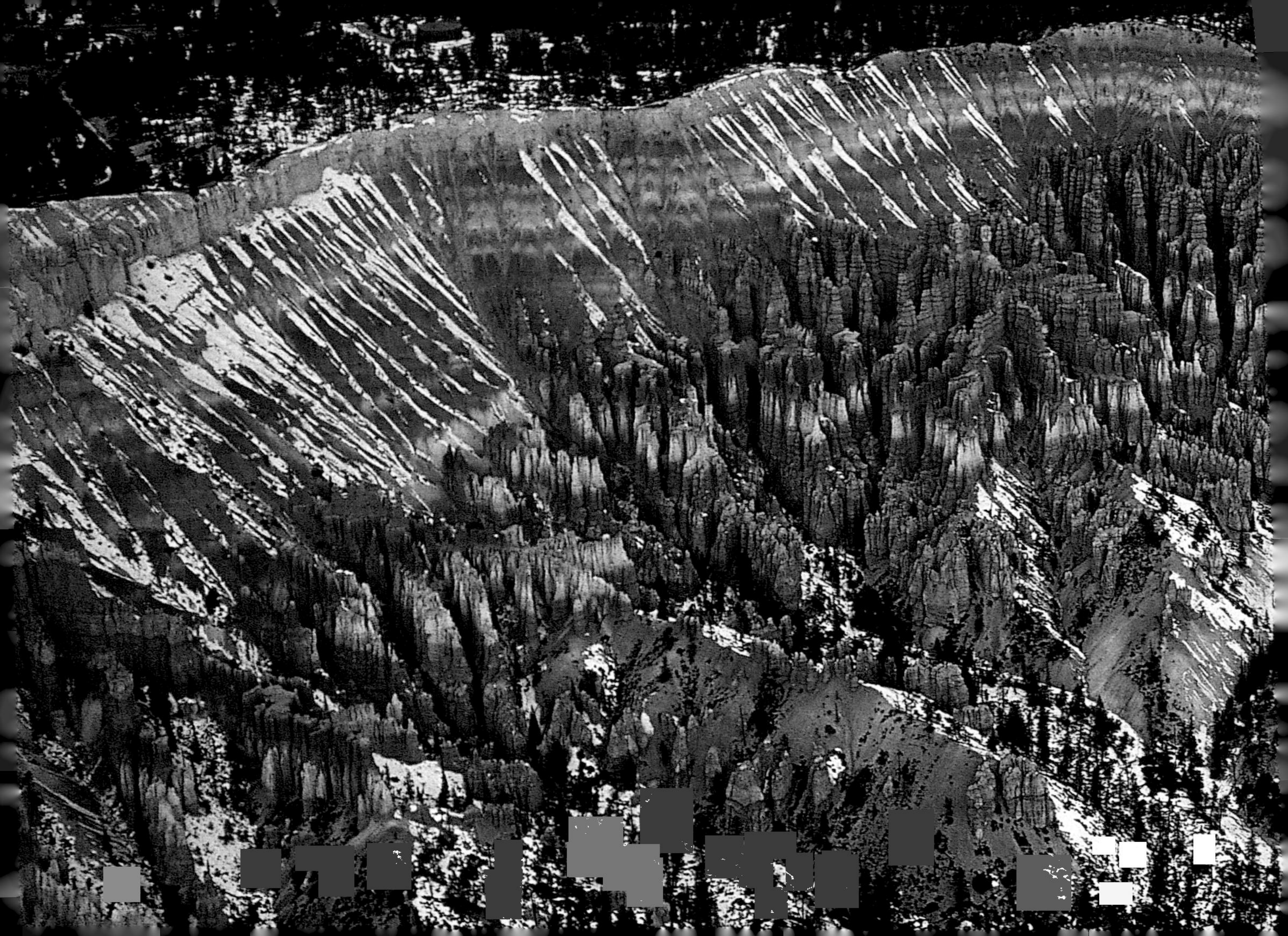

229
Morning light strikes the eroded rocks of Factory Butte, a prominent landmark in Southern-Central Utah.

Factory Butte

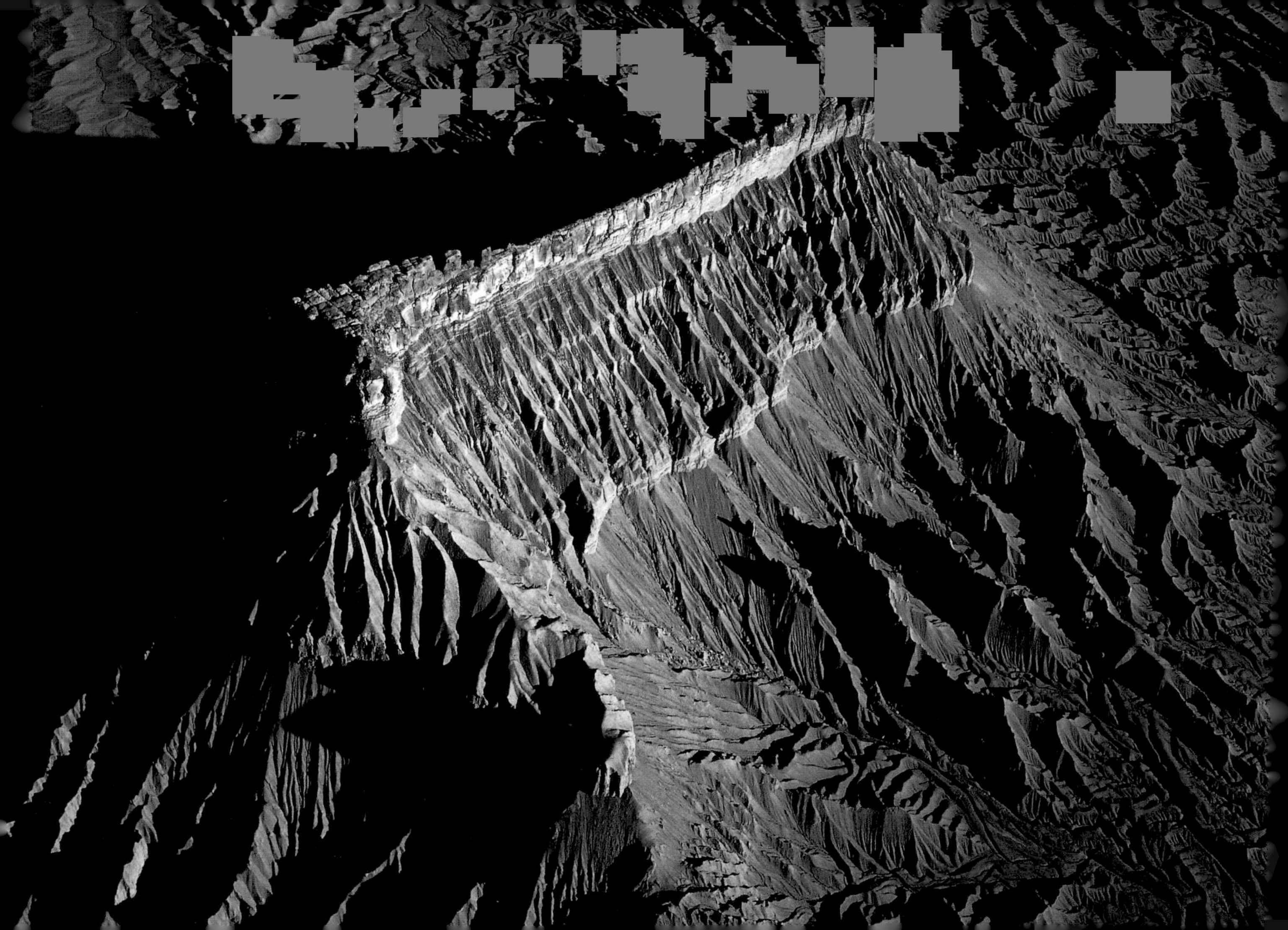

Round Rock

230-231

Round Rock, in the Navajo Indian Reservation, Apache County, Arizona, is a typical mesa of the Colorado Plateau which will in time erode to smaller spires and buttes as now exist in Monument Valley, 50 miles northwest of here.

Canyon de Chelly

232
The finger of Spider Rock aims the sky over Canyon de Chelly National Monument, Navajo Indian Reservation, Arizona.

233
Face Rock (left) and Spider Rock (right) stand at the confluence of Canyon de Chelly (left) and Monument Canyon (right).

236 and 237
The lands of Canyon de Chelly National Monument are owned, inhabited and cultivated by the Navajo tribe. Navajo Indian Reservation, Apache County, Arizona.

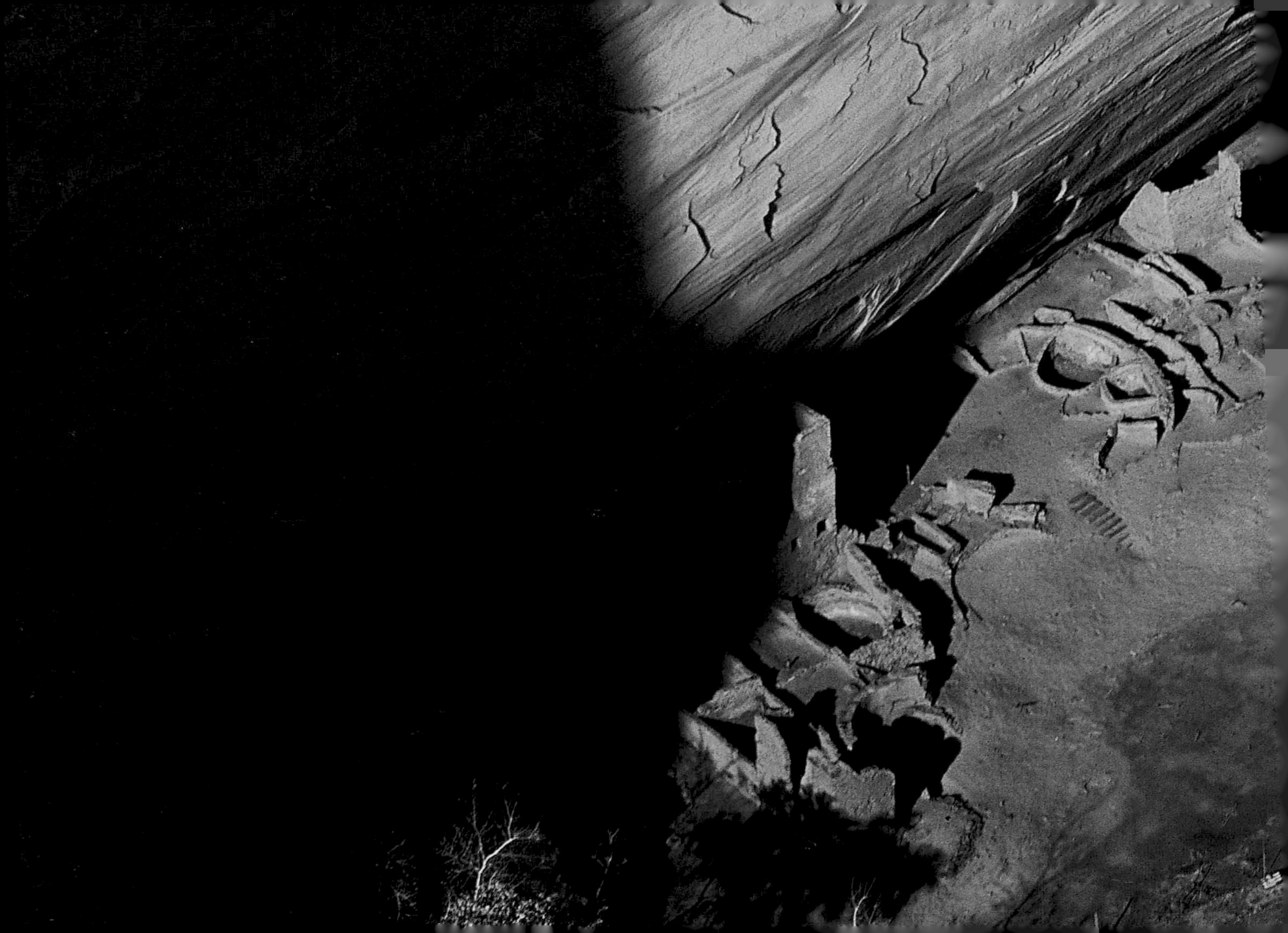

238-239
Running Antelope Ruins, in Canyon del Muerto, are remains of the ancient Anasazi culture which flourished in this area from about 500 to 1300. Canyon de Chelly National Monument.

MIRRORS OF LIGHT

FLYING HIGH

246
The shiny Blue Mouse Cove stretches in Glacier Bay National Park, Alaska.

247 left
Wachusett Inlet cuts its way across the Glacier Bay National Park, Alaska.

247 center
In Glacier Bay National Park, Alaska, tributaries stripe the surface of Skidmore Bay with sediments.

247 right
Woody islands cluster in the entrance to North Indian Pass, Glacier Bay National Park, Alaska.

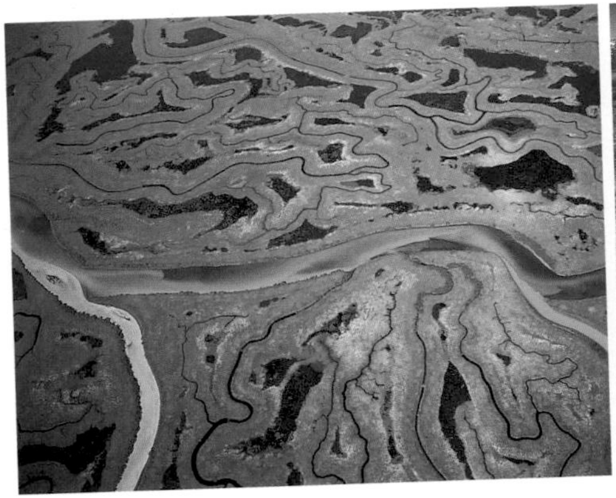

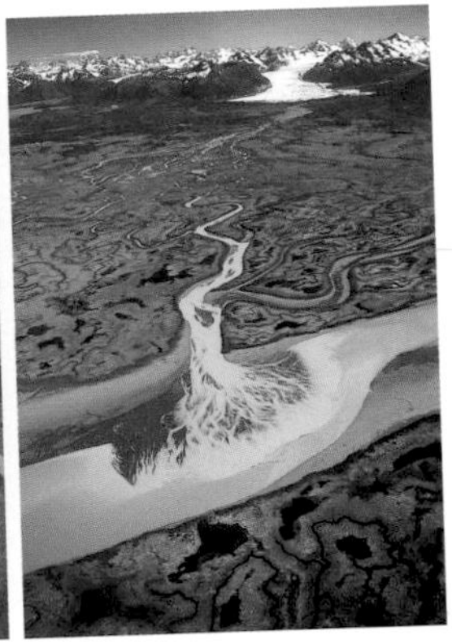

248 and 249

The Copper River Delta (left and center) creates "camouflage" patterns toward the Gulf of Alaska, near Cordova, Alaska. Chugach Mountains (right), in the distance, rise above the Sheridan Glacier in the foreground.

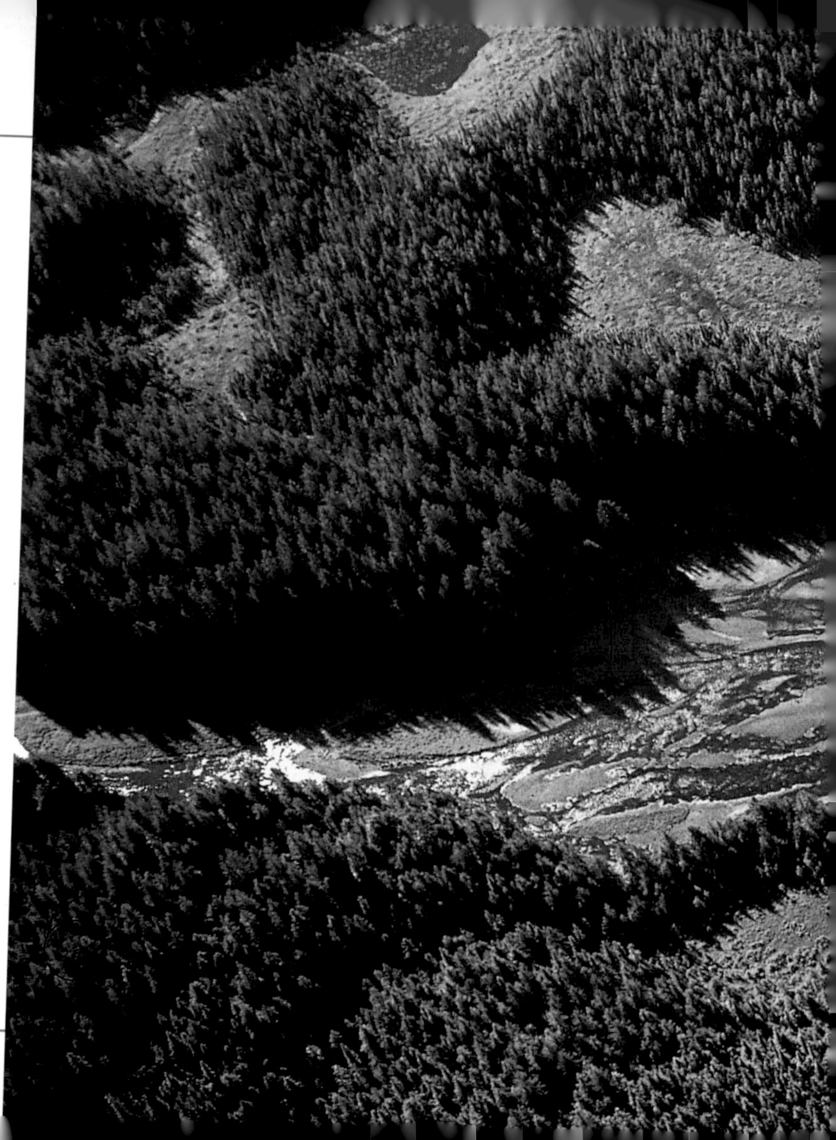

250-251
A fishing craft floats just off shore from the colorful small river delta of Jordan Creek, in Galena Bay, of Prince William Sound, Alaska.

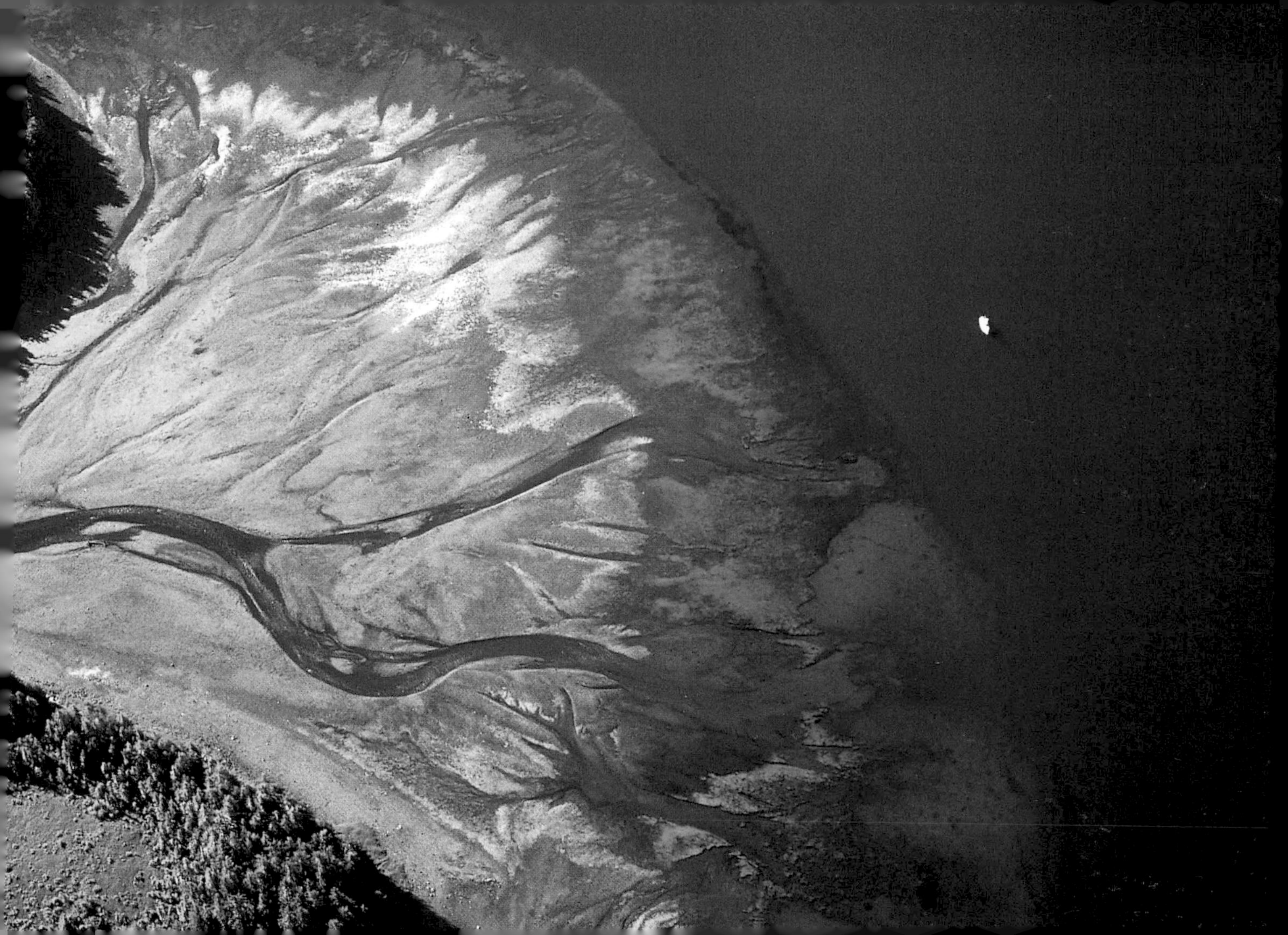

252 left

Wizard Island, a small volcanic cone, rises in Crater Lake National Park, Oregon.

252 right and 253

The Crater Lake caldera was formed about 5700 BC by the explosive eruption and collapse of Mt. Mazama. The volcanic cone of Wizard Island formed in about 3000 BC. The lake is famous for its 2000 feet depth, and its clear, incredible blue reflecting waters.

254 and 255

Yosemite Falls, in Yosemite National Park, California, are the world's fifth highest (1,430 feet) falls and have an average spring flow of 300 cubic feet per second.

256-257
Imperial Valley meets the Salton Sea in Southern California. The water which fills the saline sea and irrigates the valley all comes from the Colorado River. The Imperial Valley, which lies within the Sonoran Desert, is America's vegetable garden.

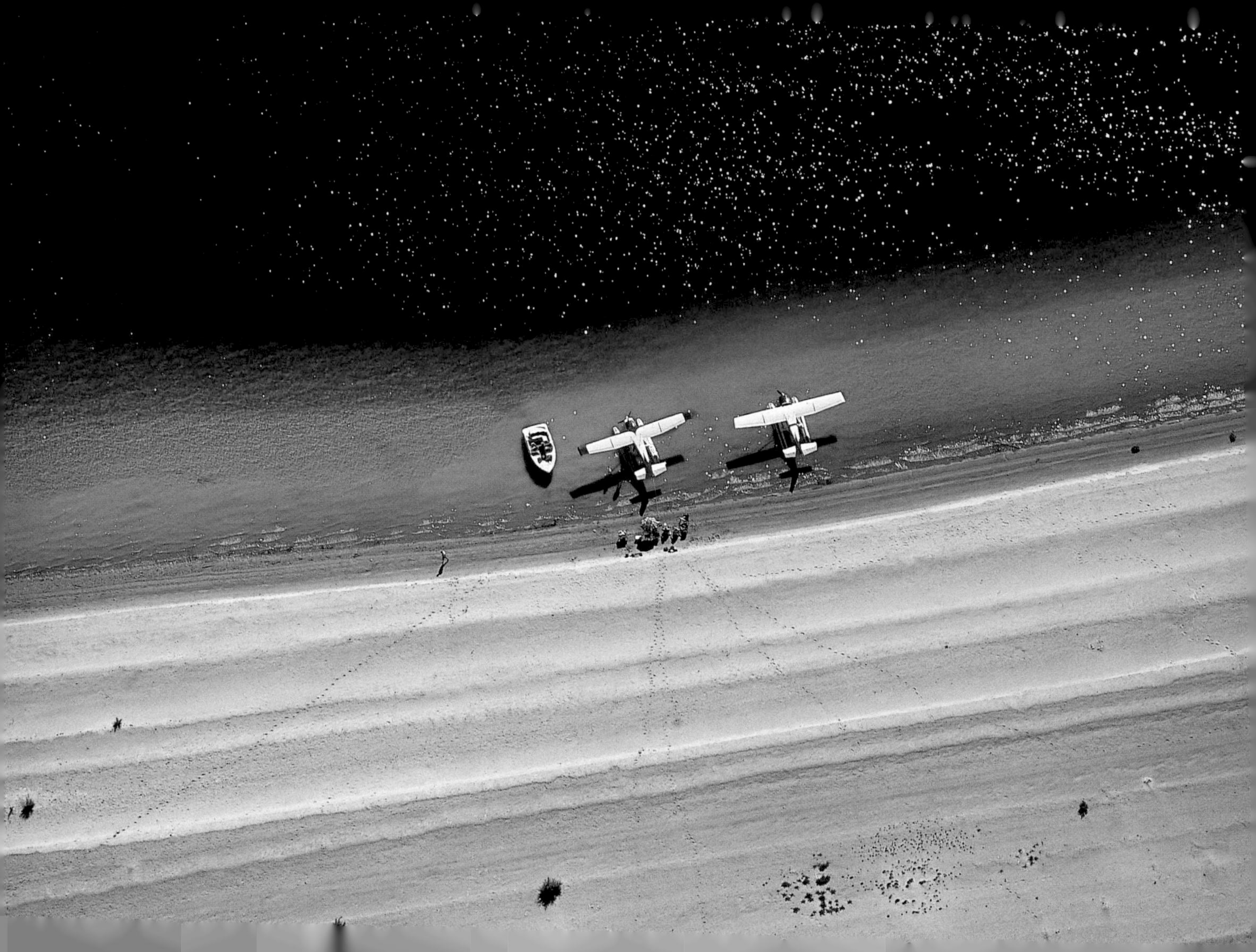

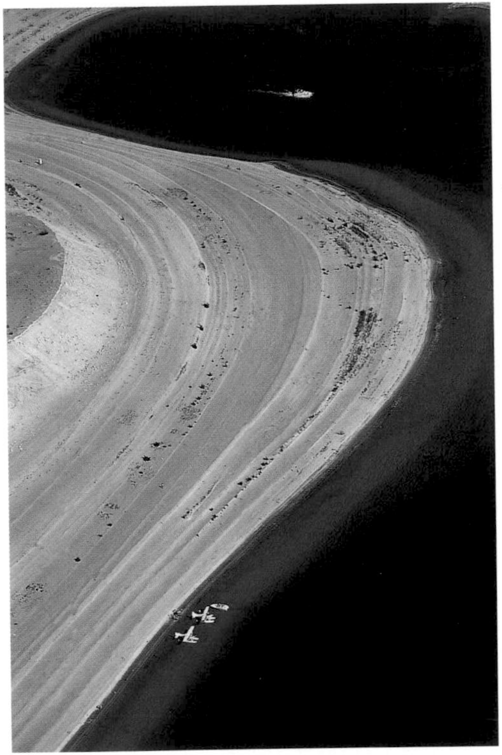

258

Lake Meade, in the Clark County, Nevada, is formed by Hoover Dam on the Colorado River. Hoover Dam, the first of the two great barrages on the Colorado River, was completed in 1935.

259

A pair of float planes enjoys the beach at the southern end of Lake Mead.

260
A railroad causeway crosses the Great Salt Lake, Utah, from Promontory Point westward. At Promontory Point on may 10, 1869 the tracks of America's first transcontinental railroad were joined.

261
Salt evaporation ponds draw geometric shapes on Great Salt Lake, Utah. The Great Salt Lake, a remnant of the giant pre-historic Lake Bonneville, is four times saltier than the oceans. Salt production is a major industry of the lake.

262 and 263 left

San Juan River arm of Lake Powell flows in great bends across Glen Canyon National Recreation Area and Navajo Indian Reservation, Utah.

263 right

Padre Bay is the largest expanse of water in Lake Powell, Utah, The lake itself was created in 1966 by the completion of the Glen Canyon Dam, Arizona.

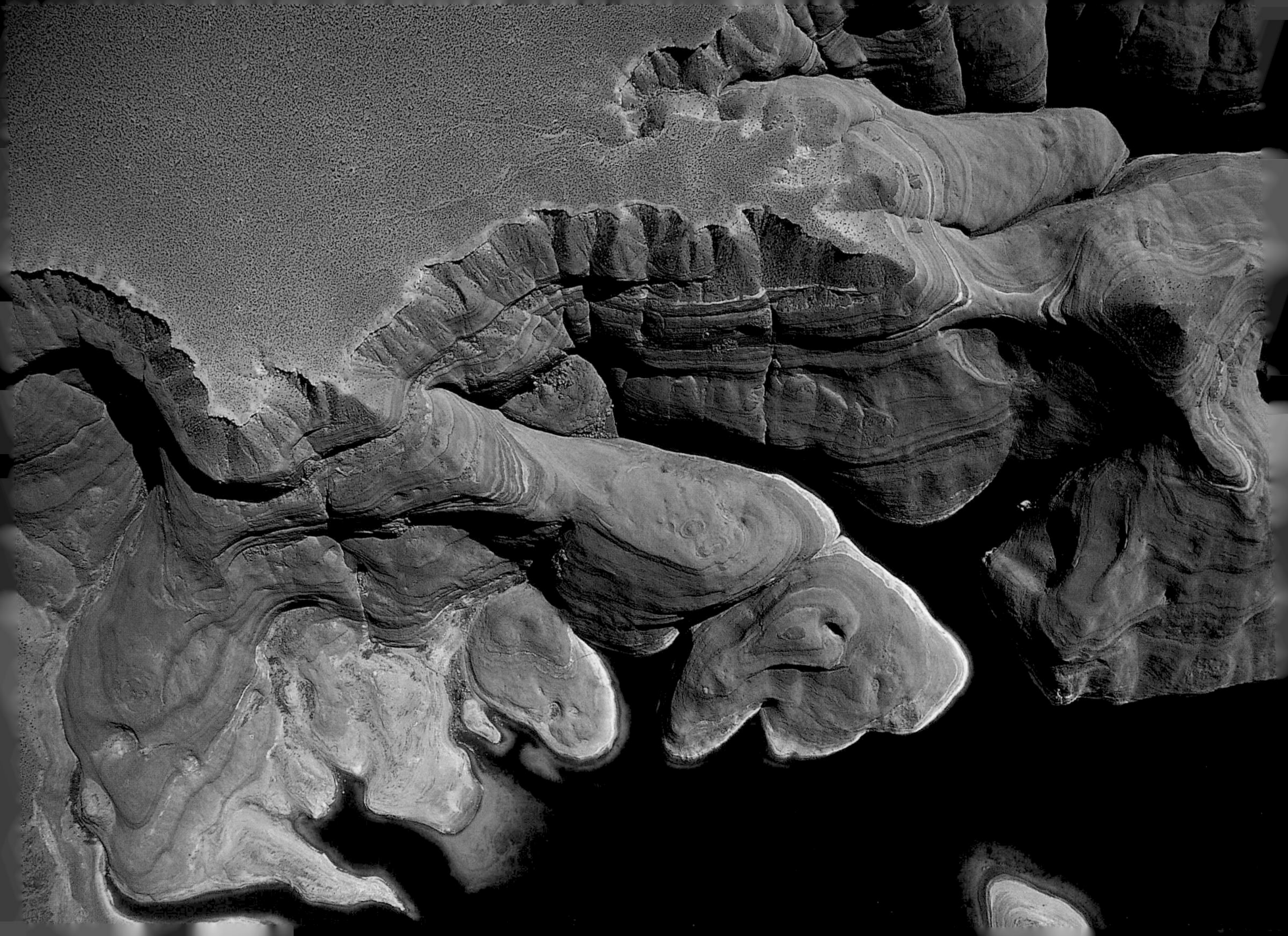

Mirrors of light

264
Bullfrog Basin on the Colorado River arm of Lake Powell is the most visited of the lake's recreation areas.

265
A small craft explores a slot canyon, Lake Powell, Glen Canyon National Recreation Area, Utah.

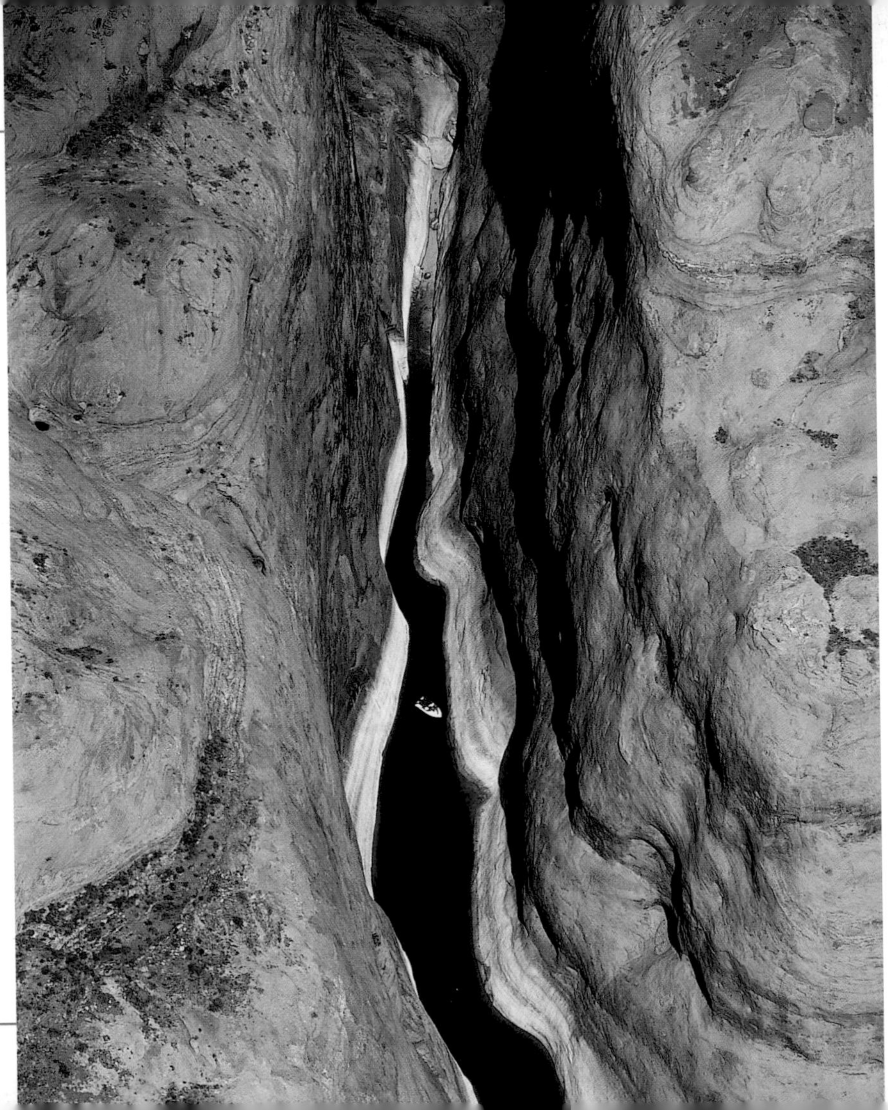

Mirrors of light

266
The Colorado River Gorge grooves deeply in rock layers southwest of Moab, Grand County, Utah.

267
River arms join at the Gooseneck, Colorado River Gorge, Grand County, Utah.

268

The Glen Canyon Dam at Page, Arizona was begun in 1956 and completed ten years later. It can generate 1.3 million kw and at peak flow passes 15 million gallons per minute through its turbines.

269

The Glen Canyon Dam backs up water in the Colorado River's Glen Canyon for more than 100 miles. The dam created Lake Powell, one of America's most beautiful natural areas.

270
Dead trees emerge from the frozen surface of Lake Pueblo, Arkansas River, Pueblo County, Colorado.

271
These dead trees were allowed to remain as Lake Pueblo was formed by the Pueblo Dam. They provide habitat for bald eagles and other large birds.

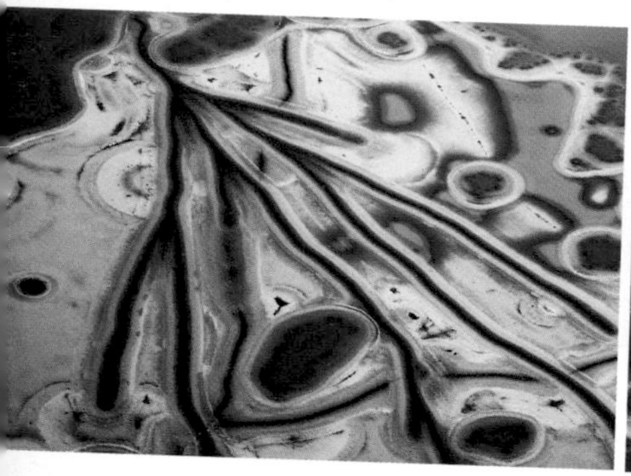

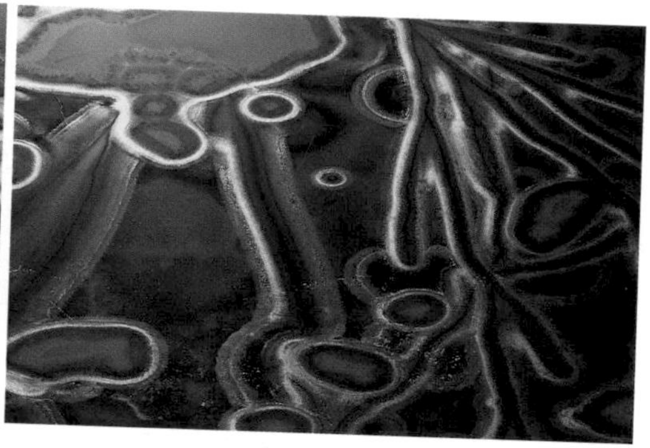

272 and 273

The ice crack patterns on the surface of Lake Pueblo, Colorado, formed when the ice cracked in extreme cold night temperatures. The water beneath then wells up through the cracks, spread out, and then quickly refreezes.

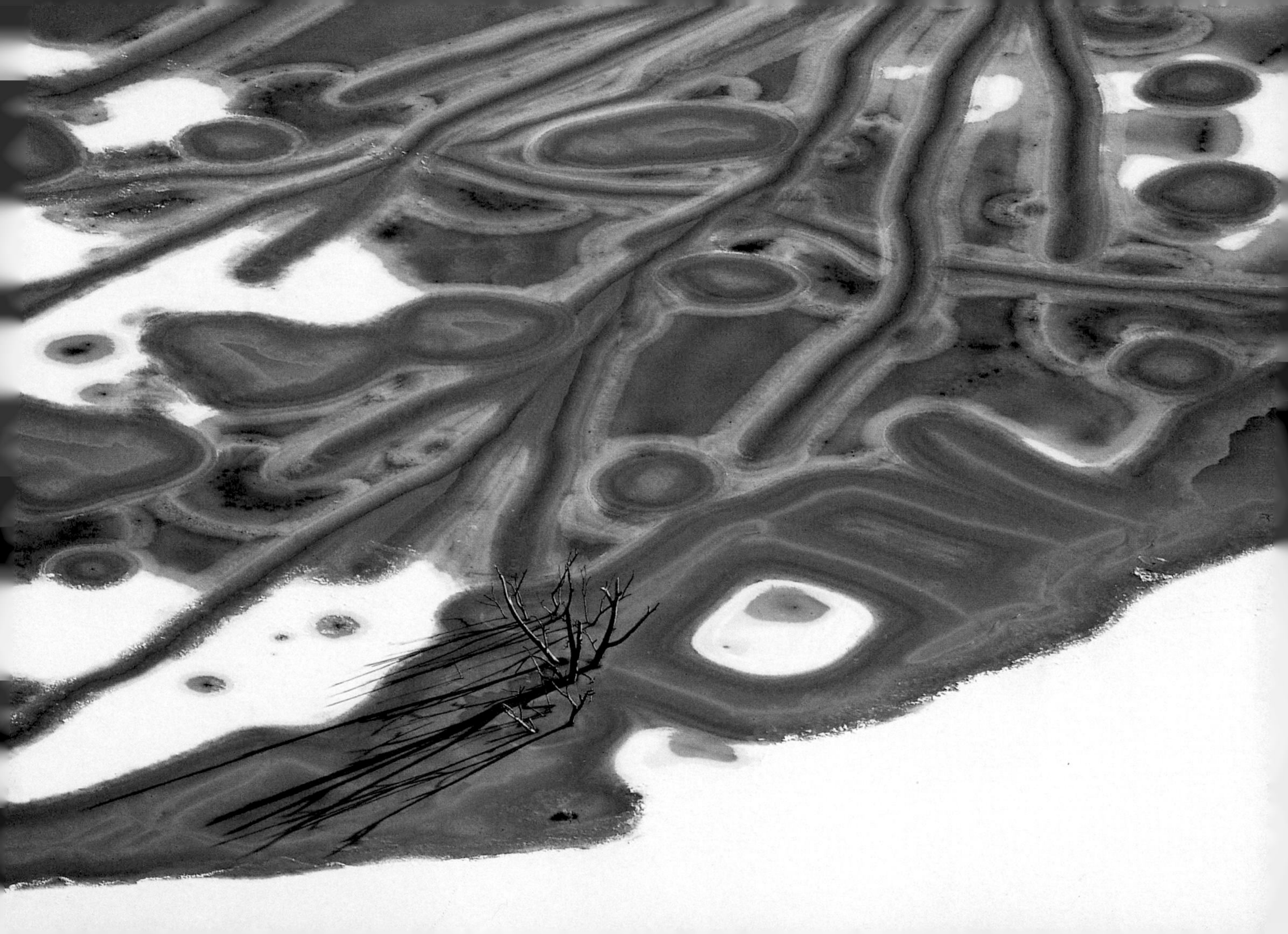

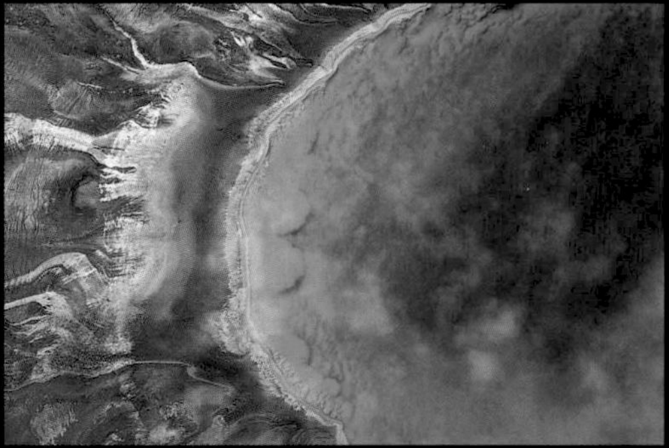

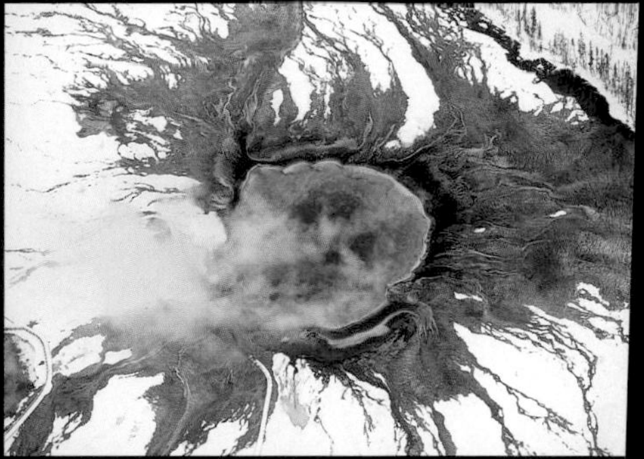

274 and 275
A boardwalk allows visitors to approach the lower geyser basin of the Grand Prismatic Spring, in Yellowstone National Park. The various colors riming the spring are from different algae species which in inhabit different temperature zones. The central blue water is too hot to support algae life.

276-277
Roaring in a snowclad gorge, the Yellowstone River tumbles over Lower Yellowstone Falls.

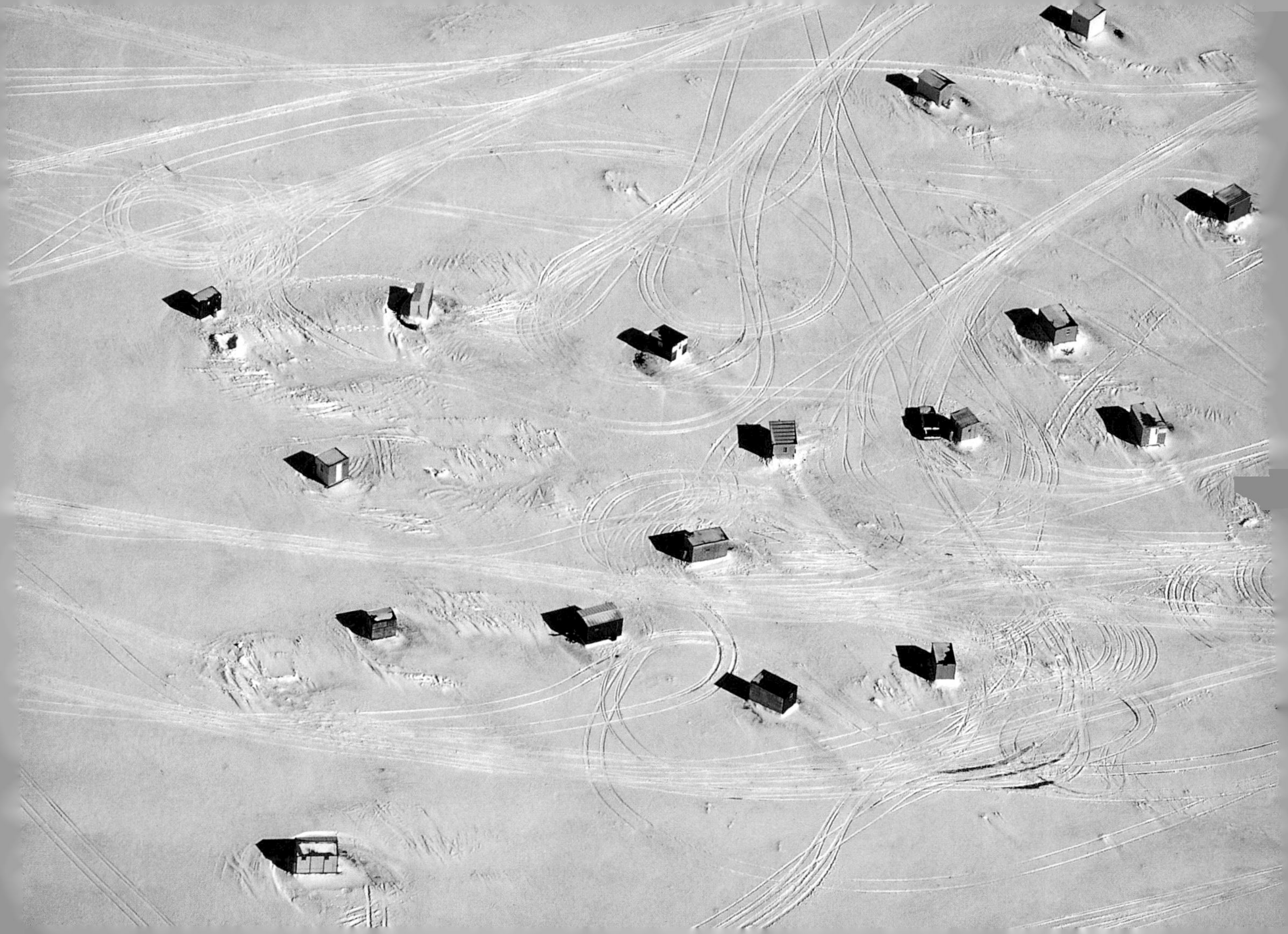

278
Fishing shacks dot Lake Bemidji, Beltrami County, Northern Minnesota. Ice fishing is a religion for some in this part of America.

279
Near Two Harbors, Minnesota, Split Rock faces Lake Superior and is the great lake's most famous and most photographed lighthouse.

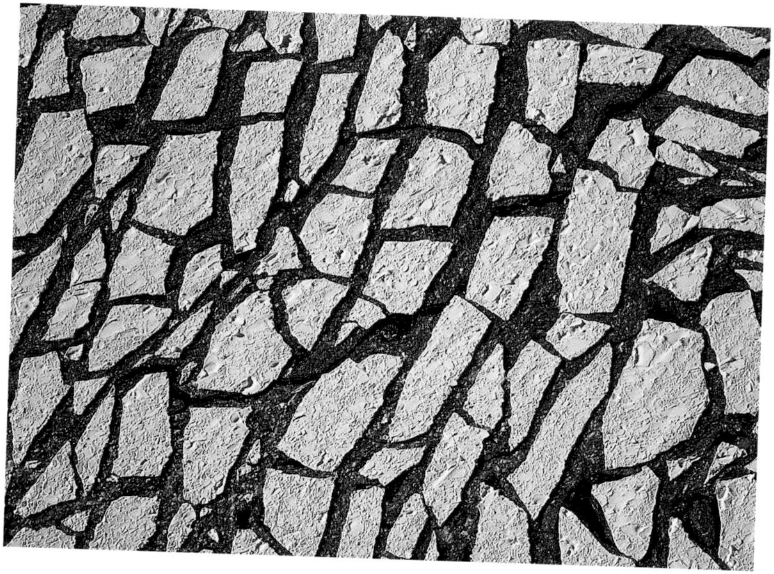

280
Lake Superior ice floes create a natural mosaic near Duluth, Minnesota.

281
At least four mid-water lighthouses are located in the Mackinac Strait, on Lake Michigan: the one above is named Lansing Shoal Lighthouse.

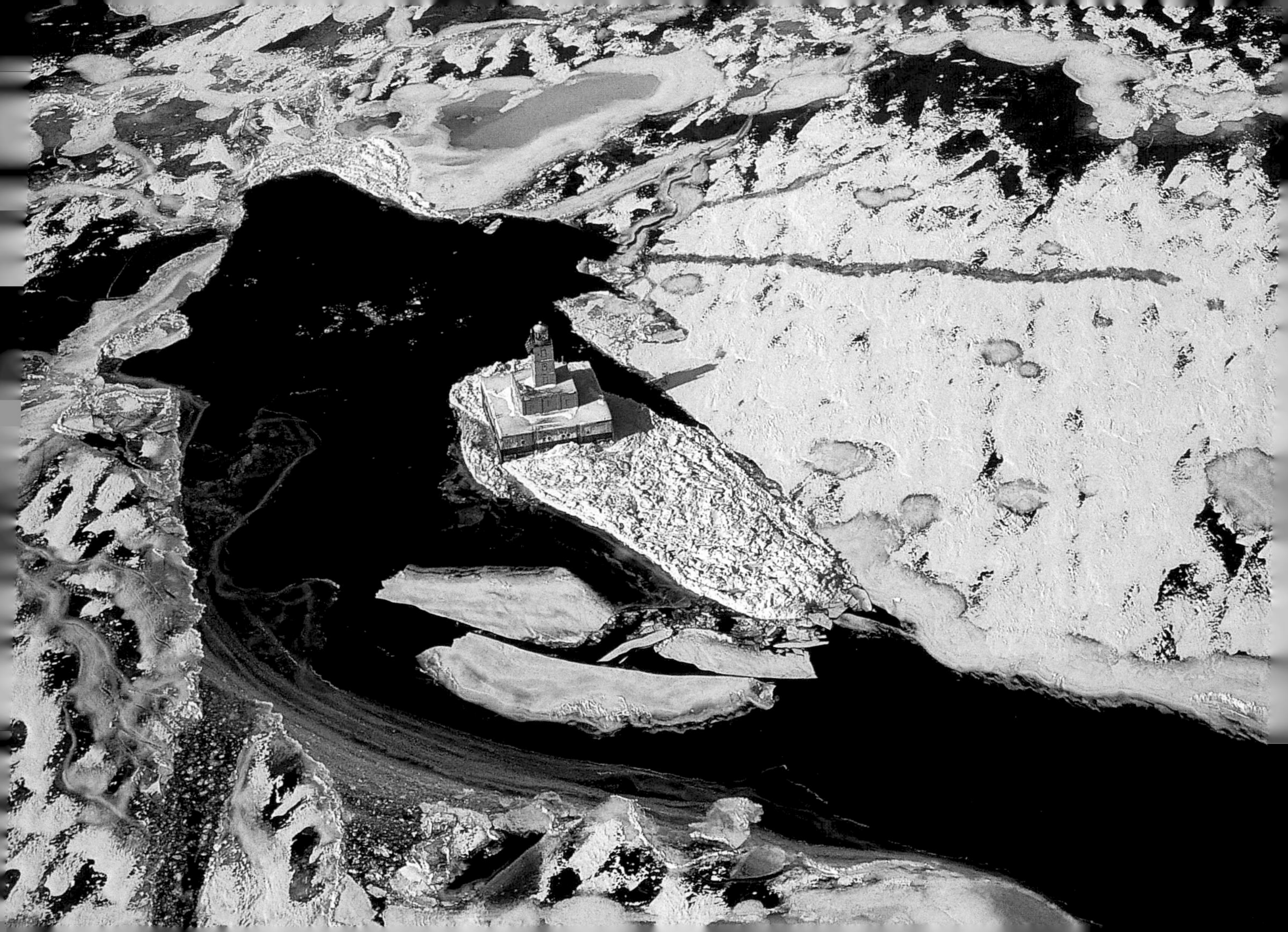

282-283
Mists linger on Pictured Rocks National Lakeshore, Lake Superior, Alger County, Michigan.

284

An inlet enters Lac La Belle, in Bete Grise area, Keweenaw County, Michigan. The Keweenaw Peninsula juts into Lake Superior like the thumb of a right hand. It is famous for its rich native copper deposits.

285

The steamship *Francisco Morazan* ran aground off the south end of South Manitou Island, Lake Michigan, Michigan.

Mirrors of light

286
Mackinac Bridge joins Michigan's lower and upper peninsulas. Its single suspension span of 8614 feet is the longest in the Americas. This five-mile-long bridge connecting the Lakes Michigan and Huron was completed in 1957.

287
Seen here from the north, Grand Island stretches on Lake Superior, Alger County, Michigan.

288

American Falls tumble into the Niagara River, New York.

289

At Niagara Falls, New York/Ontario, the Canadian Horseshoe Falls are at the top of the photo, American Falls at lower left.

290

Niagara Falls, New York/Ontario: the tour boat *Maid* on the mist near the foot of Horseshoe Falls. The falls average 170 feet in height.

291

Niagara Falls, New York/Ontario the *Maid on the mist* turns around approaching Horseshoe Falls.

292-293

Little Blue Run Dam creates the stunning lake of the same name, Georgetown, Pennsylvania.

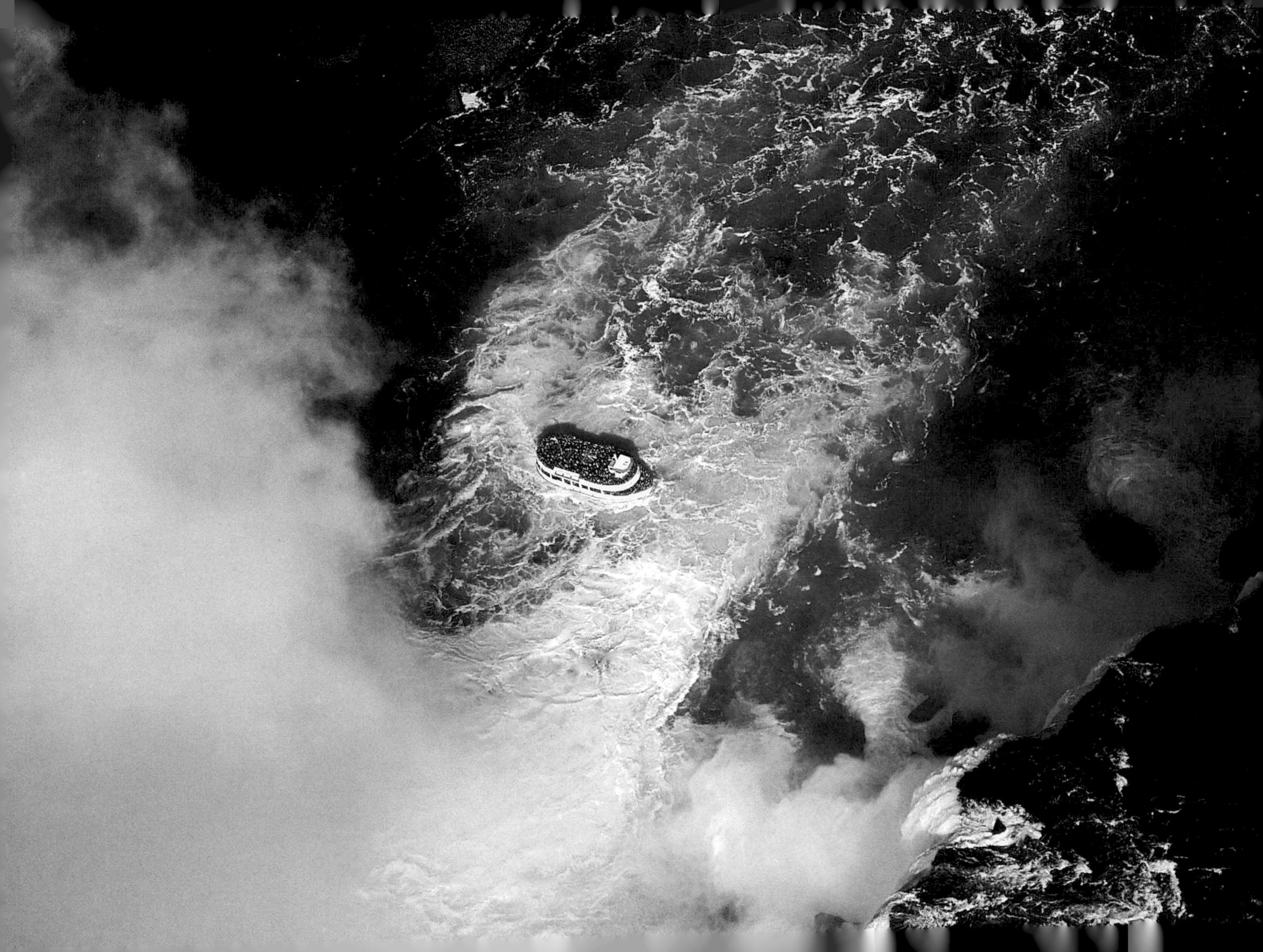

294 and 295
Coldtream and Little Cold Stream flow placidly through Penobscott County, Maine.

296-297
The unorganized territory of 380 square miles, Aroostook County, Maine, is inhabited by fewer than 500 people.

298-299
The White River meanders toward the Mississippi near Augusta, Woodruff County, Arkansas.

300
Lower Missouri River, five miles west of Washington, Missouri.

301
Osage River flows into the Lower Missouri River, Missouri.

302-333
On Lewis and Clark Lake, South Dakota, sand bars line the shore near Springfield.

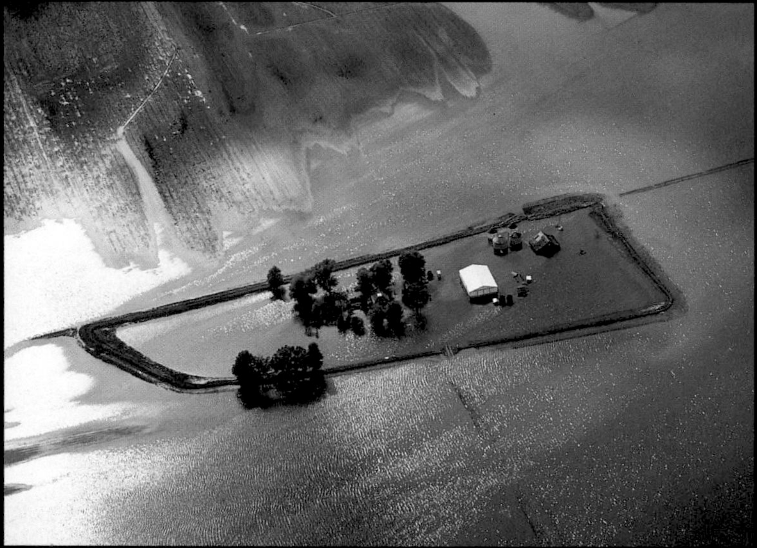

304 and 305

Flooded farms surface near Clarksburg (left) and Jefferson City (right), Mississippi River, Missouri. Flooding on the major rivers of the American Midwest is not uncommon but it is usually controlled by dikes like the one encircling the farm on the left. In the summer months of heavy thunderstorm downpours overwhelmed control structures on the Missouri and Mississippi rivers resulting in scenes like this.

306 and 307 left

Lakes like the R.L. Harris Reservoir (Lake Weedowee) near Birmingham, Alabama, with their hundreds of small coves are a resort developers' dreamworld. The Reservoir was created by a small hydroelectric dam which impounds the Tallapoosa River.

307 right

Resort homes cluster on the shores of Lake Weedowee, Randolph County, Alabama.

308-309

The Mississippi River, is seen here 15 miles south of Memphis, Tennessee. The State of Mississippi is on the left, Arkansas on the right. View looks south. The Mississippi stretches 2,350 miles from almost the Canadian border to the Gulf of Mexico.

310

Sargent, close to the the Gulf of Mexico, Texas, is a fishing and water recreation community.

311

The layout of Sargent radiates on Caney Creek. The Gulf Intracoastal Waterway passes across the top of the photo just inside the narrow barrier beach. Gulf of Mexico surf can be seen on the beach.

312

Barge fleet in the Houston Ship Canal, Houston, Texas.

313

Gulf Intracoastal Waterway at Matagora, Texas runs about 1500 miles from the southern tip of Texas to northwest Florida.

314-315

The tidal wetlands like these, in Beanfort Inlet, North Carolina, are essential to sustaining a healthy fishery.

316 and 317

The Everglades in Monroe County, Florida: the Indians called it a "River of Grass," white settlers called it a swamp. Whatever the name, it's a World Heritage treasure. Much of the Everglades is a sawgrass prairie with a river that flows 50 miles wide and one foot deep.

318-319

The Everglades are the only sub-tropical area of the continental United States, it is a place of manatees, snakes, cougars, long-legged birds, and the only place in the world where crocodiles and alligators live together.

LOFTY HORIZONS

FLYING HIGH

321
Sangre de Cristo Mountain Range rises in Colorado (left); Hopkins Inlet is a tidewater fjord in Glacier Bay National Park, Alaska (right).

Mountains are the core of the Earth boldly penetrating and intruding on human habitation and industrial activity. Only the sea and its shores exceed them as a source for recreational activity and nourishment of the human spirit. Like no other feature on the planet, mountains provide a picture and graphic representation of the Earth and its history since the beginning of its time. They provide humankind with a source of spiritual energy and material wealth like no other natural feature. Whilst both mountains and seashores are a source of spiritual renewal, mountains are the high-energy and adventure-thrusting messengers and agents. Even if we do not go to them, most of us through contemplation at some time partake of this energy.

Mountain flying is always a challenge and mountain aerial photography could be called extreme mountain flying. The mix of high winds, rapidly changing weather and reduced aircraft performance in the thin air provide a constant challenge. But for those who go there that's what mountains are about. The challenge of flying, hiking, climbing, skiing, crossing, and extracting mineral and timber wealth are all met with a special sense of accomplishment if done "in the mountains."

Mountains are formed by several processes and are present on every landmass and on every sea bottom. Orogeny is the process of mountain building which begins with forces deep beneath the Earth's crust. Huge areas, many thousands of square miles, of the Earth's surface can be thrust upward over many millions of years by these forces. The result is a faulted, folded, metamorphosed pile of rocks, which can have risen by tens of thousands of feet. Sometimes these rocks are

322
Sunrise strike a high peak in the San Juan Mountains, Colorado.

323

326-327
Mt Russell impends Chedotlothna Glacier, Alaska Range, in Denali National Park, Alaska.

328

Seen here on a rare cloud free day, Mt Mckinley, in Denali National Park, Alaska, is the highest elevation in United States, 20,320 feet.

329

In this view to the north, Mt Foraker rises in the foreground, with the huge massif of Mt Mckinley in distance, Denali National Park, Alaska.

330 left

Glaciers cut their way down the St. Elias Mountains, Alaska, Wrangell-St. Elias National Park.

330 right

Chisana Glacier stretches in Wrangell-St. Elias National Park, Alaska.

331

High in the Tongass National Forest, huge ice tongues form the Meade Glacier, near the Alaska-British Columbia border.

332
White is snow, blue is water, gray is ice in this vertical view of Kahiltna Glacier, in Denali National Park, Alaska.

333
The rugged surface of Chisana Glacier, in Wrangell-St. Elias National Park, Alaska, is scattered with blue glacial lakes.

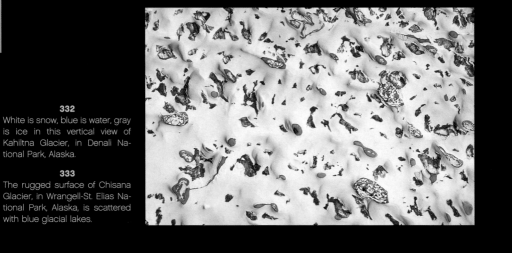

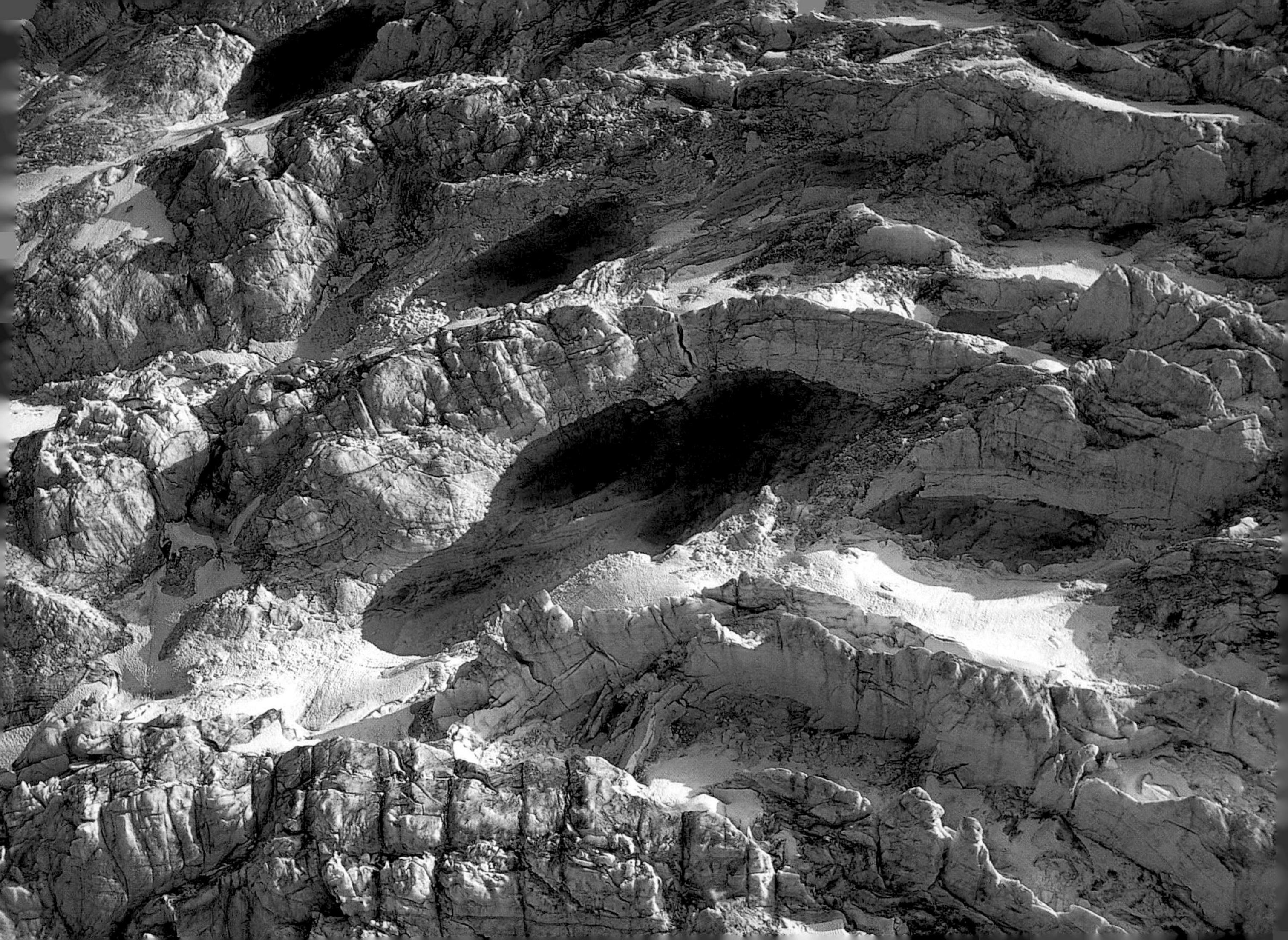

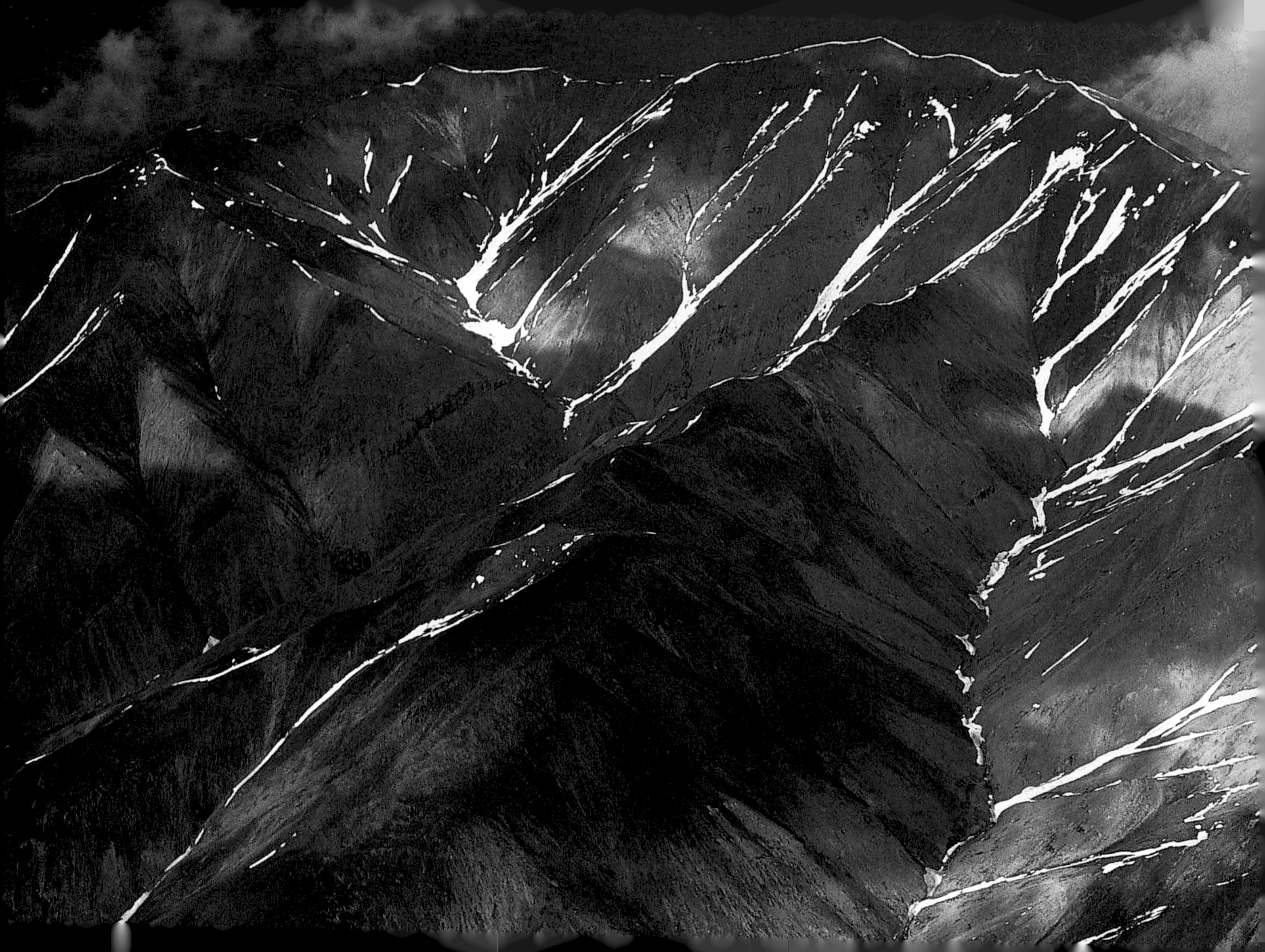

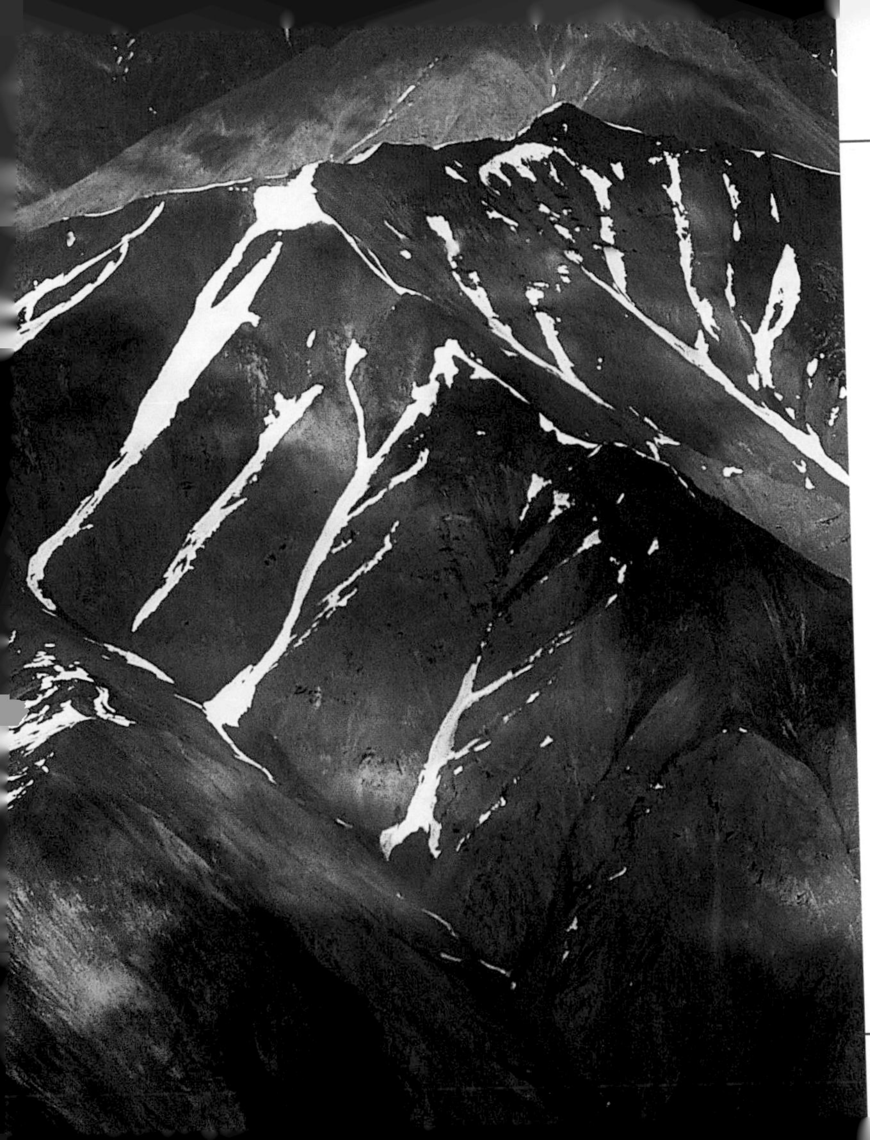

334-335
Ribbon-like snow fields mark the slopes of Smith Mountains, in the Brooks Range, Northern Alaska.

336

Mt. St. Helens Crater shines in pure white and blue at dawn, in Mt. St. Helens National Volcanic Monument Cascade Range, Washington.

337

Mount Hood reaches 11,235 feet in altitude above the Hood River Wilderness, Oregon.

338-339
An orange-colored sky at dawn may recall the volcanic fire: the eruption of 18 May 1980 stripped 1,314 feet from the top of Mt. St. Helens, lowering its elevation from 9,677 to 8,363 feet.

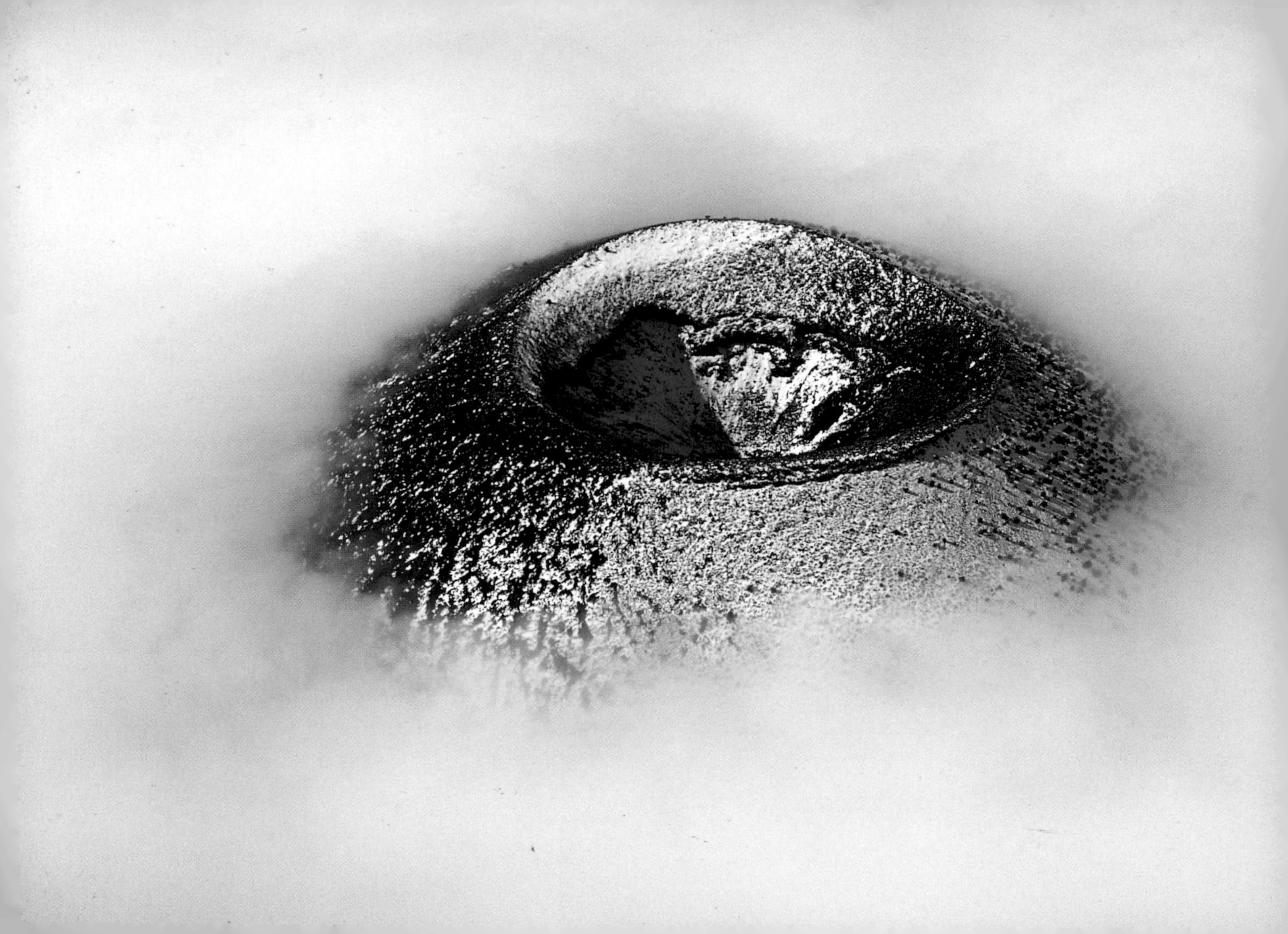

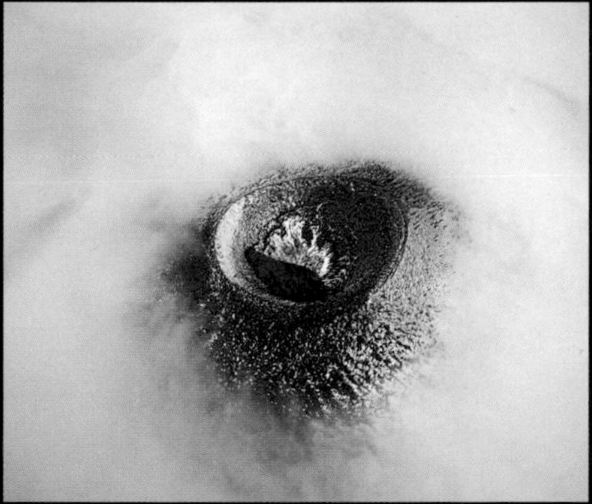

340

One of the Strawberry Craters surfaces the mists in the San Francisco Volcanic Field, Coconino County, Arizona.

341 left

The San Francisco Volcanic Field has more than 600 craters 50.000 to 100.000 years old.

341 right

The Humphreys Peak, in the background, is seen here from above the cinder cone of Sunset Crater. This volcano was formed about AD 1065 and is the youngest one in the United States. Sunset Crater Volcano National Monument, Coconino County, Arizona.

342
The volcanic core of Devils Tower, in Devils Tower National Monument, Crooks County, Wyoming, stands 900 feet above its base. In 1906 president Teddy Roosevelt made it America's First National Monument.

343
Cochise Stronghold, in the Dragon Mountains, is where the Apache Chief Cochise with a band of 200 warriors held out against the U.S. Army from 1861 to 1874. Cochise County, Southeast Arizona.

344 and 345

The crest of the Chinese Wall forms a segment of the continental divide of the United States and seperates waters flowing to the Atlantic and Pacific Oceans. The Wall also forms part of the Rocky Mountain Front. Bob Marshall Wilderness, Flathead County, Montana.

346

Grand Teton Peak (13770 feet) is the apex of Grand Teton National Park, Teton County, Wyoming.

347

Clouds shroud some of the Lesser Peaks of the Teton Range.

348
Day breaks on Humboldt Peak (14,064 feet), Custer County, Colorado.

349
The peaks in this photo, part of the Sangre de Cristo Range, between Custer and Saguache Counties, Colorado, are all above 13,000 feet.

350-351
Flanked by the Crestone Needles, Crestone Peak culminates at 14,294 feet in the Sangre de Cristo Mountains.

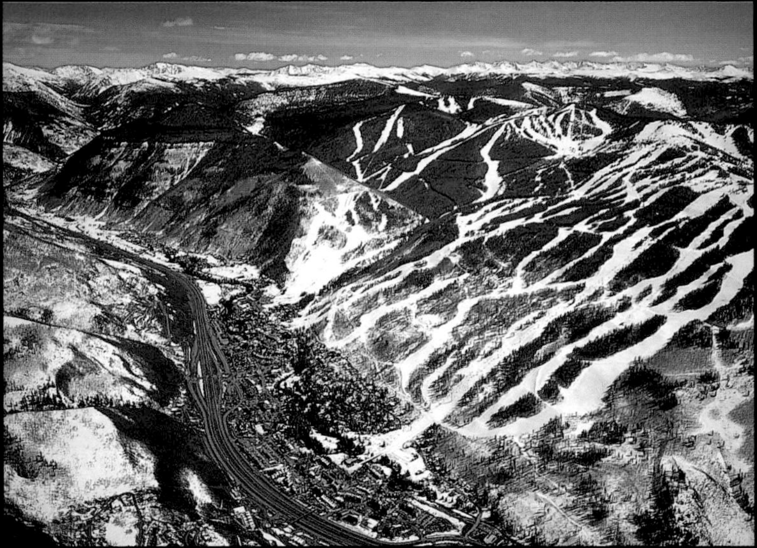

352 and 353

Both the Beaver Creek Ski Area, in Eagle County, Colorado (left), and the town of Aspen with its ski runs, in Pitkin County, Colorado (right), are in the heart of Colorado's ski country.

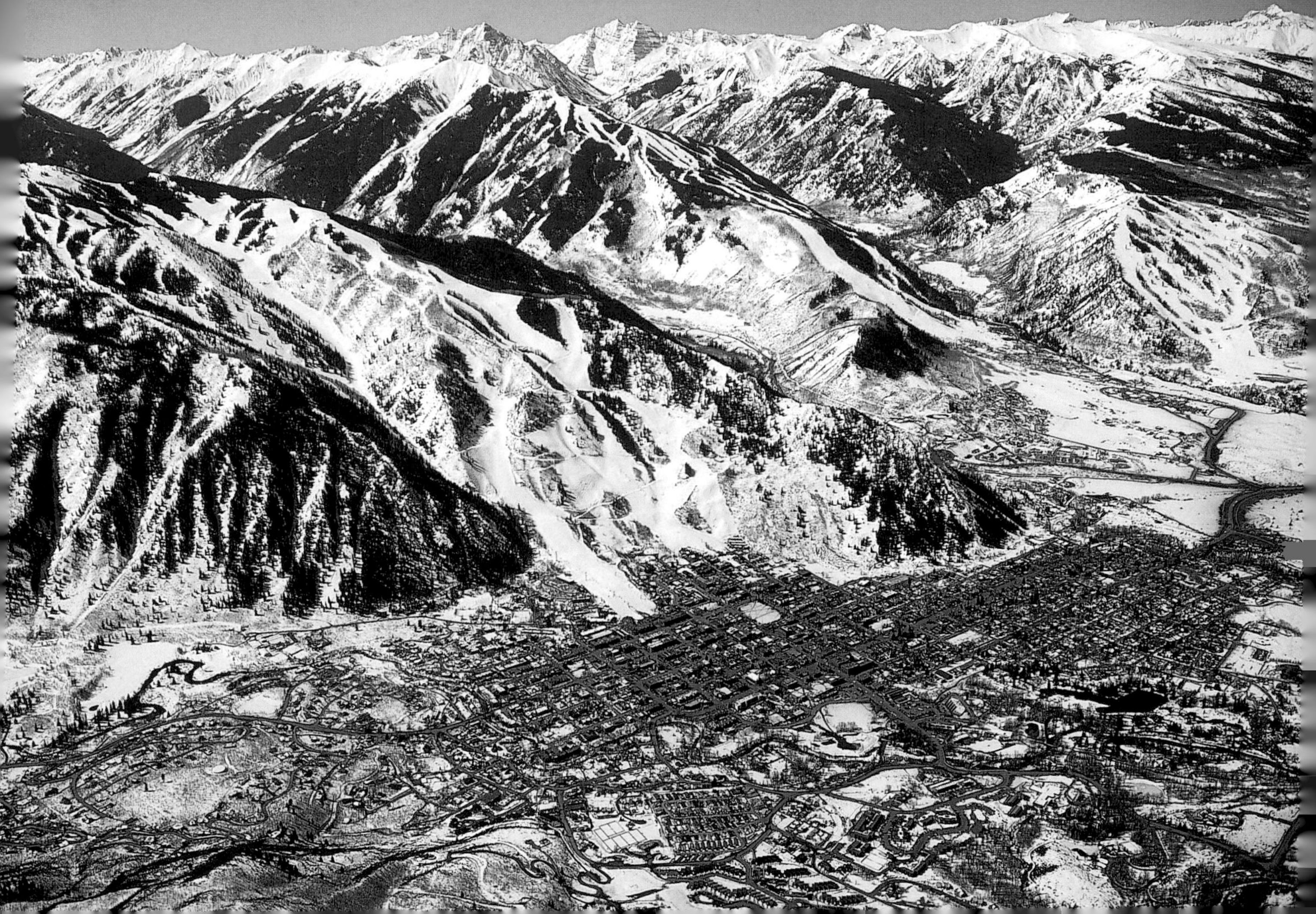

356-357
A mid-winter dawn lights up Colorado's Continental Divide, Hinsdale County, Colorado.

358 and 359
Mauna Kea northeast slope (left), and Mauna Kea "White Mountain" summit (13.796 feet) are seen here after heavy wintersnows. Big Island, Hawaii.

THE REALM OF EMPTINESS

FLYING HIGH

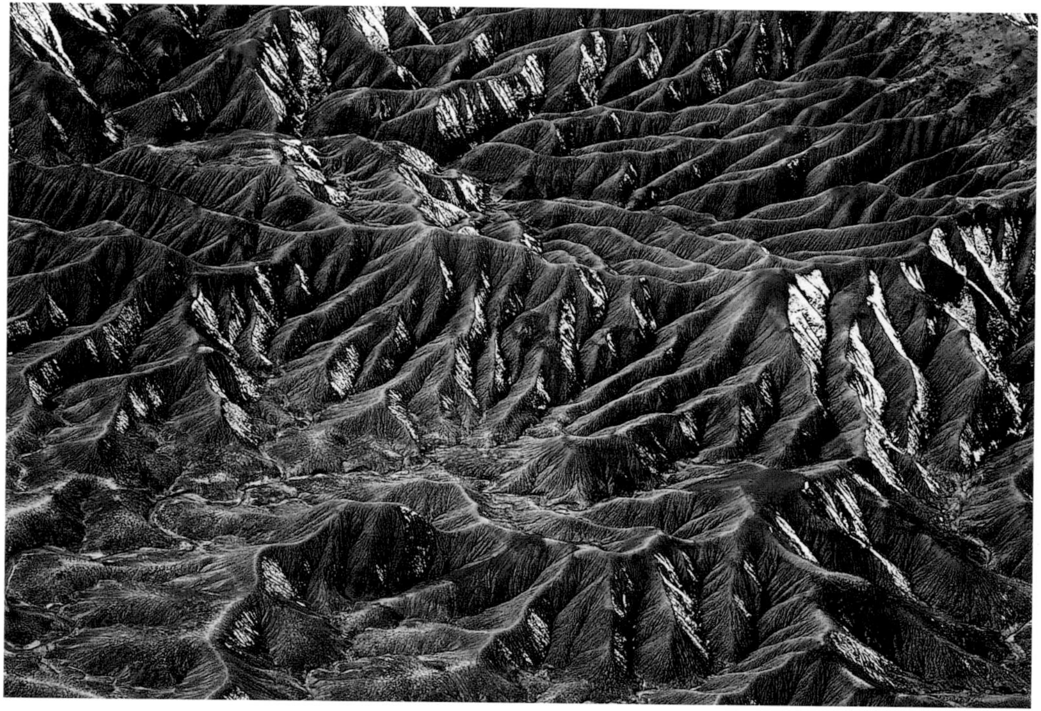

363
A volcanic plug emerges from Hopi Buttes Area, Arizona (left); Little Harcuahala Mountains rise in the northern fringe of the Sonoran Desert, Arizona (right).

Four named deserts cover a large part of the American West. The Sonoran Desert straddles the Arizona-Mexico border. Just east of this is the higher elevation Chihuahuan Desert, also straddling the Mexican border in Arizona, New Mexico and Texas. The largest of the American deserts is the Great Basin Desert that covers all of Nevada, much of Utah, and small portions of Arizona, Idaho and Colorado. This is a colder, wetter, higher desert with elevations averaging between 4000 and 6000 feet. Seasonal temperature swings of 100F, and daily swings of 50°F are common. Rainfall is less than 10 inches in most years but can come in torrential downpours in the summer monsoon season. Travelers are constantly cautioned to be alert for flash floods that can come roaring out of small canyons without warning.

The smallest, yet most famous of the American deserts is the Mojave. Located at the southern tip of Nevada and in a small adjacent part of California it is the home of Death Valley National Park. Death Valley is a land of extremes. The lowest point in the United States is Badwater Basin, elevation 282 ft below sea level. Just a short distance from this lowpoint the land rises 12,000 ft to the top of Telescope Peak. The area receives only two inches of rainfall in an average year and summer temperatures can rise above 130°F. In the late 1800s it was thought Death Valley would be a prosperous mining district. At least eight mining camps sprang up between 1875 and 1904. Most of these were gold and silver camps but the most profitable product extracted was probably the salt mineral, borax. Panamint City

364
Snow sprinkles an expanse of badland hills in Painted Desert, Petrified Forest National Park, Arizona.

365

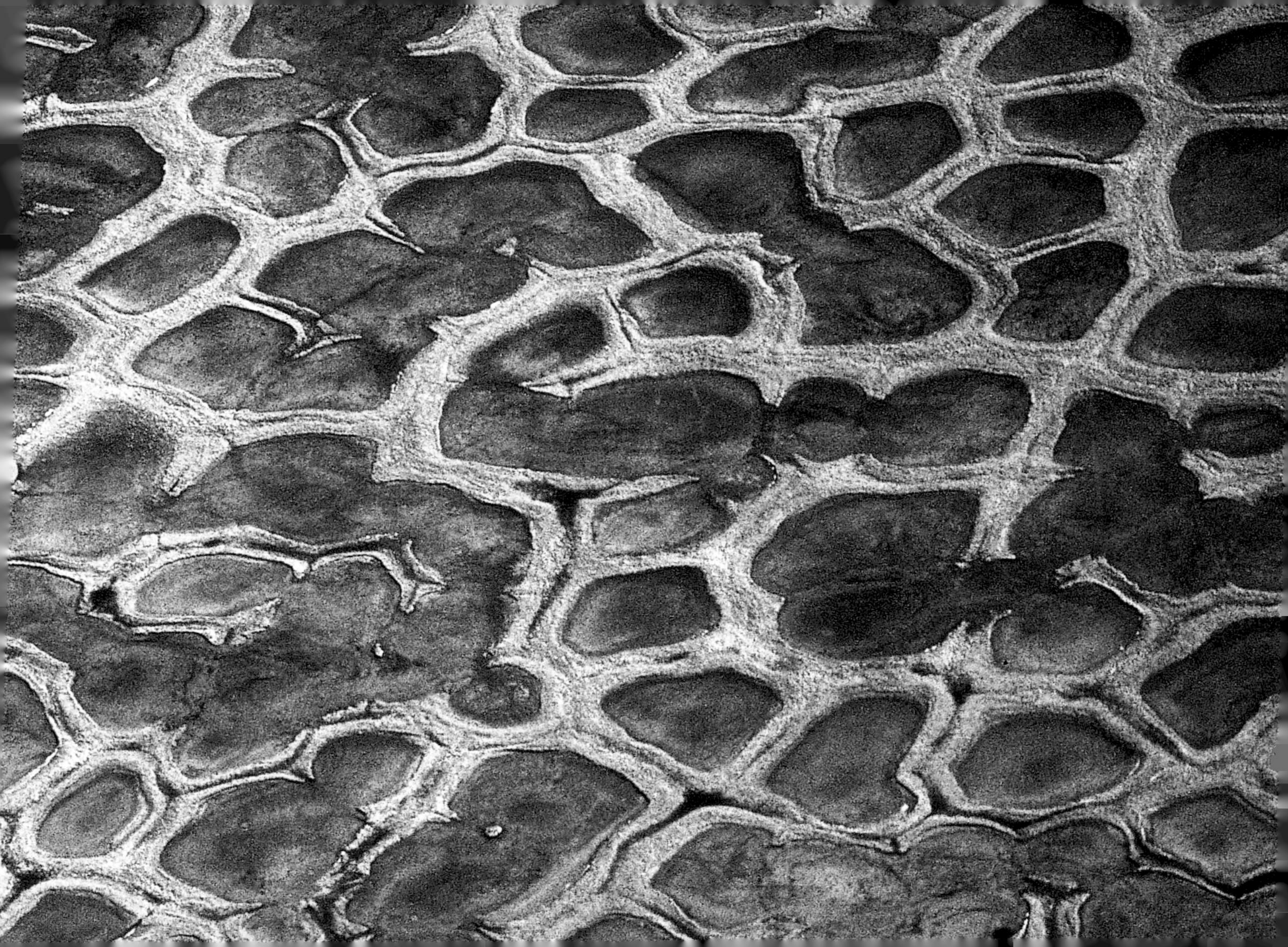

372 and 373
Now almost completely arid, the harsh surface of Death Valley National Park was sculpted by rainwater, wind and gravity only in "recent" geological times. Mojave Desert, California.

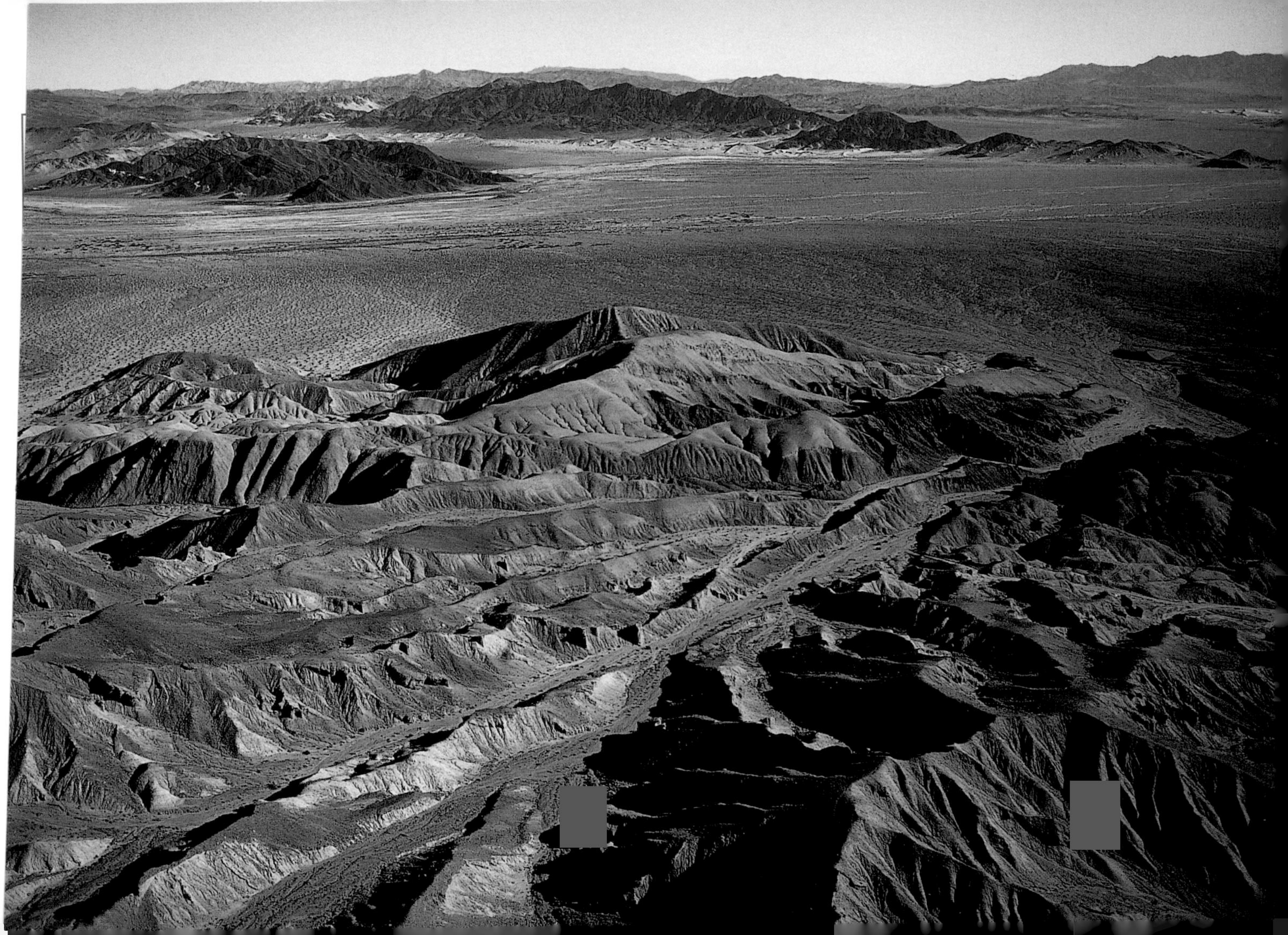

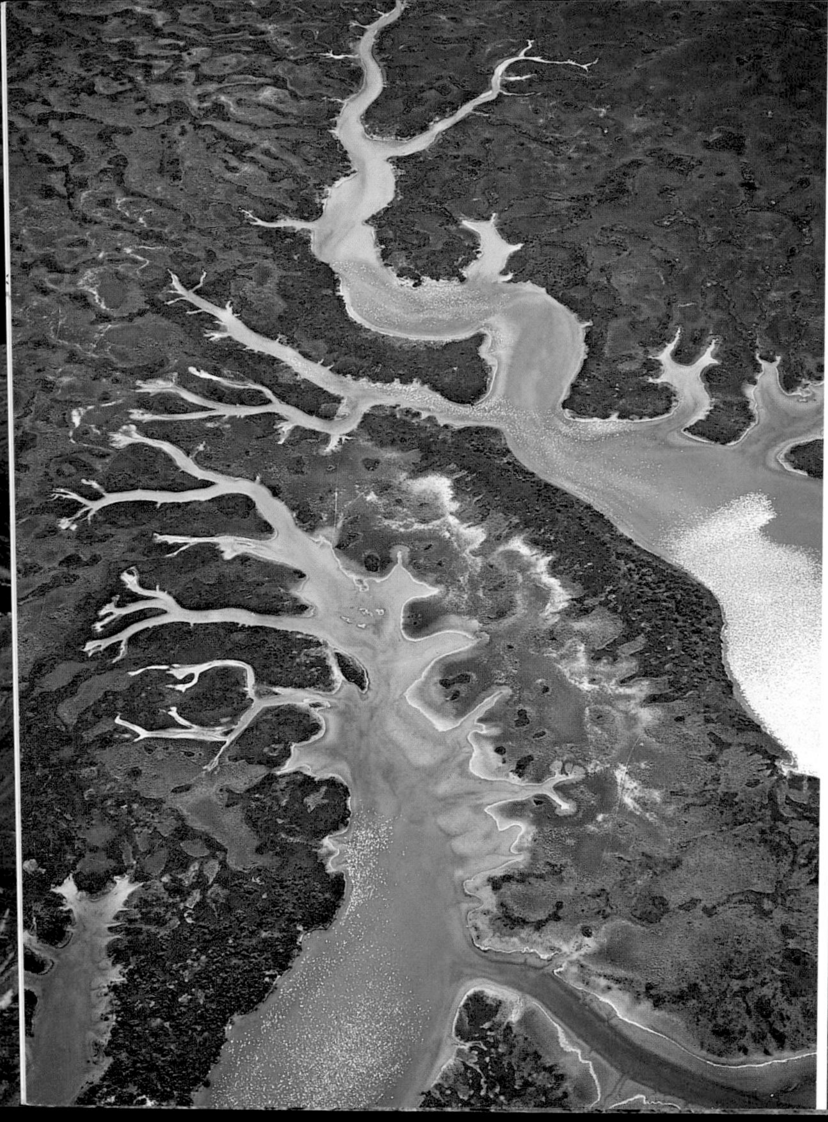

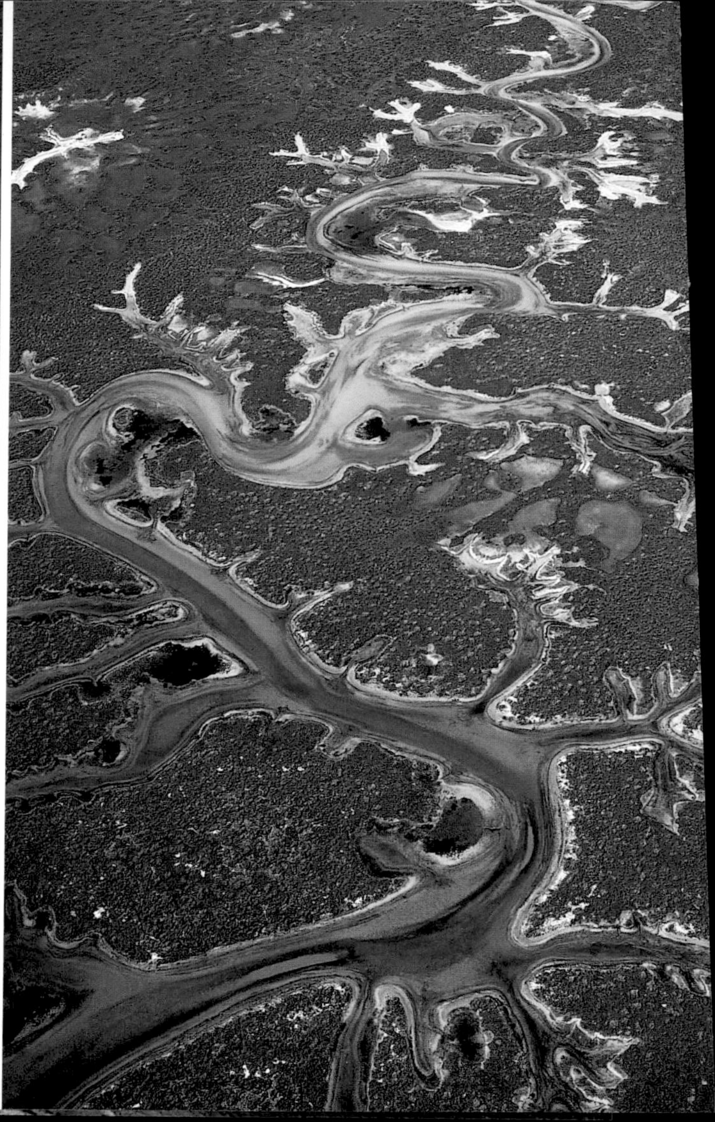

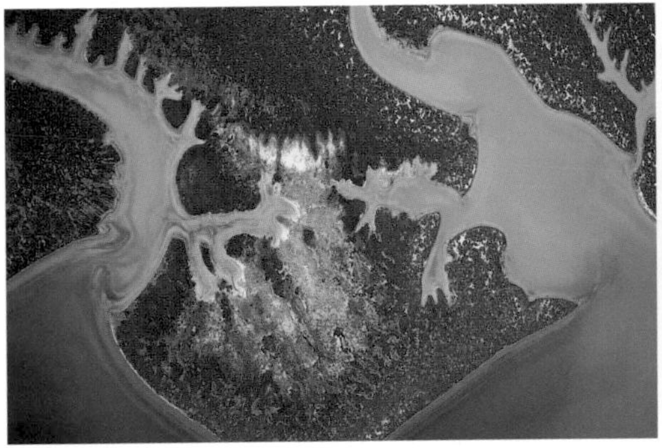

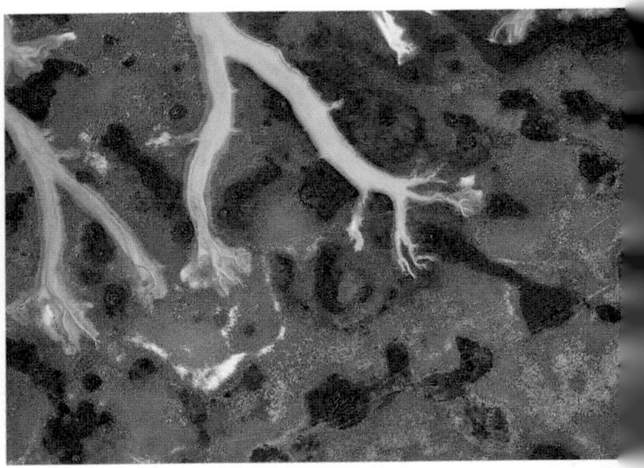

380 and 381
This is what the lake wetlands in Soda Lake area look like after springtime rains. Carrizo Plain Natural Area, San Louis Obispo County, California.

382
Crescent dunes create a huge "X" shape in Big Smoky Valley, Nye County, Great Basin Desert, Nevada.

383
Alluvial outwash radiates from Virgin Mcuntains, Great Basin Desert, Clark County, Nevada.

384-385
Now an abandoned home, once this was a proud passenger rail car, Johnson Mesa, Colfax County, New Mexico.

386
On the right side of the photo there is Tank Mesa, on the left there is Comb Ridge and the Monument Upwarp, La Sal Mountains in the distance. Great Basin Desert, San Juan County, Utah.

387
Small aeolian sand dunes are formed in alignment by prevailing winds. Henry Mountains rise in the distance. San Rafael Desert, Wayne County, Utah.

390

The scrub vegetation scattered amid small sandunes finds pockets of water in Salt Wash, Grand County, Utah.

391

Desert sand washing up against a sandstone outcrop provides a place for moisture to accumulate enabling heartier vegetation to grow in Salt Wash.

392

Looking southeast across the San Rafael Reef, Factory Butte and The Henry Mountains overlook Great Basin Desert, Wayne County, Utah.

393

This bird's eye, or mapping, view shows desert erosion in Red Desert, in Wayne County, Utah.

394 and 395

San Rafael Swell, in Wayne County, Utah, is seen here by the front side of the eastern flank (left) and the back side of the range. The San Rafael Swell is one of America's Premier Geological Areas.

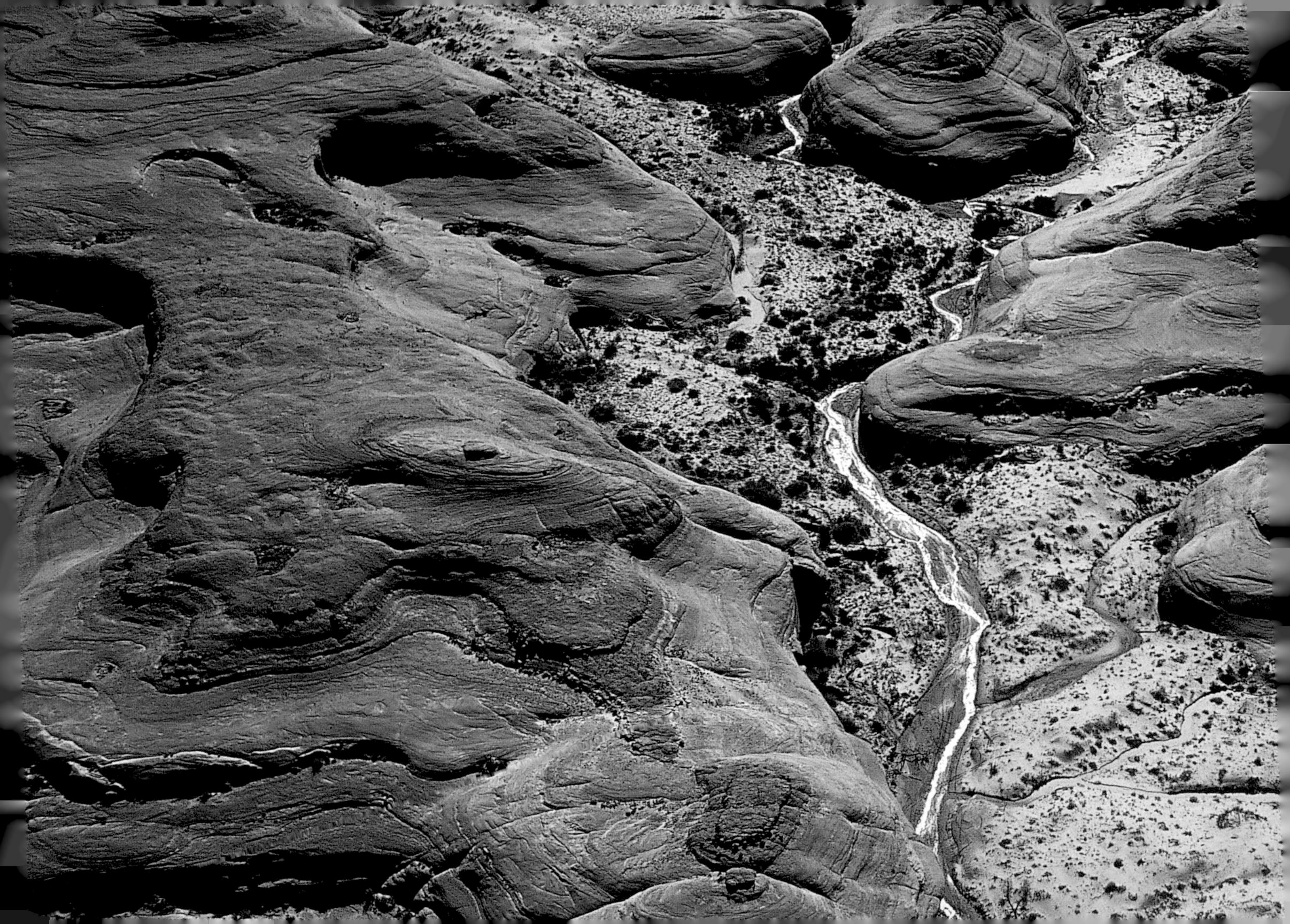

396-397

A small canyon cuts through the red sandstone of the Wheeler Desert, San Rafael Swell Area of Wayne County, Utah.

398
Moenkopi Plateau meets the Painted Desert, Navajo Indian Reservation, Coconino County, Arizona.

399
Dinnebito Wash meanders across Moenkopi Plateau, Hopi Indian Reservation, Coconino County, Arizona.

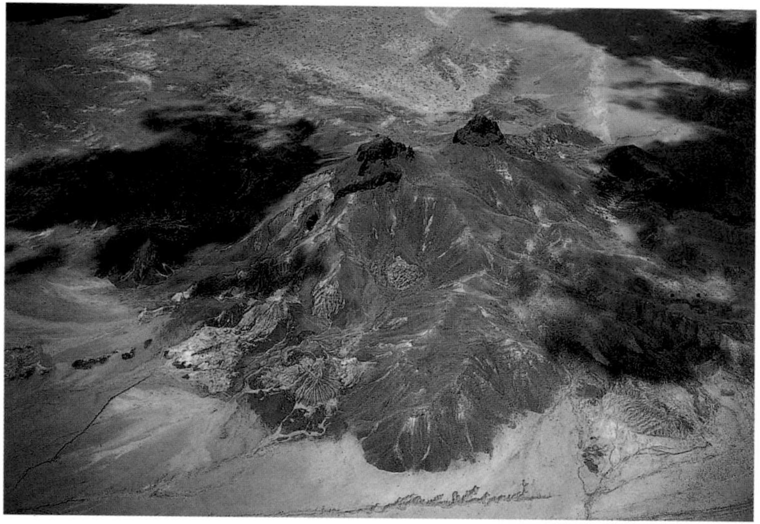

400

A volcanic plug protrudes from the soil in Hopi Buttes Area, Navajo Indian Reservation, Navajo County, Arizona.

401

A boundless landscape characterizes Hopi Buttes Area near Dilkon, Navajo Indian Reservation, Great Basin Desert, Navajo County, Arizona.

402

Desert recreational campers make a stop near the town of Quartzite, Sonoran Desert, Arizona.

403

Created by a meteorite impact, Barringer Meteor Crater was formed 49,000 years ago in today' s Canyon Diablo, Conconino County, Arizona. Mt. Humphreys (12.633 feet) is in the distance.

The realm of emptiness

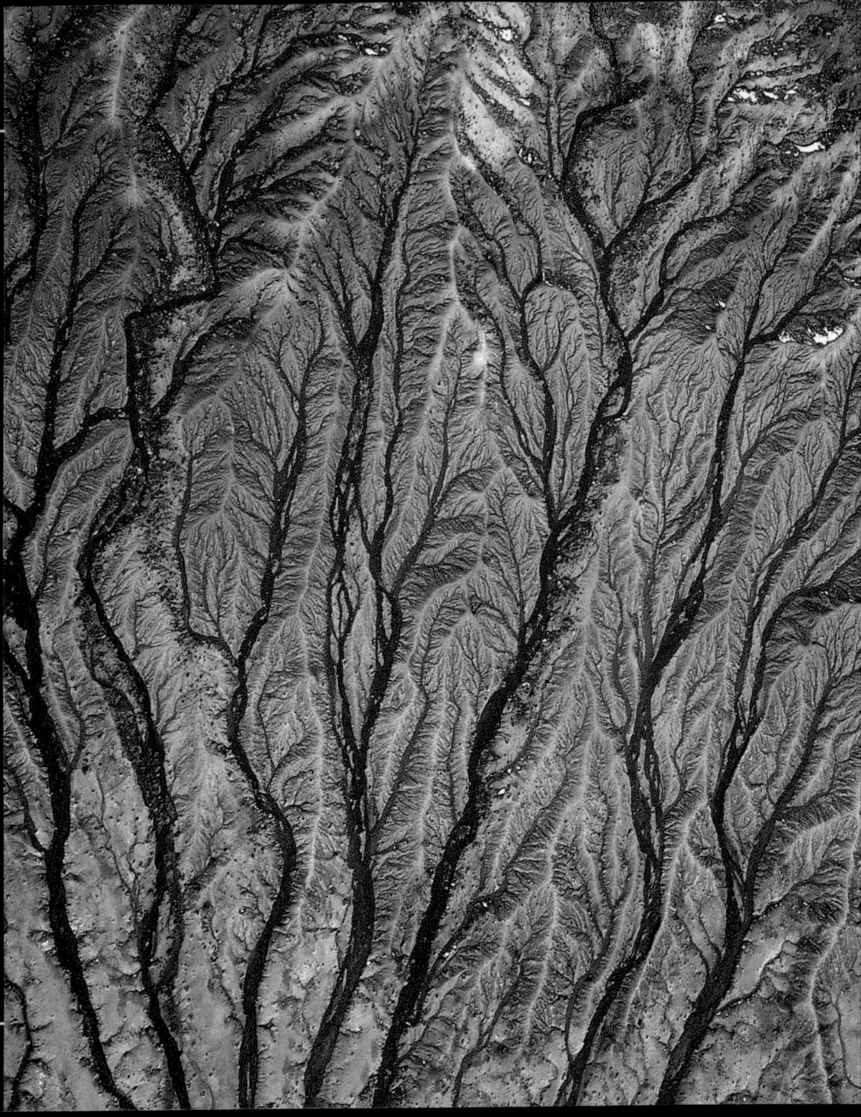

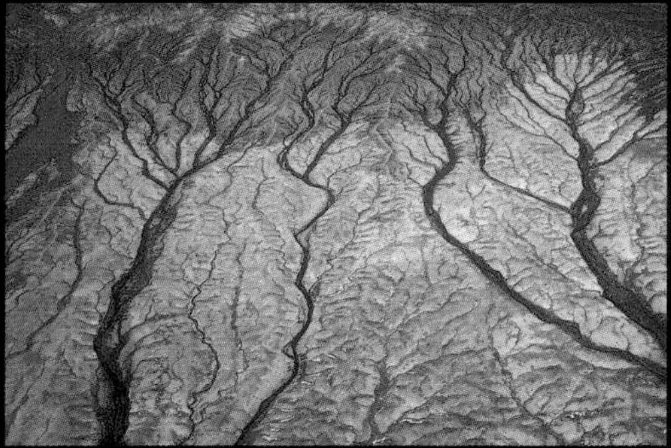

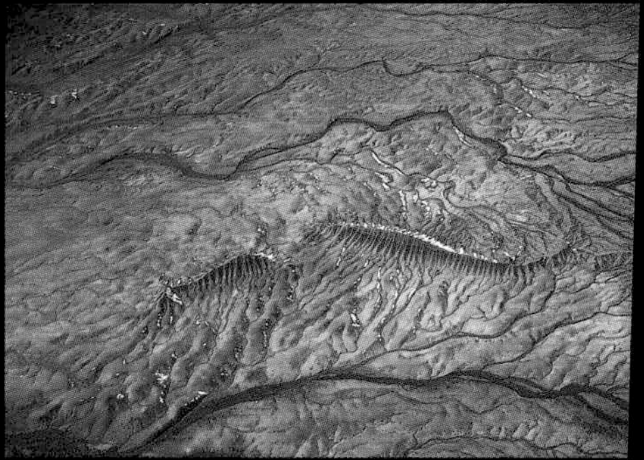

404 and 405
Erosional patterns break the Painted Desert area of the Petrified Forest National Park, Apache County, Arizona.

406 and 407

Complex erosional fissures create a "Red Planet-like" topography in the Red Rock Mesas, Chinle Valley, Navajo Indian Reservation, Apache County, Arizona.

408-409

Sagauro cactus grow near Harguahala, Sonoran Desert, Lapaz County, Southwestern Arizona. A typical nature saguaro will stand about 30 feet tall and have five or more arms. In its hydrated state a nature plant can expand to hold up to a ton of water.

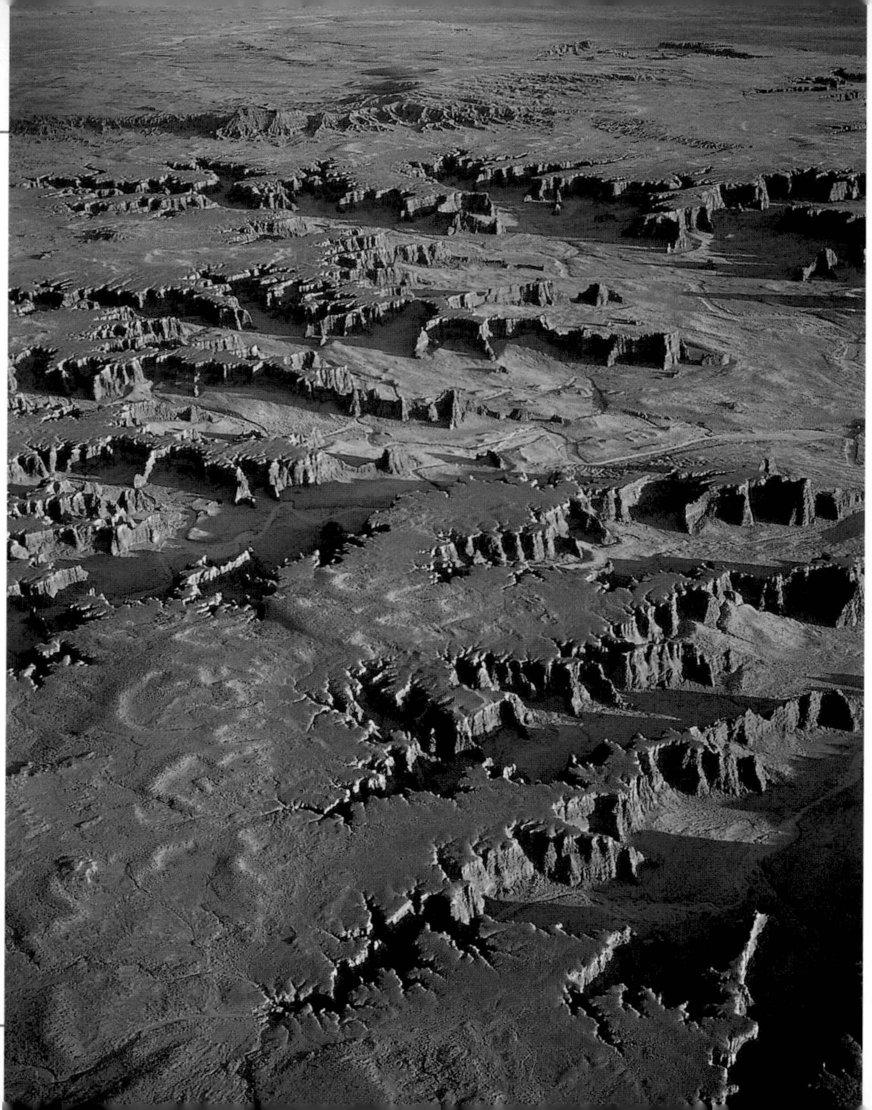

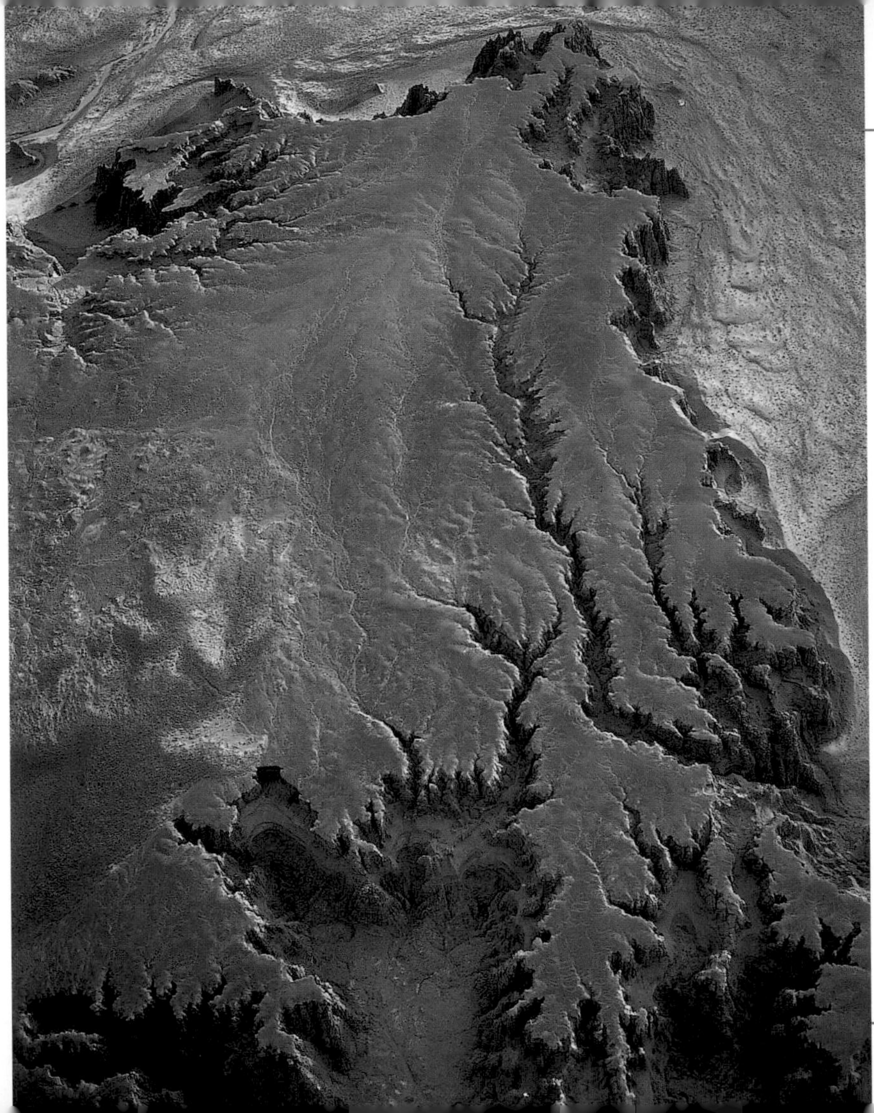

410 and 411

In Pueblo County, Colorado, lightning strikes at sunset. Desert rains are infrequent but in the summer monsoon season they come in the form of intense thunderstorm downpours wich rapidly deepen the few existing drainages.

412 and 413

Heavy spring thunderstorms over the eastern plains threaten Las Animas County, Colorado.

414-415

The High Plains Prairie is a semiarid, often desert-like landscape which cannot support farming without irrigation. Near Avondale, Pueblo County, Colorado.

The realm of emptiness

416-417
The Pawnee Buttes area of the High Plains gets enough spring and summer moisture to support rich grasslands. Prior to the late 1800s it was the land where the buffalo roamed. Pawnee National Grassland, Weld County, Colorado.

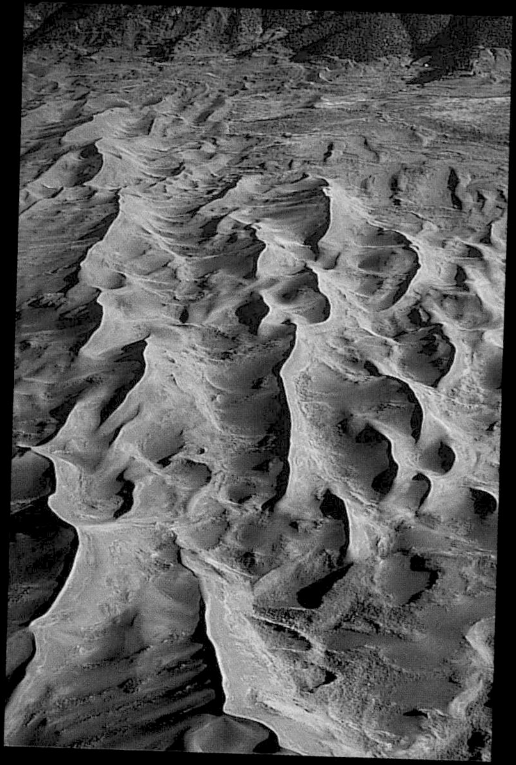

420

This near-bird's eye view of the Great Sand Dunes, Colorado, shows the sloping windward face, and the steep lee side of the individual dunes.

421

Strong prevailing winds are continually reshaping the sand of the Great Sand Dunes National Monument, Colorado. In some areas pockets of moisture support sparse vegetation.

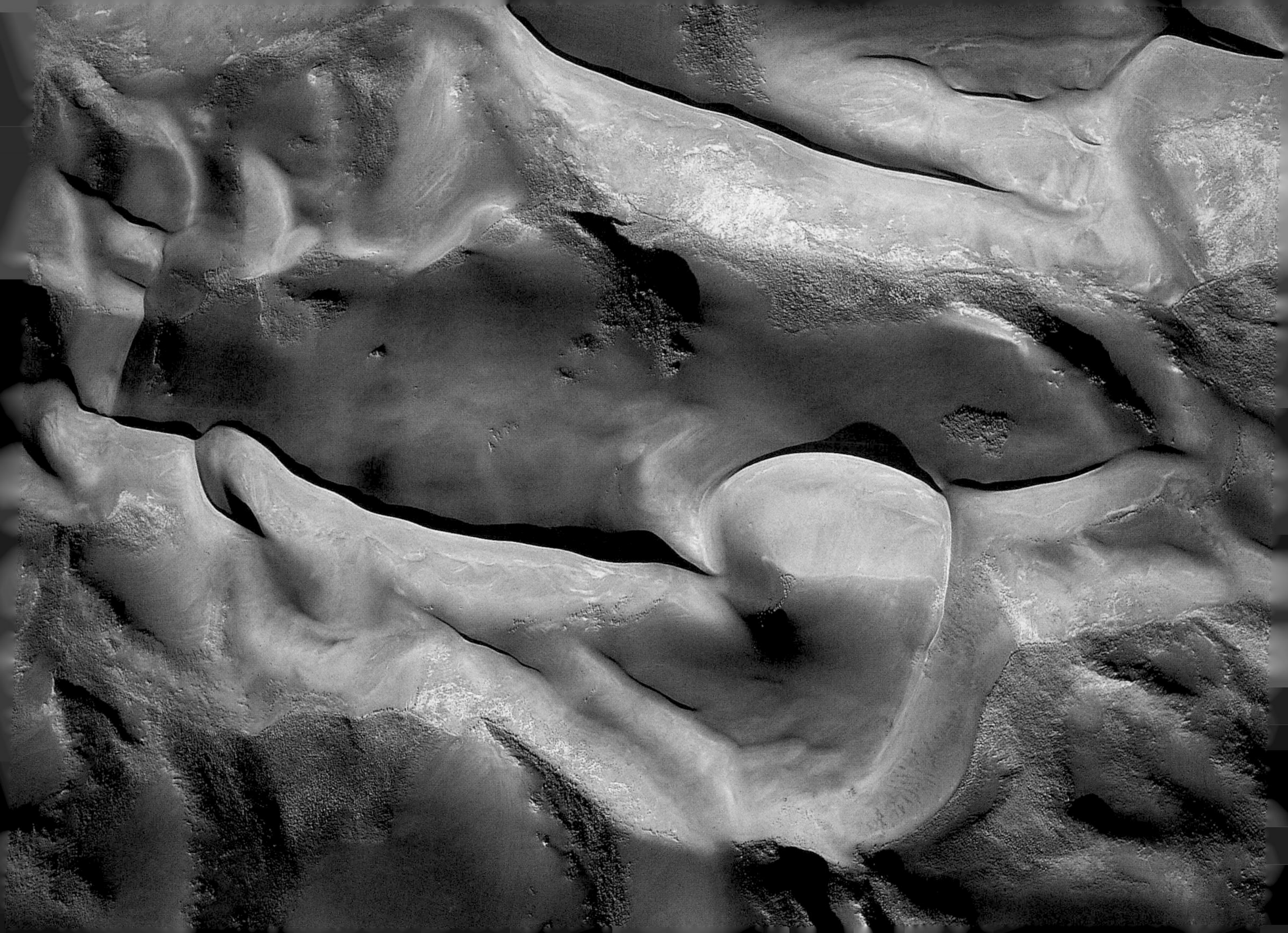

AMBER WAVES OF GRAIN

FLYING HIGH

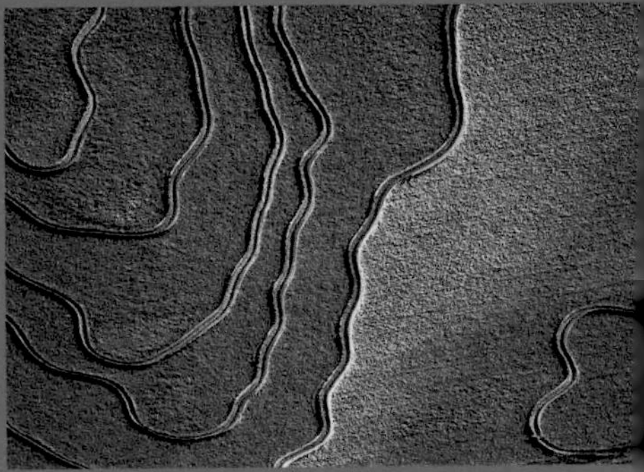

423
Typical American Midwest farm. Near Joliet, Illinois (left);. irrigated and terraced crop fields near Parkin, Arkansas (right).

In the late 1700s, an estimated 90% percent of American workers were farmers. In the northern states, farm production was mostly for local consumption, while in the South, large plantations were an overwhelming economic force producing commodities for export. In 1800, American agricultural exports were $23 million, 75% of the total export value. In 2000, those numbers were $50 billion and 6%, produced by 2.6% of the workforce.

By the mid-1800s, factors such as railroads, steamships and early farm machinery, plus westward expansion which made great rivers available as transportation routes, were beginning to shape the future of American agriculture. The South would continue to produce cotton and tobacco. The Northeast would have a limited role in dairy production and small crops. The Midwest would become the corn and dairy belt. The Great Plains and further west was to be wheat and cattle country, and what was once the Desert Southwest of America became, through the miracle of irrigation, a cornucopia of fruit and vegetable production.

The history of modern American agricultural development begins in the 1600s, when small land grants were given to individual settlers for the purpose of the establishment of private farms.

The Land Act of 1796 first made private ownership of relatively large tracts of land for farming possible by providing for the purchase of up to 160 acres at two dollars per acre.

424
A summer thunderstorm in Avondale, Pueblo County, Colorado, has just passed over the area. These irrigated farms produce a variety of vegetables including chili peppers.

425

Amber waves of grain

In 1803, President Thomas Jefferson completed the Louisiana Purchase of 800,000 square miles from France. This $ 15 million expenditure was the essential element in ensuring America's future prosperity. The area encompassed the Mississippi River Valley from the Gulf of Mexico to the Canadian border and west to the Rocky Mountains. It was to become, literally, the breadbasket of America.

Following this, in 1819, the government of Spain ceded Florida to the United States, a place destined to become the fruit basket of America. By 1850, successful farming of the prairies had begun, but the real boom came in 1862 when the Homestead Act granted 160 acres free to any settler who could work the land for five years. This was the ticket to the American dream for thousands of recent immigrants from Europe, and the key to the prosperous agricultural development of the vast American Midwest. As the homestead farms edged westward into Colorado and Wyoming they, metamorphosed into huge cattle operations that grazed freely over millions of acres of open rangeland. By 1880, most of the humid land was settled, and by 1890, the era of frontier settlement had ended. The last big hurdle for American agriculture came in the 1930s in the form of worldwide depression and prolonged drought. By 1950, the formative years were past and the population of American farmers had shrunk from 90% to 12% in 150 years.

All of this came naturally to America. The combination of temperate climate, huge areas of rich soil with abundant moisture, and easy access to transportation has made America a food provider for the World on a scale not achieved by any other country. This is not to say that there are not agricultural problems to deal with. In the 1930s the western prairie states were so devastated by prolonged drought that a huge section of the country became known as the Dust Bowl. Ruins of abandoned homesteads can still be found on the

Amber waves of grain

plains of eastern Colorado. Lesser droughts continue to occur, but the tapping of huge underground aquifers has mitigated their effect. The manifestation of this can be seen in the photos of circular irrigation patterns that are created by a rotating sprinkler arm attached at the pivot end to a deep water well and pump.

In the irrigated areas of the American Southwest, most of the water comes from the few rivers traversing the area. These water sources are either being depleted, as in the case of the Midwest aquifers, or stretched to their limit, as is the case for the rivers of the Southwest.

Continued efforts at planning and engineering are needed to maintain the present agricultural bounty of these regions.

The colors, patterns and textures of the agricultural landscape of America are extraordinary. Images of cranberry and blueberry farms and fields in New England and the beautifully crafted fields and buildings of Pennsylvania Amish farms dominate the agricultural photos of the Northeast. In the Corn Belt of the Midwest, mainly Wisconsin, Iowa and Illinois, it is rectilinear and sinuous patterns of cornfields and roads that dominate. In the Great Plains states, from Colorado to Kansas, and Montana to North Dakota, wheat fields dominate with irrigation patterns and unusual geometries of plowed fields to be seen. These wheat field patterns are visible, too, in the Pacific Northwest states of Washington and Oregon. Also in the Pacific Northwest, random shapes of bright yellow canola fields make wonderful views. In the Southwest states of Arizona and California, it is irrigation circles, rectangles, and the angles, patterns and curves of the water delivery systems that make compelling photos

The substance and patterns of American agriculture provide a rich source of material for the aerial photographer. One cannot view these photographs without realizing that a miracle for and of mankind is at work here.

428-429
This New England dairy farm appears in the green fields of Orleans County, Vermont.

Amber waves of grain

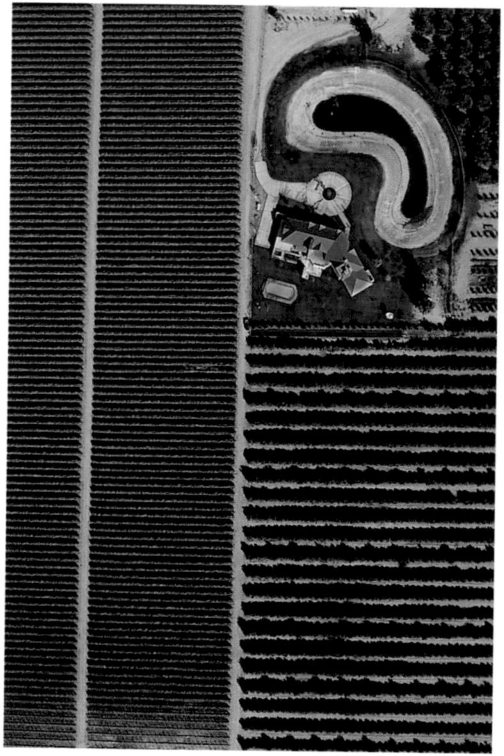

430
The geometric patterns reveal a date farm near Indio, Riverside County, California.

431
This suggestive view shows few corn farms near Mount Pleasant, Van Buren County, Iowa.

432

An airplane shadow can be seen over a hay raking tractor, Houghton County, Michigan. The hay swathes are being turned over to promote drying. Hay must be reasonably dry before it can be baled.

433

A tractor photographed while mowing and swathing hay in Stanley County, South Dakota. After mowing, the alfalfa (hay) is allowed to dry before baling.

434 and 435
Corn (yellow) and milo (striped) are being stockpiled at Montezuma, Gray County, Kansas. This grain is used mainly for livestock feed. It is being stored outside for lack of silo storage space, this is evidence of an overbundant harvest.

436 and 437

spectacular images is depicted harvest in Baca County, Col- This area of America's grain belt ed by dry land method.

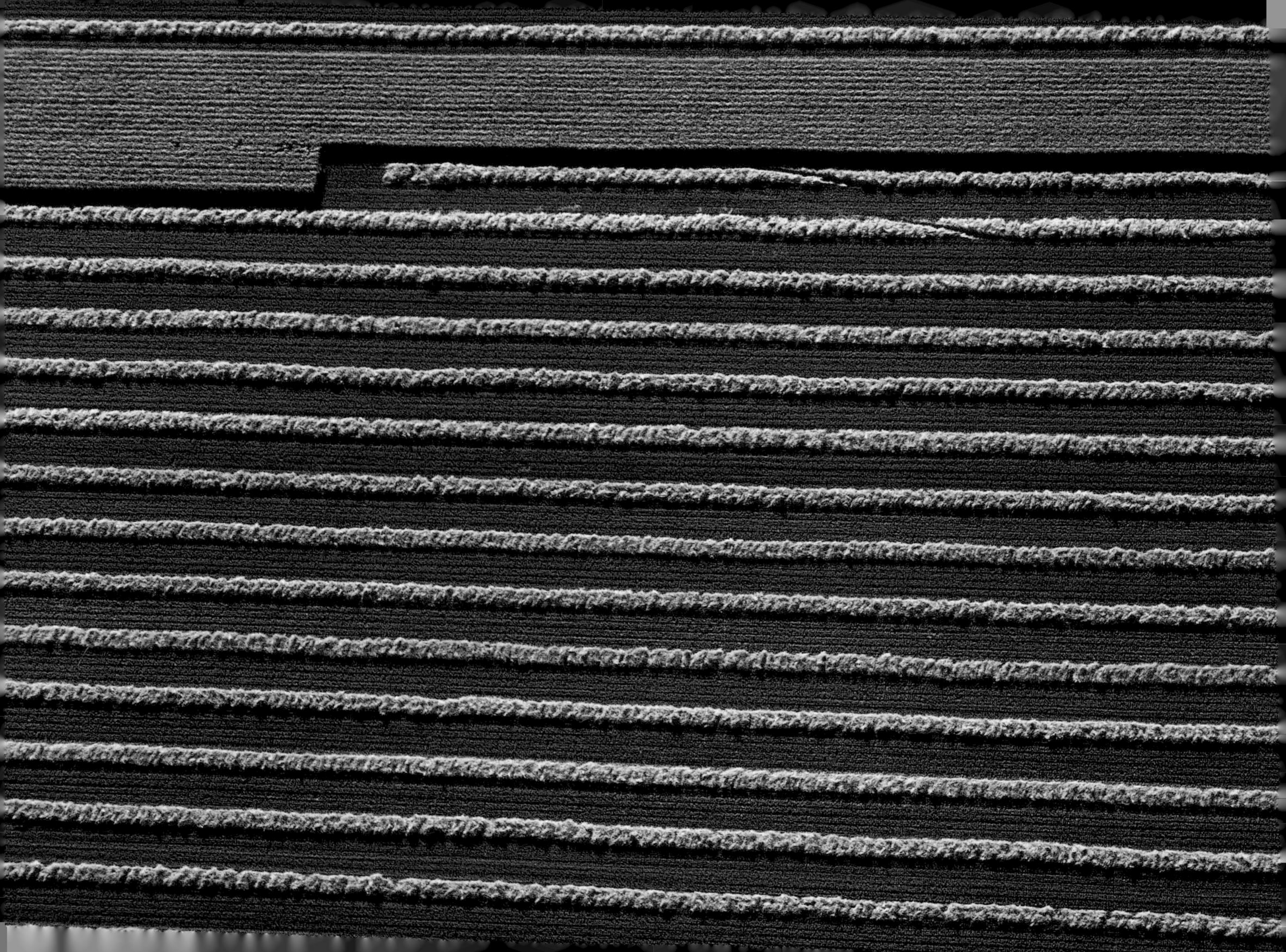

438

In this singular geometrical photograph is presented a partially harvested corn field, in Pueblo County, Colorado. The corn will become livestock feed and the swathed material will be used as fodder for adding filler to livestock feed.

439

The strips of dry land wheat fields in this photograph taken in Lincoln County, Colorado, may be used to alternate between spring and winter wheat.

440

These tilling harvested wheat fields are situated near Anthony, Harper County, Kansas.

441

Contour plowing in these fields in Harper County, Kansas controls soil erosion and helps to capture and preserve rainfall.

442

These farms on Mississippi River bottomland are located near Prairie du Rocher, Randolph County, Illinois.

443

The field patterns in Mississippi River bottomland near Prairie du Rocher, Illinois, are representative of the random land surveys of early 1800 America.

444 left

Irrigated wheat fields, Colorado.

444 right

This irrigated wheat field is located near Lamar, Walla Walla County, Washington State. The sprinkler arm can be seen across the center of the photo.

445

This well set in the center of the field and a sprinkler arm that rotates around – a common irrigation system – is near Florence, Pinal County, Arizona.

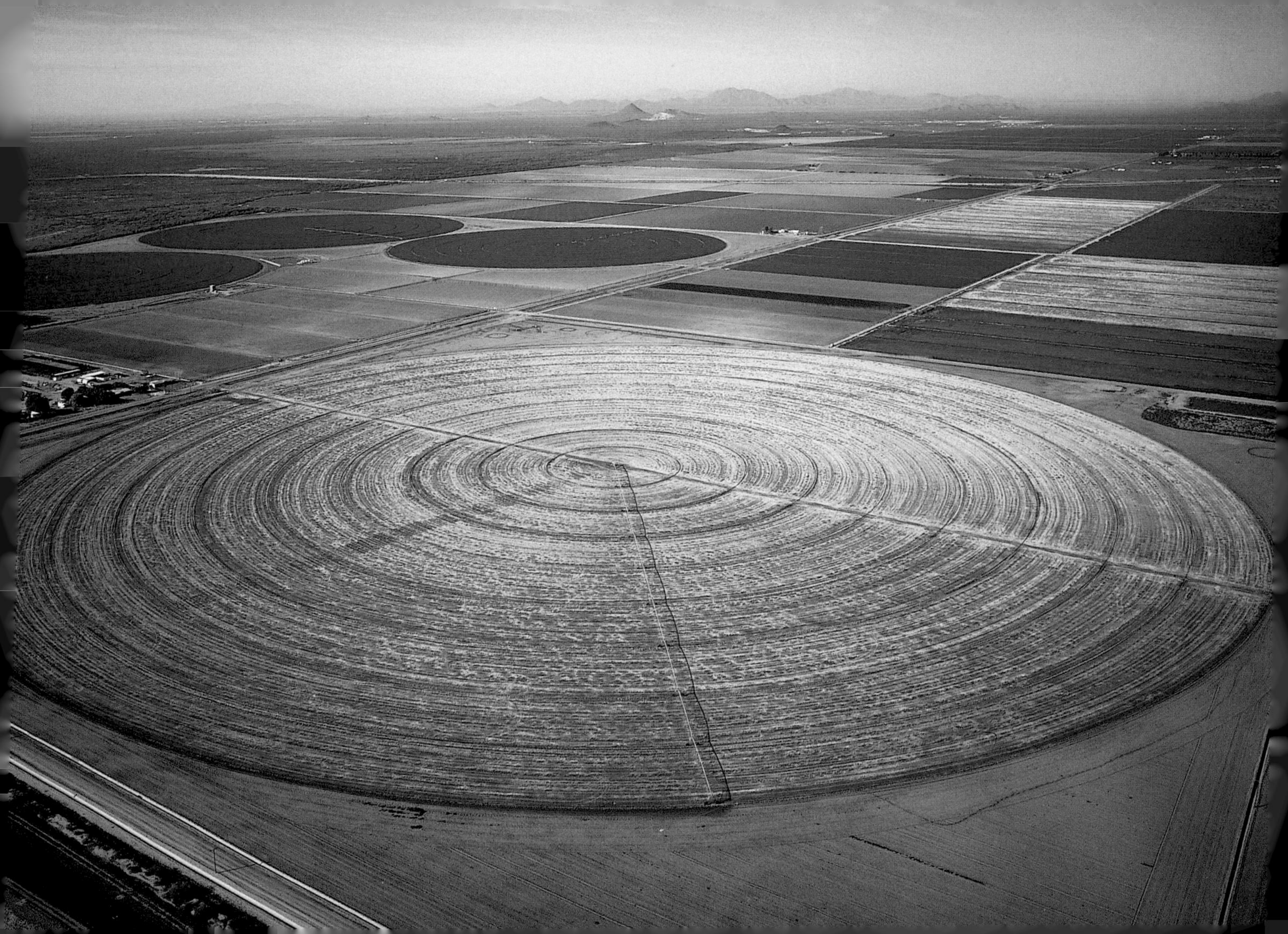

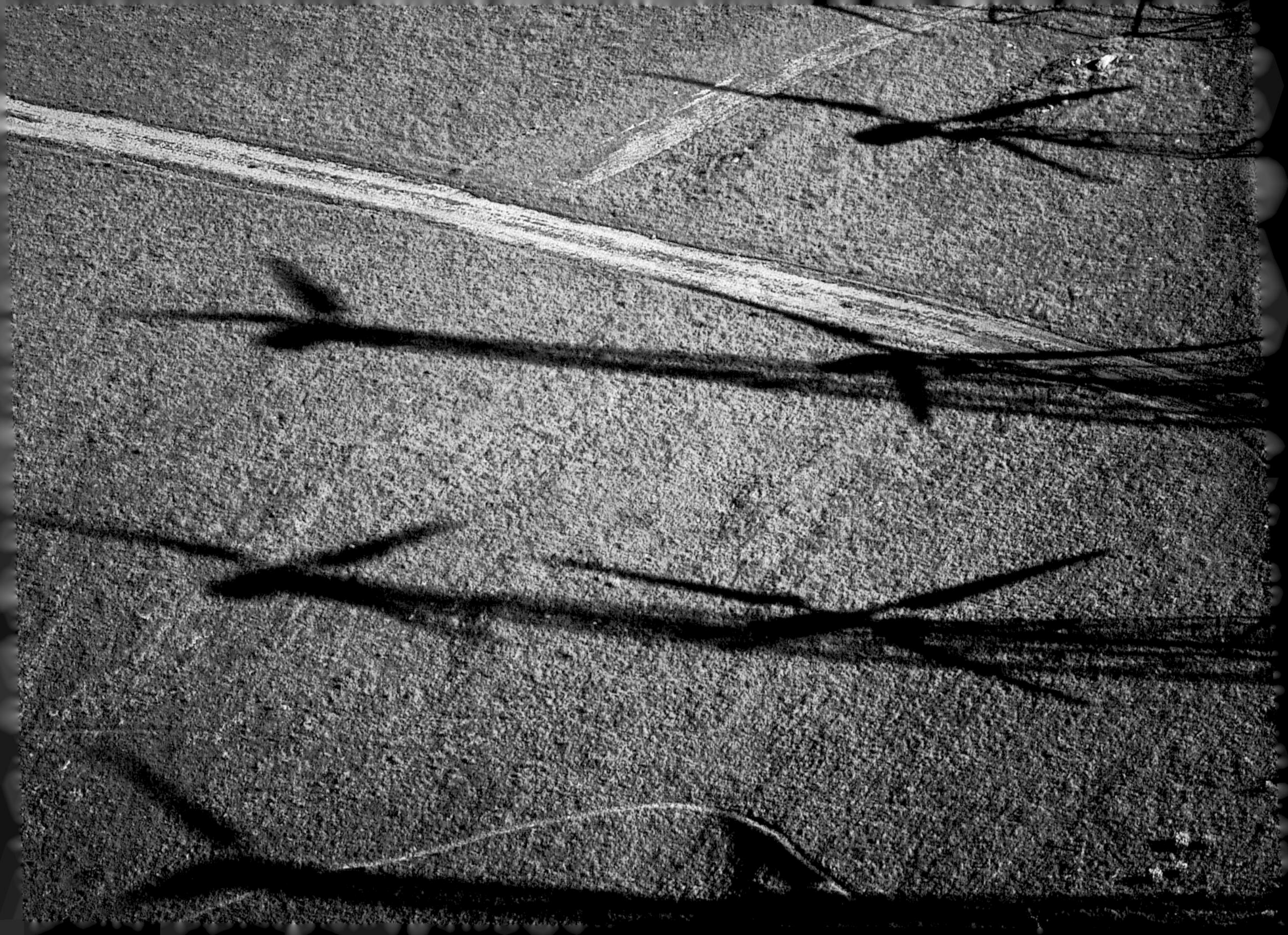

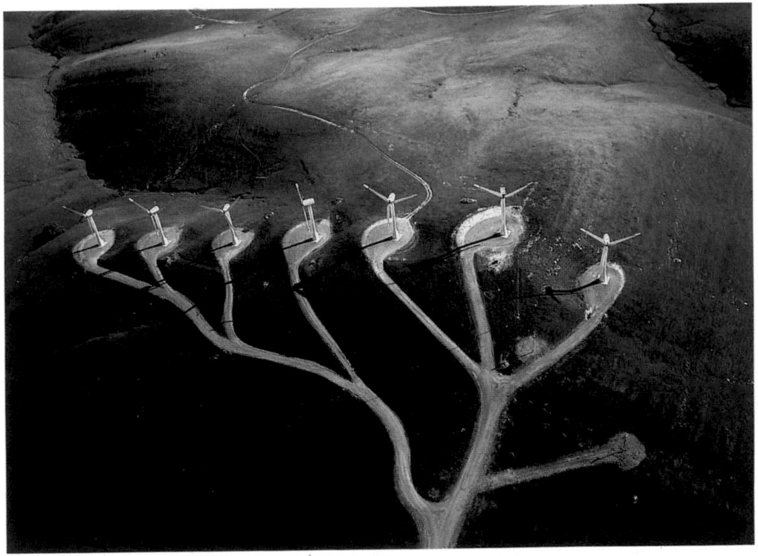

446

This photograph taken in San Ramon, Contra Costa County, California shows shadows cast by power-generating windmills. .

447

In 2000 wind power – in the image is a hilltop windfarm in San Ramon, California – amounted to about 0.1% of U.S. electric power consumption. Coal-fired generation amounted to 52%, nuclear generation about 20%.

448 and 449

The Imperial Valley, in Imperial County, California, is irrigated by diverting water from the Colorado River. This has turned a region of the Sonoran Desert into America's vegitable garden.

450-451

It looks like the flowers of a flower farm near Thermal, Riverside, California, maybe serve as an interim resource while a citrus orchard matures. The small trees will also provide some wind protection for the flowers.

452
The view shows a cranberry bog at harvest time near Biddeford, York County, Maine.

453
The berries, here in a cranberry farm near Biddeford, Maine, grow low to the ground in fields like those surrounding the pond. When the berries ripen, the field is flooded. The berries are raked and float to the surface from which they are collected.

Amber waves of grain

454 and 455

In America farmers are paid to keep some land out of production. This helps reduce surpluses and benefits the land by resting it. These images show strips of corn and fallow land, or land planted with a cover crop in Lancaster County, Pennsylvania.

Amber waves of grain

456-457
These farm headquarters are located in an area not reached by the circular irrigation patterns. The man product in this region – San Luis Valley, Alamosa County, Colorado – is potatoes.

458 and 459

The images realized respectively near Wray, Yuma County, Colorado (left); near Fort Morgan, Morgan County, Colorado (center); near Farmington, San Juan County, New Mexico. Center show pivot irrigation patterns: a water well is drilled at the center of each circle and a sprinkler rotates about it.

460

After cutting, the swathed tows are allowed to dry before baling. The photograph was taken near Riceville, Howard County, Iowa.

461

This photo shows raking swathed hay from a center-irrigated field near Dillon, Montana. The raking is proceeding from left to right and it appears that the last row is being worked.

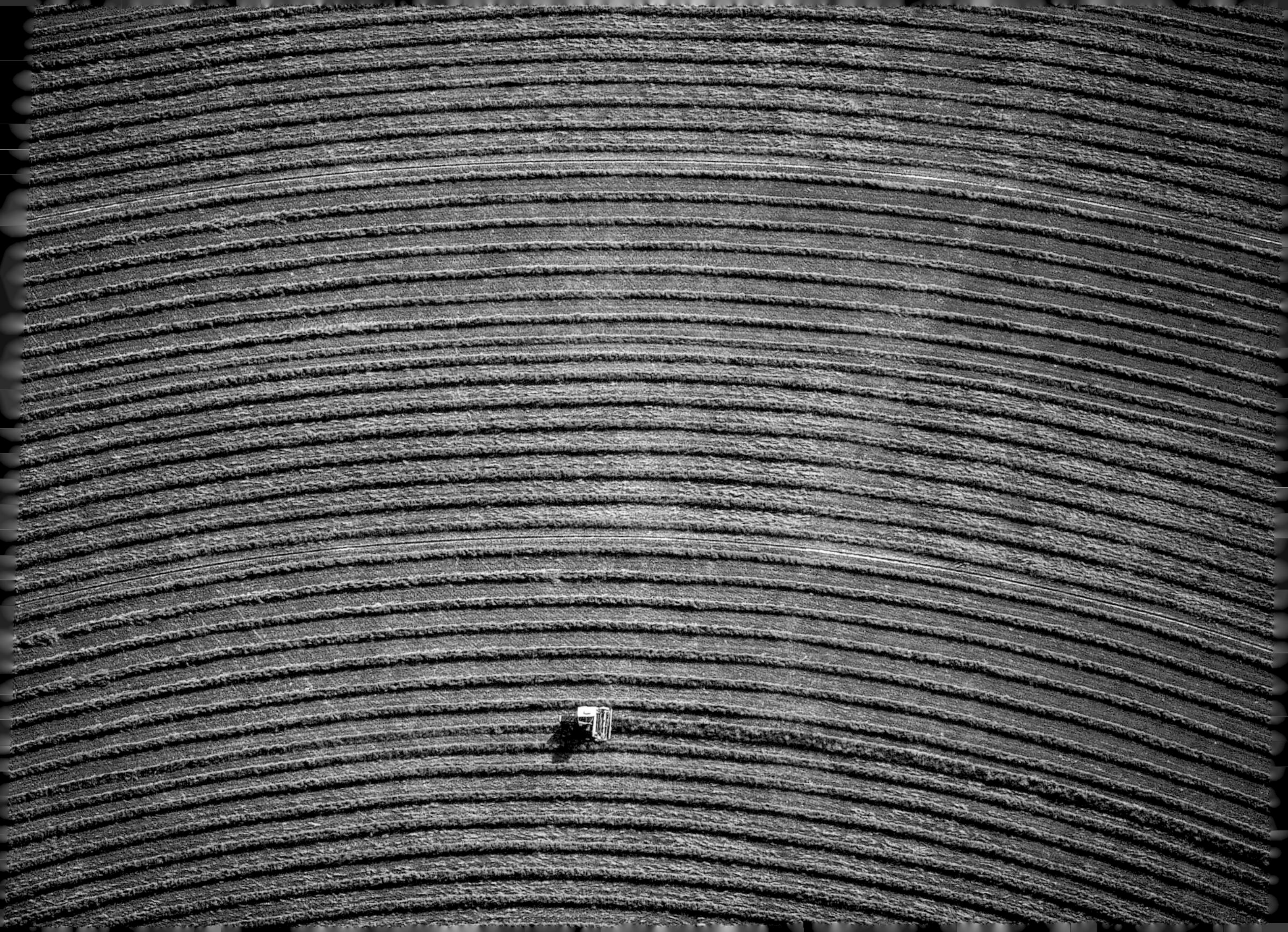

462 and 463

Canola or rapeseed near Nez Perce, Northern Idaho (left), near Palouse, Washington State (center), and near Nez Perce, Idaho (right), is grown extensively. It is used to make canola oil which is used as a light industrial oil and a cooking oil.

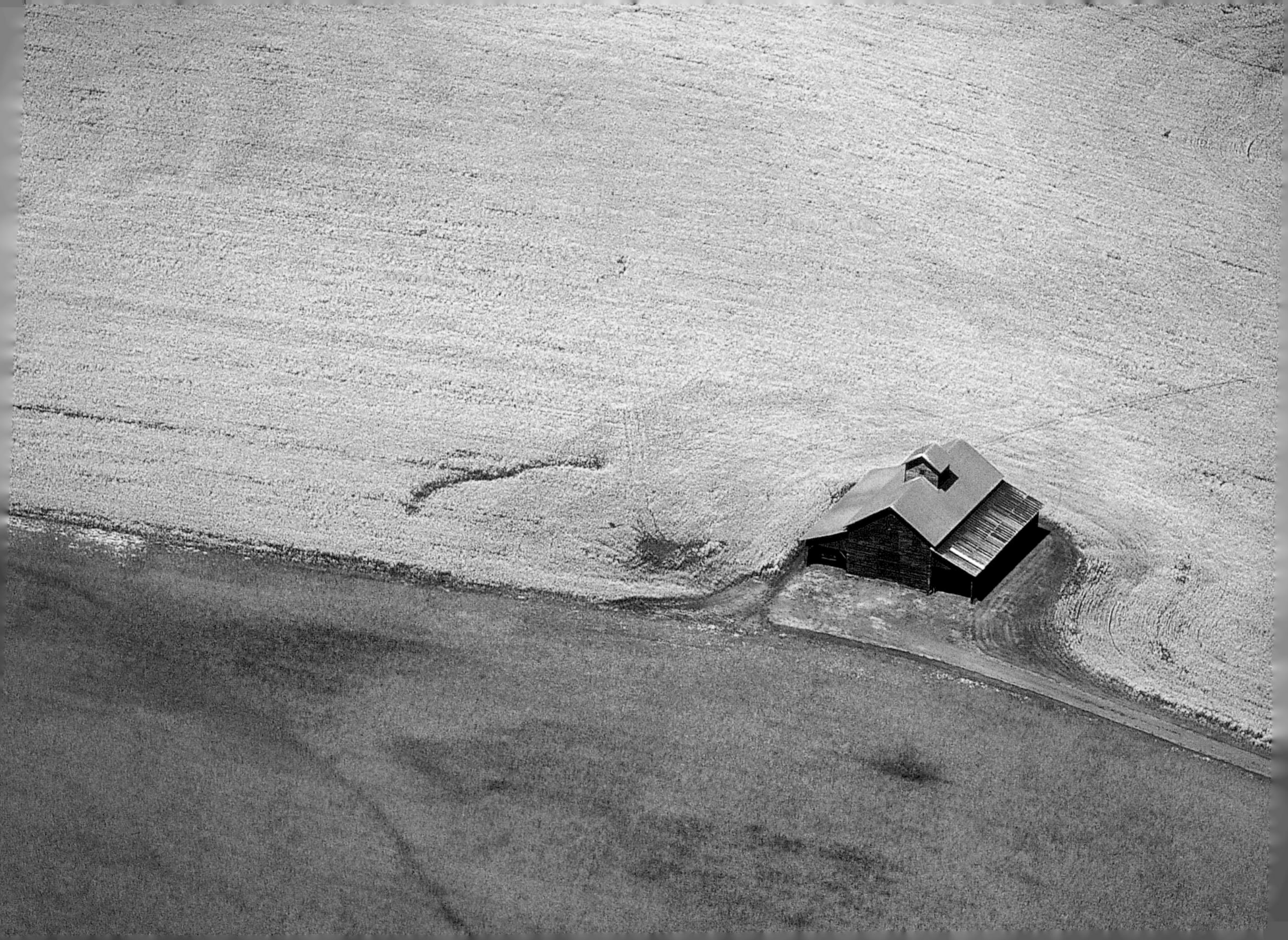

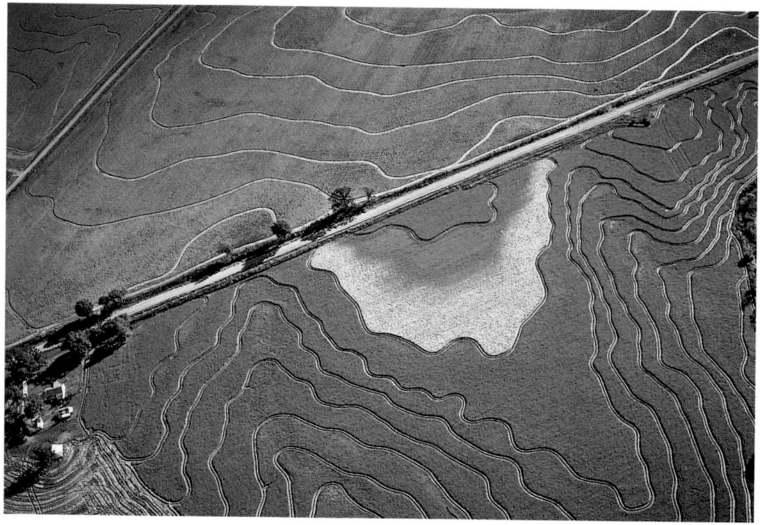

464 and 465

These irrigated terraces are located near Parkin, Cross County, Eastern Arkansas.

466-467

Earth berms create terraces to control irrigation and runoff. These are near Parkin, Arkansas.

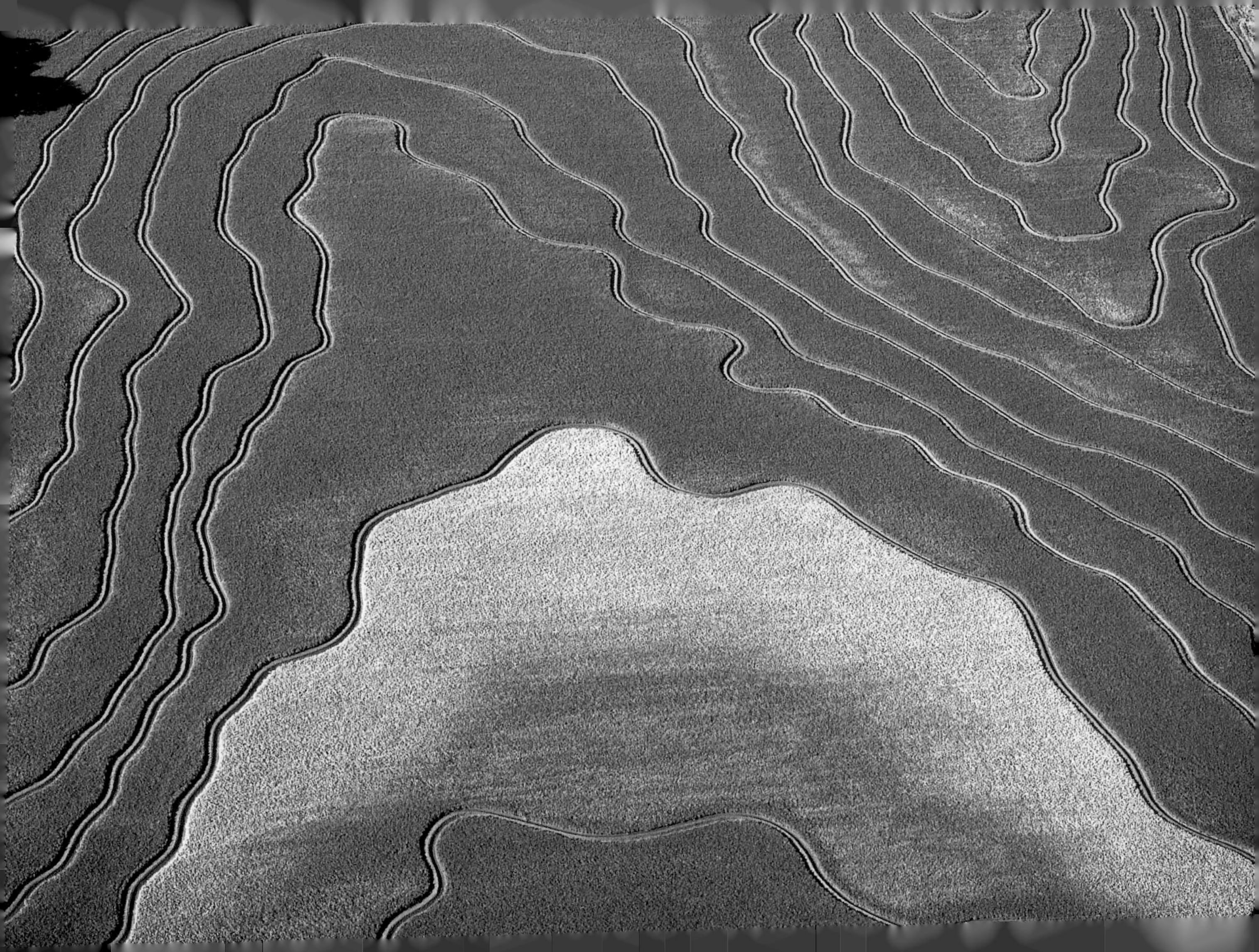

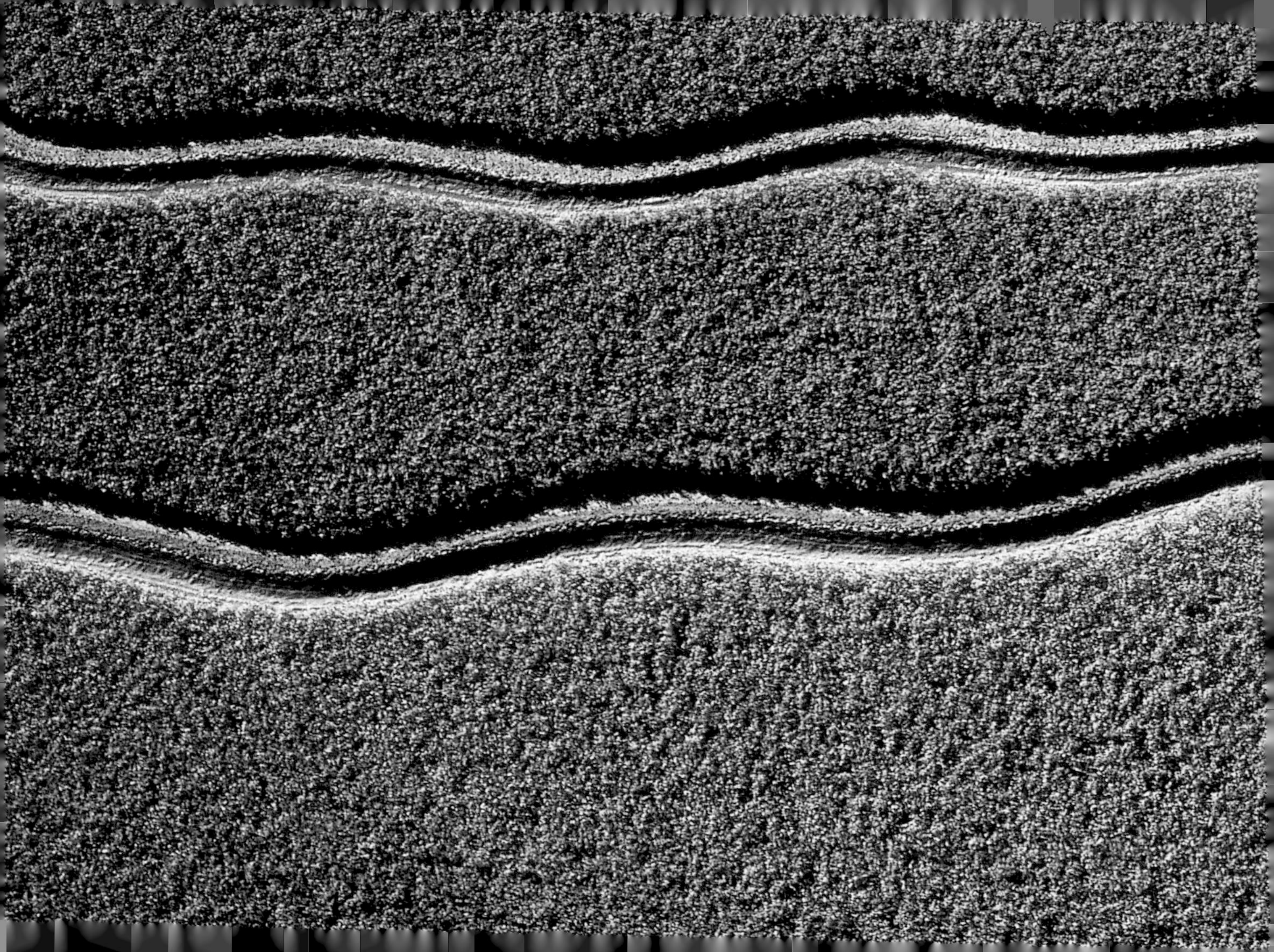

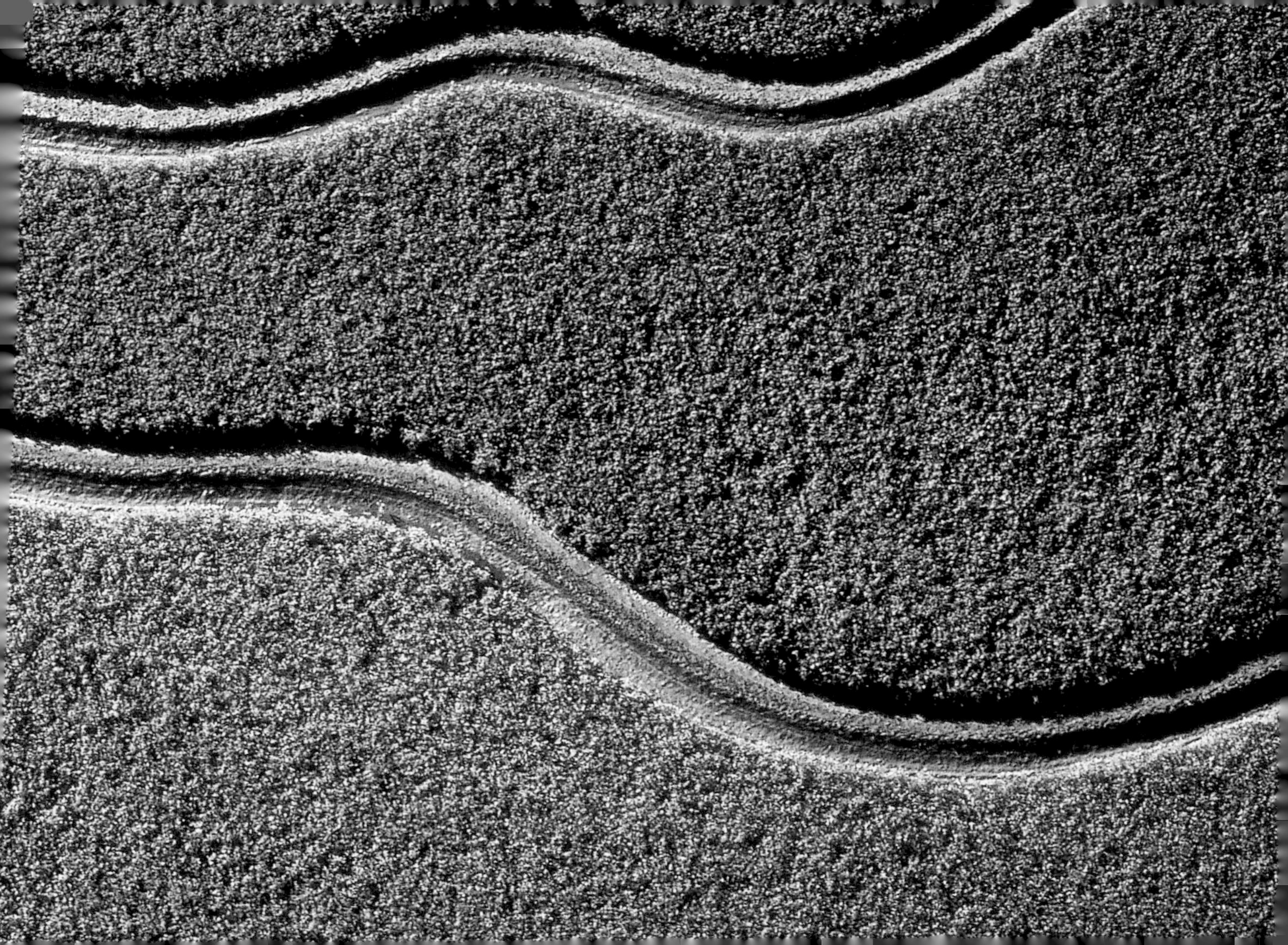

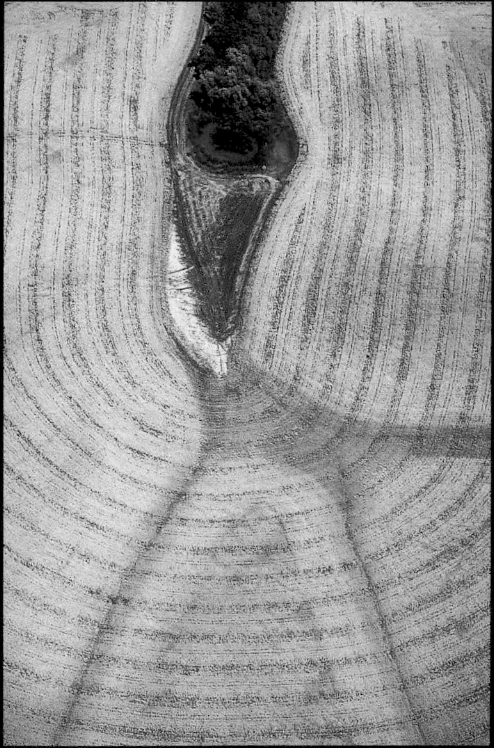

468 and 469

The two images shows contour cultivation of canola fields near Nez Perce, Idaho. The farm on the right has preserved a small island of troos. Such preservations provide small areas of wildlife habitat.

470-471

These small graineries for wheat storage are in Kremlin, Hill County, Montana.

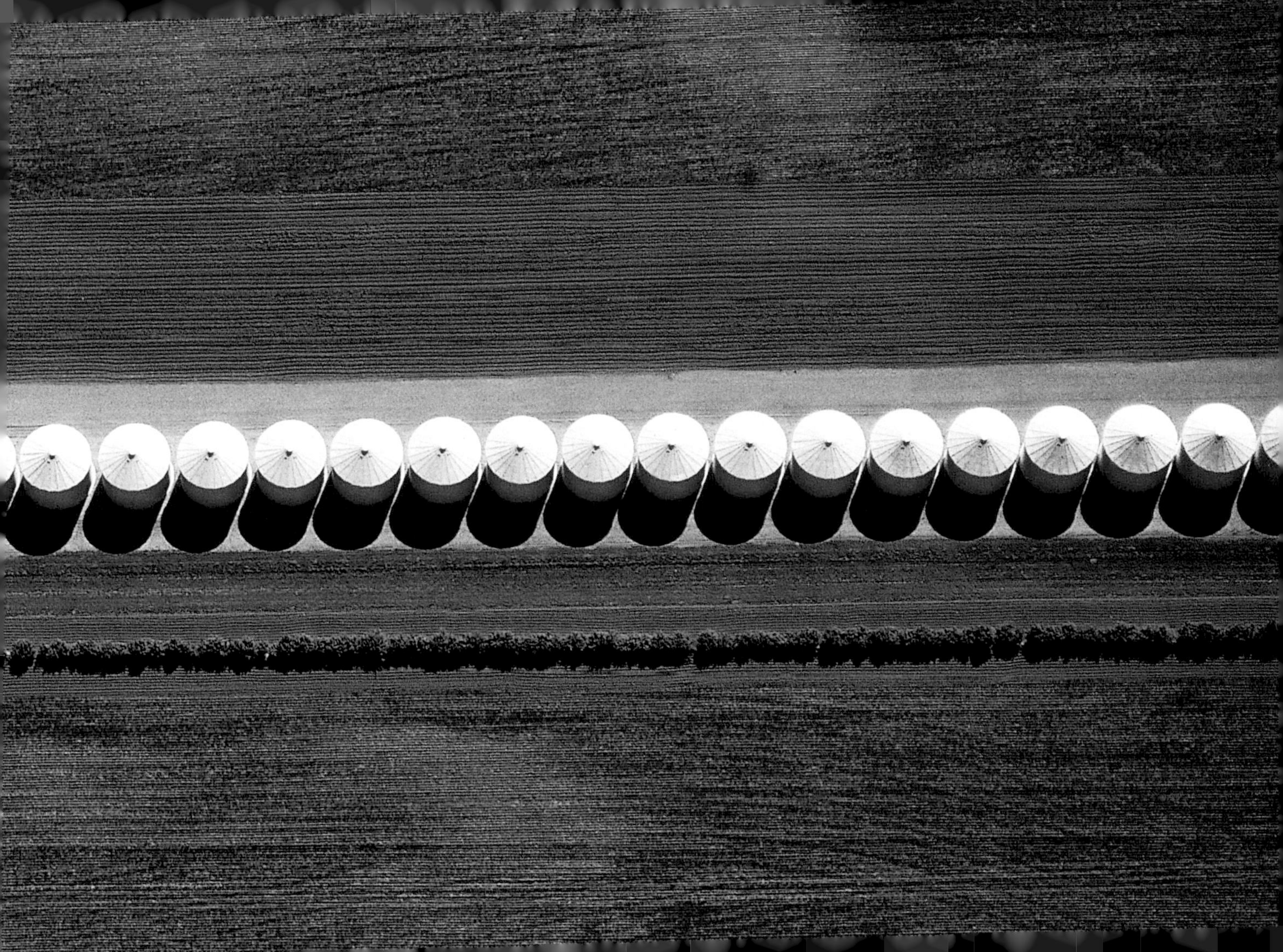

472
The geomtric image shows an apple orchard situated near Rochester, New York.

473
An anti-frost air fan dominates a citrus orchard in Casa Grande, Arizona. By keeping air in circulation around the trees the threat of freezing is lessened.

474 and 475
The colored lines reveal corn growing in Lancaster County, Pennsylvania (left) and in Carol County, Maryland (right).

476

A Midwest farm in Correction Ville, Woodbury County, Iowa, uses filter belts. The green strips are set in the natural drainages. Runoff from higher ground must pass through these low points. Sediments and some chemicals are filtered out. This results in better stream and river water quality.

477

A small lake and stream at upper right is the receptor for runoff from this farm in Correction Ville, Woodbury County, Iowa.

478 and 479
Contour plowing and terrace berms in an area near Woodbine, Harrison County, Iowa, are methods of controlling and capturing precipitation runoff. The shelter belts provide water treatment and wildlife habitat.

480 and 481

These images present two unused and historically preserved old barns: The one of the left is near Circle, McCone County, Montana, the other is near Palouse, Whitman County, Washington State.

482 and 483

These small clusters of farm buildings – Wisconsin dairy farm (left), Penobscott County, Maine (center), Port Clinton, Ottowa County Ohio (right) – seems cantilevered into their cultivated fields.

484
Crop strips photographed near Lenore, Idaho County, Northern Idaho.

485
These crop patterns located near Palouse, Whitman County, Washington State, are all designed to reduce soil erosion from wind and runoff.

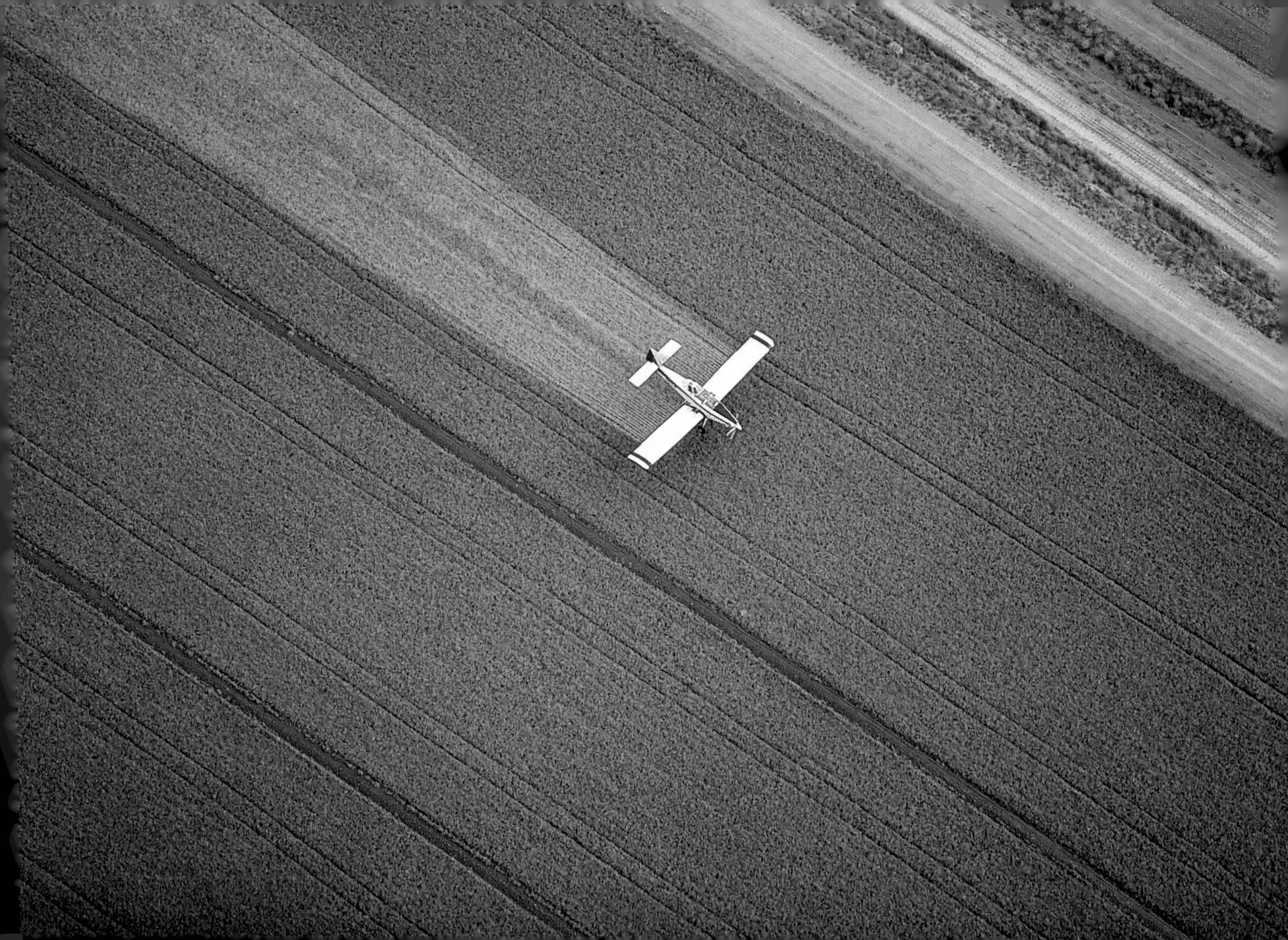

486 and 487

Crop spraying of irrigated vegetable fields near Florence, Pinal County, Arizona. A large irrigation canal runs across the upper part of the photo on the right. Crop sprayers were once guided by flagmen who moved after each pass. Now guidance is provided from a cluster of 24 earth sattelites known as the global positioning system (GPS).

488
This interesting bit of crop art is located near Anthony, Kansas. This may have been achieved by keeping the creen portions cut so they do not mature.

489
This image shows strips of planted corn and alfalfa near Lafayette County, Wisconsin.

490
Round barns – the one here is at Bucklin, Ford County, Kansas – were introduced in Kansas in the early 1900s. They were promoted as a more efficient way to stall draft horses. this was true but the advent of the farm tractor soon made them obsolte.

491
This image showing the tilling of a wheatfield was made near Steptoe, Colfax County, Washington State.

BLUE BOUNDARIES

FLYING HIGH

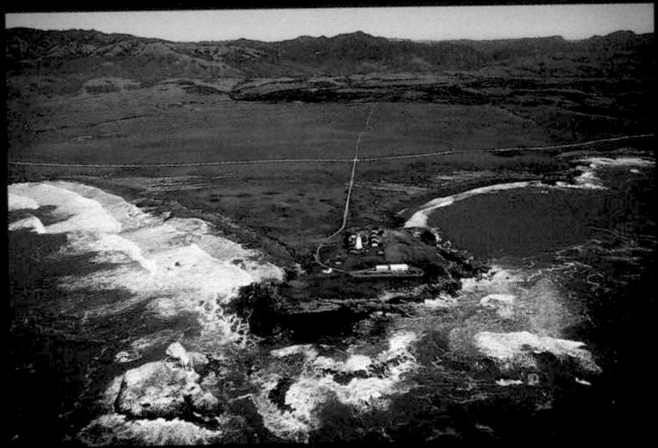

493
Piedras Blancas Light, San Luis Obispo County, California (left); Sheffield Island, Connecticut (right).

494

A coastline is a simple concept. It is where the water meets the land. The realities of coastlines are not that simple. Coastlines are difficult to compare and comprehend as to their length. What is called the general coastline of the Atlantic United States is 2,069 miles. What is referred to as the tidal shoreline is 28,700 miles – fourteen times longer. The combined general coastline of all of America's ocean coastal states is 12,383 miles and the combined tidal shoreline is 88,633 miles, a ratio of just over 7:1. Coastlines come in a multiplicity of forms: harbors, bays, inlets, estuaries, cliffs, rocky beaches, sandy beaches, barrier islands and tidal wetlands. Each will have its own distinct economy and ecology. The shoreline/coastline ratio is a measure of the relative size and frequency of bays and inlets. Harbors, bays and inlets are most hospitable to commerce and habitation, so this is where the cities and towns take root. Beaches and barrier islands are the places of recreational and resort communities. Rocks, cliffs and tidal marshes are best left to their role as nurturing areas for wild life and as sanctuaries for the human spirit.

An examination of the coastlines of three states can show us how these different factors of geography and human activity come into play. Maine is a state with a very complex coastline of continuous bays, harbors and islands. These features are, however, mostly small and rocky. This has resulted in a profusion of small villages that began as fishing and whaling ports. If we define a small city as having a population of 100,000, Maine has none despite its

495
The Point Reyes Lighthouse at Point Reyes National Seashore, California, was built in 1870 to guide ships into San Francisco Bay.

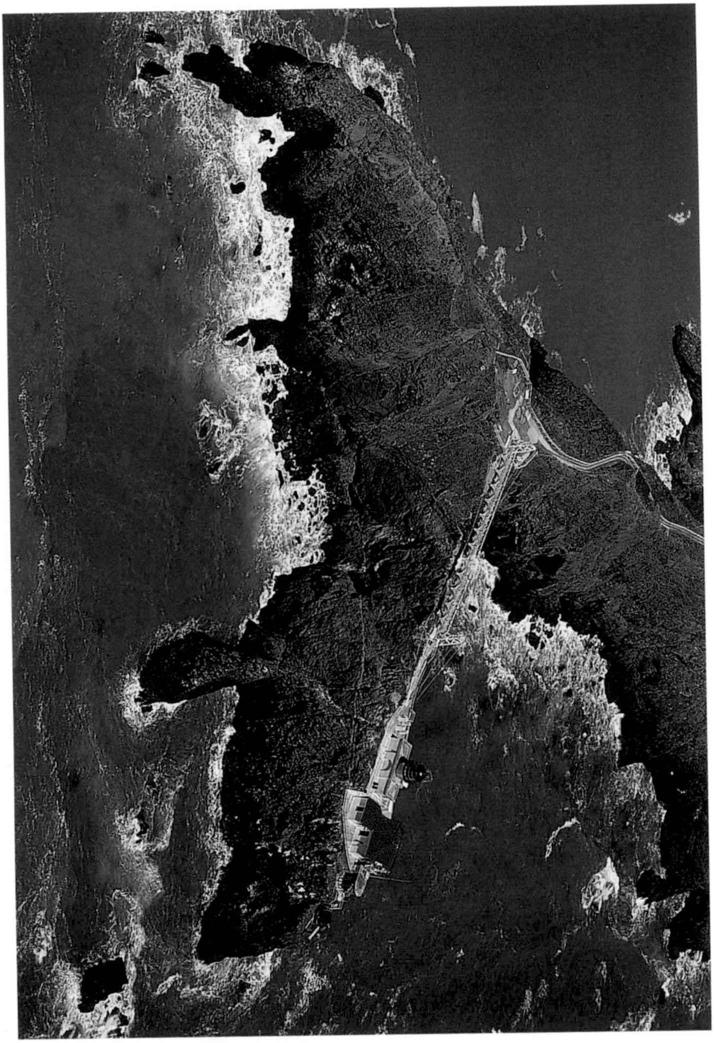

Blue boundaries

being one of the earliest settled regions of the United States. From an aerial photographer's point of view, the Maine coastline is a cornucopia of compelling scenes of rock-bound shores, lighthouses and quaint harbors. The Maine general coastline is only 228 miles; its tidal shoreline measures 3,500 miles – a ratio of over 15:1.

The California coast is the exact opposite of Maine's. Its general coastline of 840 miles is almost four times that of Maine's, however, its tidal shoreline of only 3,400 miles is less than that of Maine, and a ratio of only 4:1. In contrast to Maine's hundreds of small bays and inlets hosting small towns, California has one huge bay, San Francisco Bay, which hosts a population megalopolis of commerce and industry. Lesser bays host Los Angeles, San Diego and Montery. The remainder of the California coastline is relatively unpopulated. Notwithstanding the compelling natural beauty of the California coast, it does not offer the aerial photography opportunities of many of the other major coastal states. The island state of Hawaii is an interesting anomaly. It has by far the longest general coastline (750 miles) for its geographic size than any of America's other twenty-three ocean coastal states; yet its tidal shoreline is a scant 1052 miles, a ratio of only 1.4:1. This is more than three times the Maine coastline length and less than one-third its shoreline length. Hawaii's one area of big sheltering bays and harbors is on the Island of Oahu. The rest of the islands have none. Even small coves and inlets are rare. Though other factors are at work here, this is a principal reason that Hawaii has only one city of over 100,000 population – Honolulu. Notwithstanding that the many coves and inlets of Maine are the stuff of compelling aerial photography, Hawaii's shores make up for this with incredibly hued coral reefs, lava cliffs and plunging coastal waterfalls.

Most folks think of coastlines as being fixed boundaries of continents, countries and islands that, unlike political boundaries, will not change with time. However, on a geologic time scale there are no perma-

Blue boundaries

nent coastlines. The generally accepted theory of continental drift concludes that as recently as 200 million years ago the Earth's landmass was constituted into one giant continent called Pangaea. From that landmass the continents began to slowly separate with ever changing shapes and coastlines. This process, though imperceptible on a human time scale, will continue throughout the ages of geologic time. Of direct and immediate concern to coastal inhabitants, habitats and economies are the day-to-day forces of nature such as storms, tides, wave action and coastal currents. All coasts are under constant attack from these elements, and sometimes even from human activity. Global warming and the consequent melting of polar ice caps are a credible but uncertain threat. Those who subscribe to this theory think that a sea-level rise of three feet in the next 100 years is probable. While such cycles of climate change have been common occurrences in the Earth's history they are thought to have occurred over thousands of years giving ecosystems time to adjust. A 3-foot rise in sea level over the next hundred years would have significant negative economic and environmental impacts on America's coastal habitations. A seldom-considered but real coastal threat is the tsunami. The Alaskan earthquake tsunami of 1946 did great damage to Alaska and Hawaii. Lesser tsunamis came out of Alaska in 1957, 1958 and 1964. A 2001 report by a team British and American scientists warns of a monster tsunami which could be generated by the eruption and partial collapse into the sea of the Canary Island volcano of Cumbre Vieja. The predicted tidal wave of this event would reach the coast of Florida with a crest height of 120 feet. Events of this nature are so infrequent in the short term that they seldom affect our thinking about coastlines anywhere. Slow change is inevitable, rapid change is possible, but whatever the future holds for coastlines they will continue to play a dominant role in America's economy and ecology, and they will always be a compelling source of photography of all kinds.

498-499
Cape St. Elias, the western tip of Kayak Island, Alaska is juts 25 miles west into the Gulf of Alaska.

500

Kayak Island, Alaska, left, viewed westward from close to its east; end right, image is viewed eastward from Cape St. Elias. The lighthouse and keeper's station can be seen at the very bottom of the photo on the right.

501

Like all U.S. lighthouses the one at Cape St. Elias, Alaska, in these photos is automated, however the keeper's house can be rented by adventure tourists. It was probably the most remote lighthouse in U.S. Service.

502 and 503

At Cape Suckling, northwest of Yakutat, Alaska, is this wreck; it appears to have been a construction barge, possibly used in offshore oil-platform construction.

504

Cape Resurrection at the entrance to Resurrection Bay leading into Seward, Alaska.

505

Homer Spit, Alaska, is a fishing boat harbor.

507 left

North Head Light, at Cape Disappointment, Washington, is one of the windiest places in America. One gust was recorded at 121 mph as the equipment was destroyed. The houses are beautifully restored.

507 right

The image shows Washington State coastline, near Grays Harbor County, Quinault Indian Reservation. Bottom to top are: Tunnel Island, Hog Back, Little Hogback.

508

This spectacular image shows the famous Big Sur Coast and coast highway (El Camino Real), north of Point Sur, California.

509 left

This small beach is situated north of Point Sur in San Benito County, California.

509 right

Big Sur Point and lighthouse are part of the Big Sur State Historic Park, California.

510
El Jaro Point is located north of Santa Cruz, in Santa Cruz County, California.

511
Big Sur Point Lighthouse is part of Big Sur State Historic Park, in San Benito County, California.

512 and 513
These spectacular photographs show on the left homes on the edge of beach cliff erosion and, on the right, Shell Beach, in San Luis Obispo Bay, California.

514

This photo of the western end of Santa Catalina Island, California, also shows Catalina Harbor on left and Isthmus Cove on right.

515

Santa Catalina Island. The harbor, is privately owned and still has much of the wilderness character of 1800 Southern California. It was first visited by Europeans in 1542. Later it became a sealing harbor and by 1900 it was a tourist destination.

516
The apparently endless Pismo State Beach at Oceano, California.

517
Pismo Dunes and the city of Oceano, in California.

519
A buggy tests the dunes at Pismo Dunes State, Vehicular Recreation Area, California.

520

The lighthouse at Piedras Blancas Point, California, is one of two tall lighthouse structures on the coast. It was built in 1875 to guide whaling ships into San Simeon Bay.

521

Cypress Point in the Monterey Peninsula in Monterey County, California is famous for its professional golf courses.

522
The image has captured a sail on San Francisco Bay, California.

523
A small plane flies over surf near Morro Bay, California.

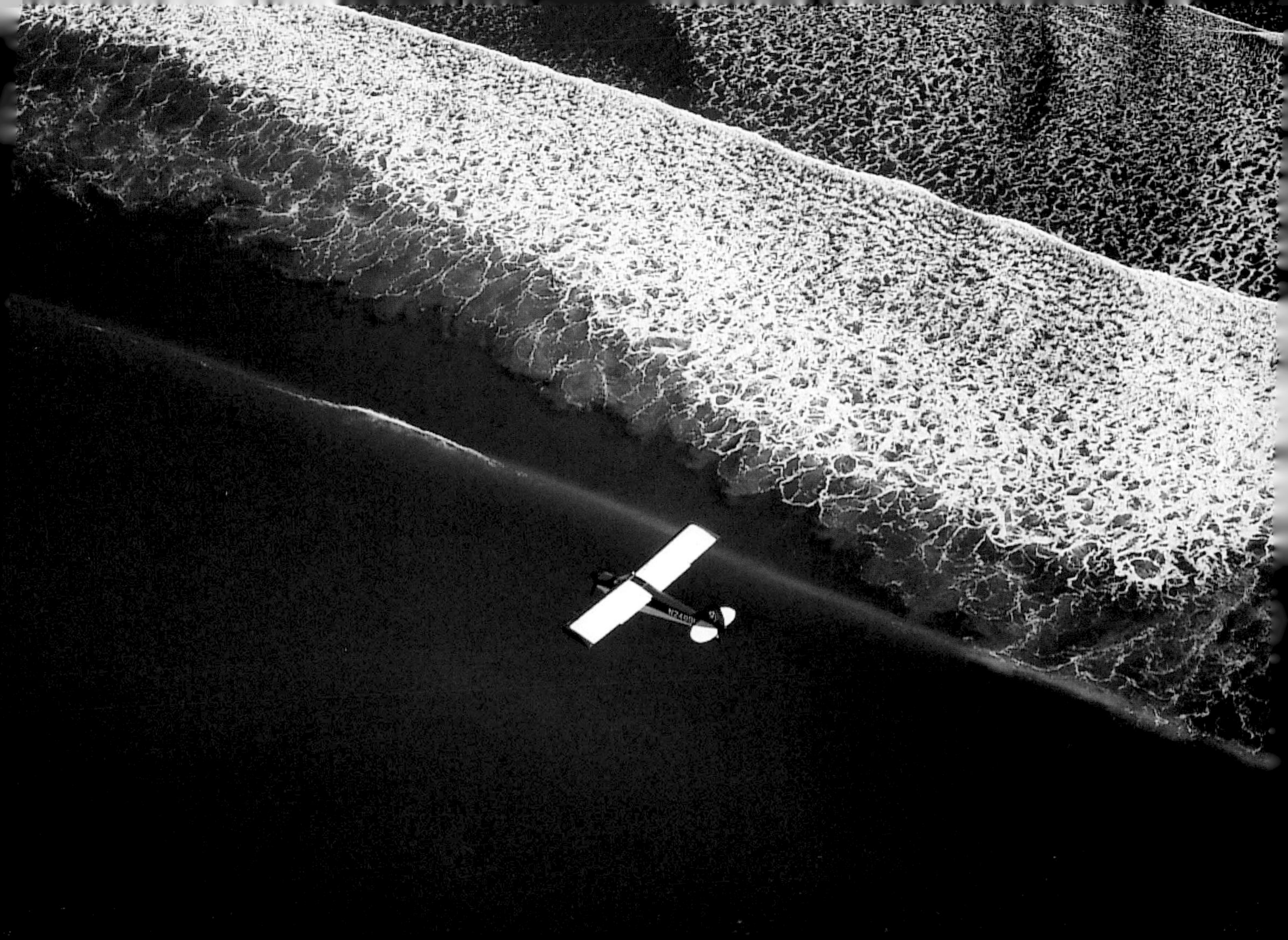

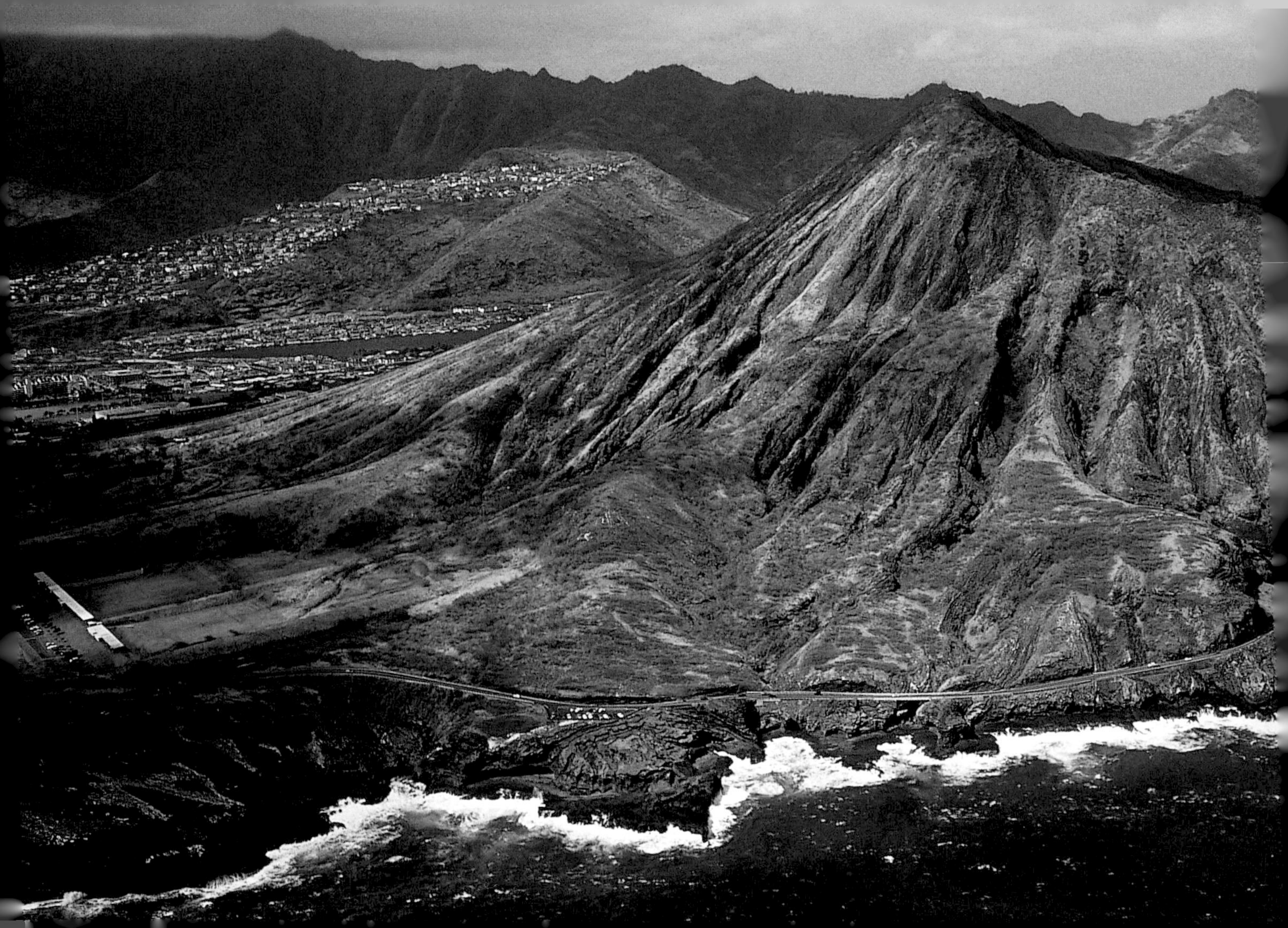

524-525
Kohelepelepe and Koko Crate on the island of Oahu, Hawaii. Koko and Damond Head are small volcanoes 70 to 500 million years old. The volcano which formed Oahu is estimated to be 3 million years old. Koko Crater is 10 miles east of Honolulu.

526
Pauwalu Point on the Northeast Shore is located on the east side of Maui Island, Hawaii.

527
Puu Koae Point in on the north-east shore of Maui Island, Hawaii.

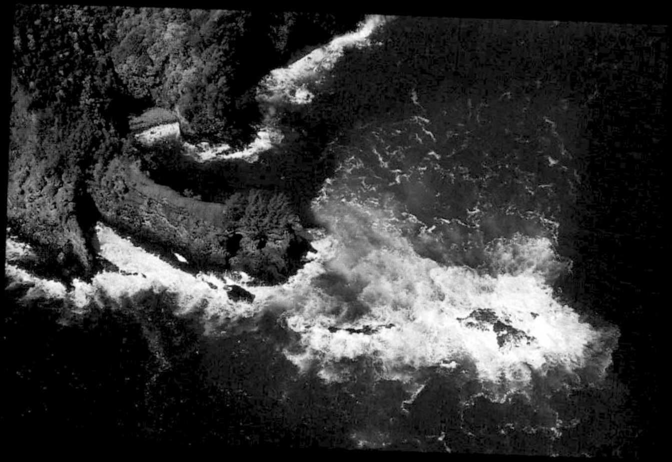

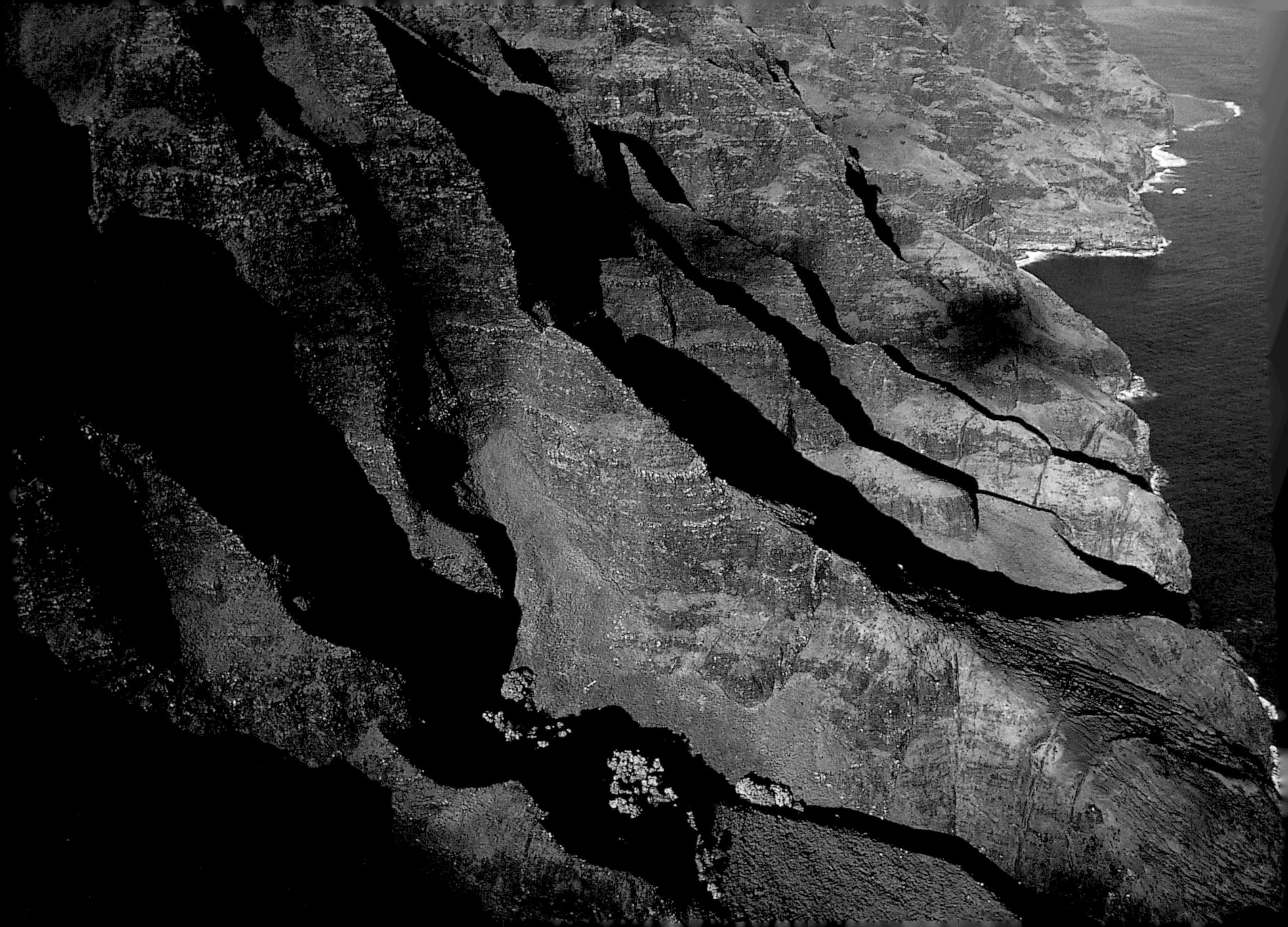

528

Napali Coast State Park, on the island of Kauai, Hawaii, is an area of 2000 cliffs and waterfalls which can only be reached by 10 to 15 mile hikes over steep ridges and valleys.

529

Trails to the Napali Coast were first constructed in the late 1800s and were rebuilt in the 1930s. The shoreline has many small beautiful beaches.

530-531

Lanai Island, Hawaii, here can be seen the northwest coast, is almost all privately owned. Beginning in about 1900 it was developed for pineapple plantations. Lanai is now a tourist destination which features the Manale Bay Hotel at the south end of the island. Most of the island is roadless and undeveloped, as in this photo.

532 and 533

These spectacular images show coral reefs on the north end of the island of Maui, Hawaii.

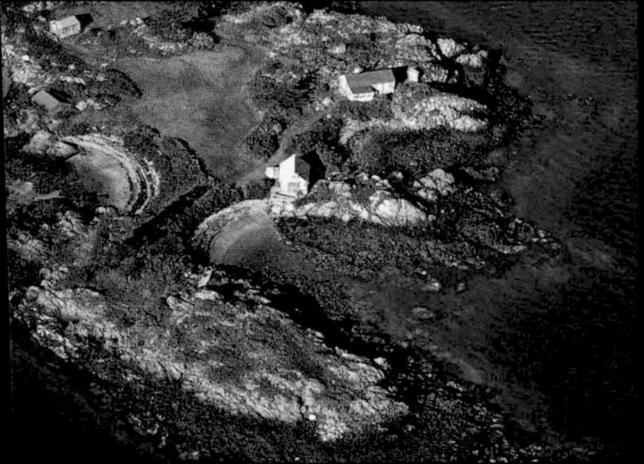

534 left
Close to Penobscot Bay, Maine is a small inhabited island.

534 right
West Quoddy Head Light, at Lubec, Maine sits on the easternmost point of the United States,. The present structure was built in 1858.

535
Cape Neddick Light, Maine, is also known as Nubble Light, and was erected in 1874.

536
Stonington is a tyical Maine coast fishing port.

537
Libby Island Light, in Maine, was established in 1824.

538

Cape Cod, in Massachusetts, loses four acres a year to beach erosion which will eventually reduce most of the Cape to a shoal.

539

Salisbury Beach, in Massachusetts, is a town built on the beach between the ocean and tidal wetlands.

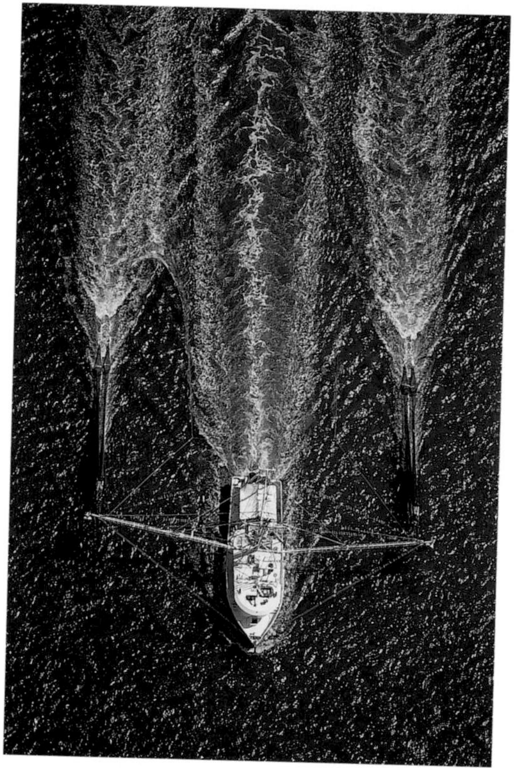

540
A fishing boat has been photographed near Port Royal Sound, North Carolina.

541
This extraordinary view shows the shoals at Martha's Vineyard, Massachusetts.

542-543
A small boat and an airplane shadow dots Cape Cod shoals.

544-545
Cape Cod is a sandy peninsula formed by glaciers about 23.000 years ago.

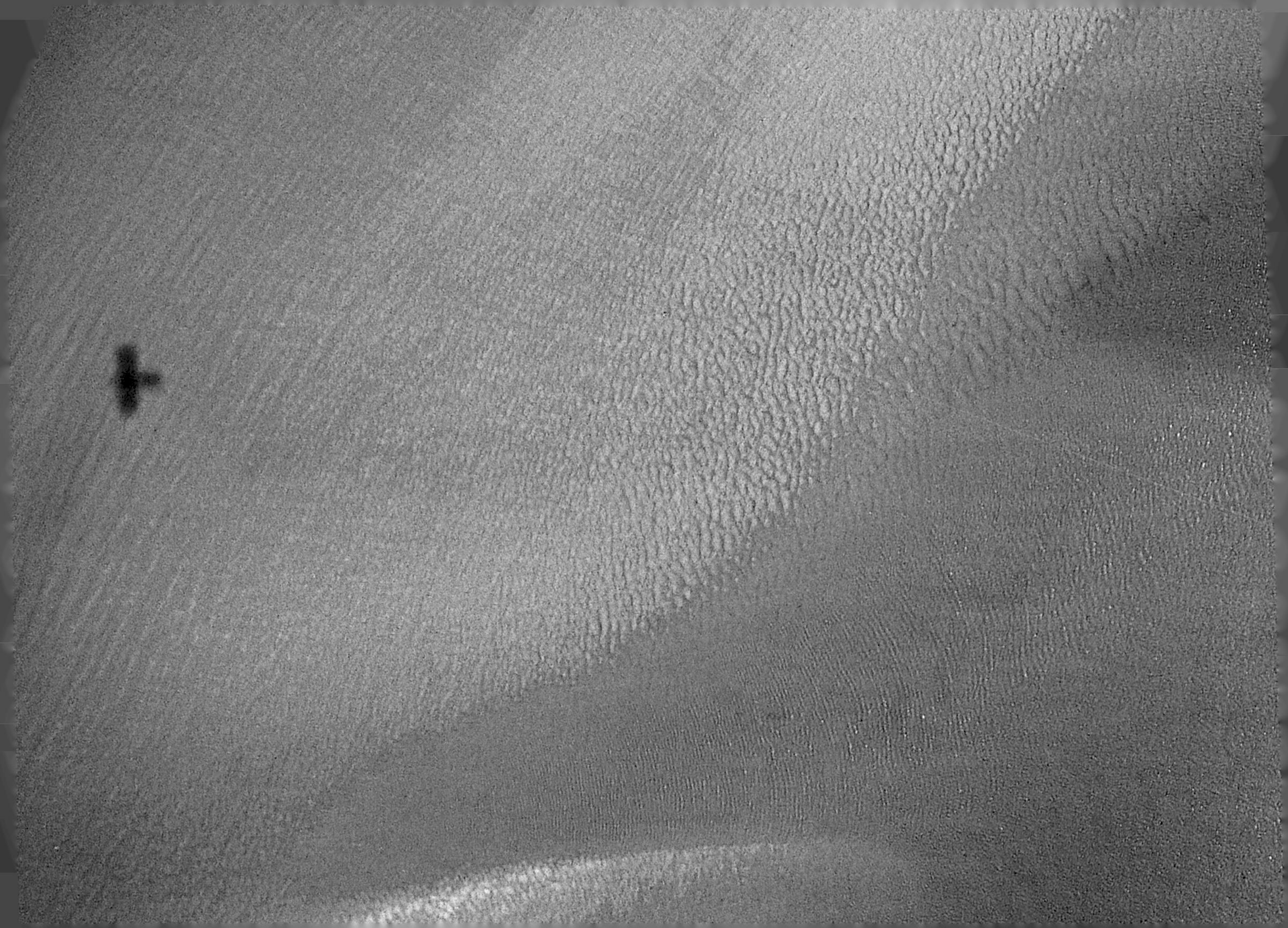

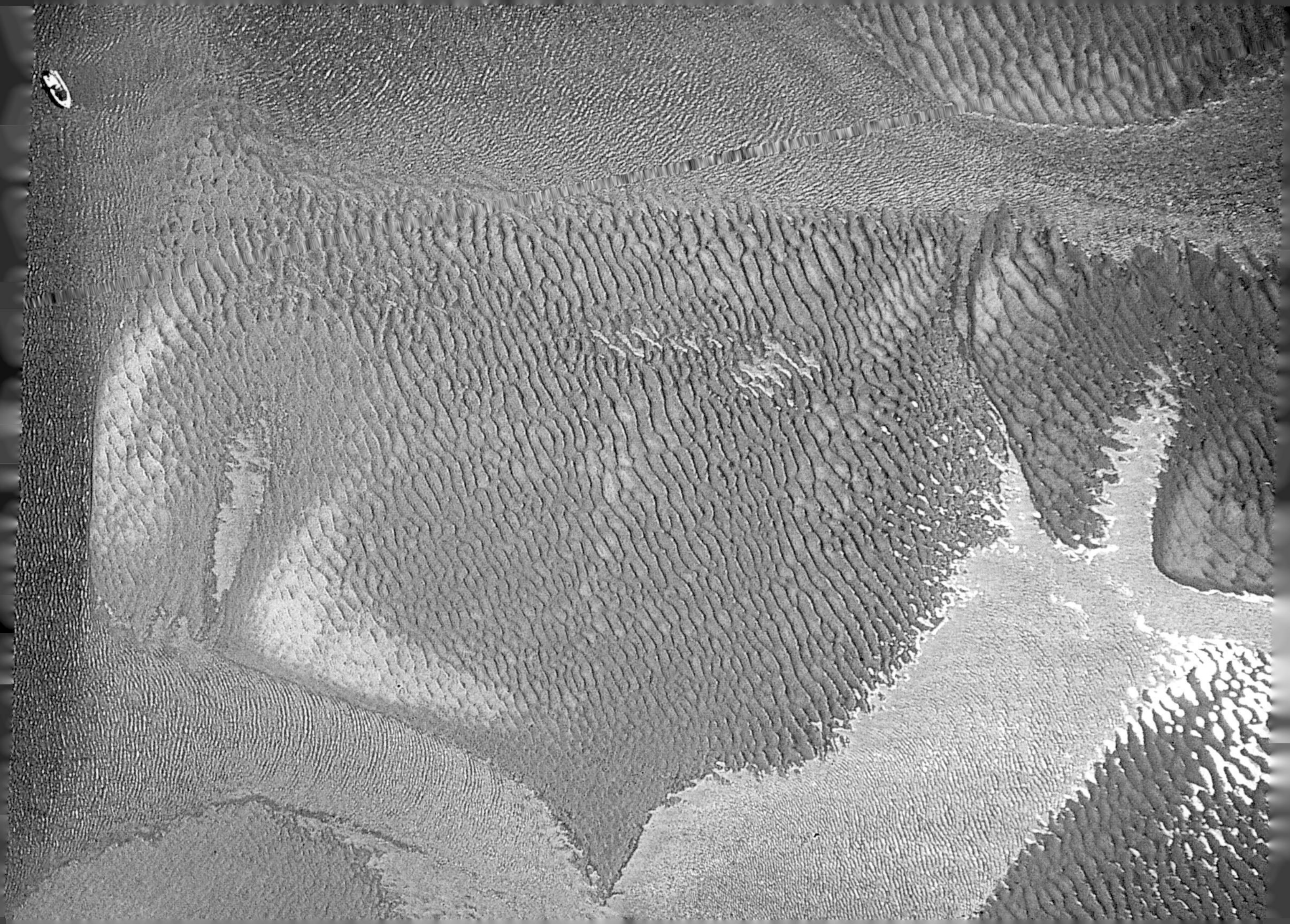

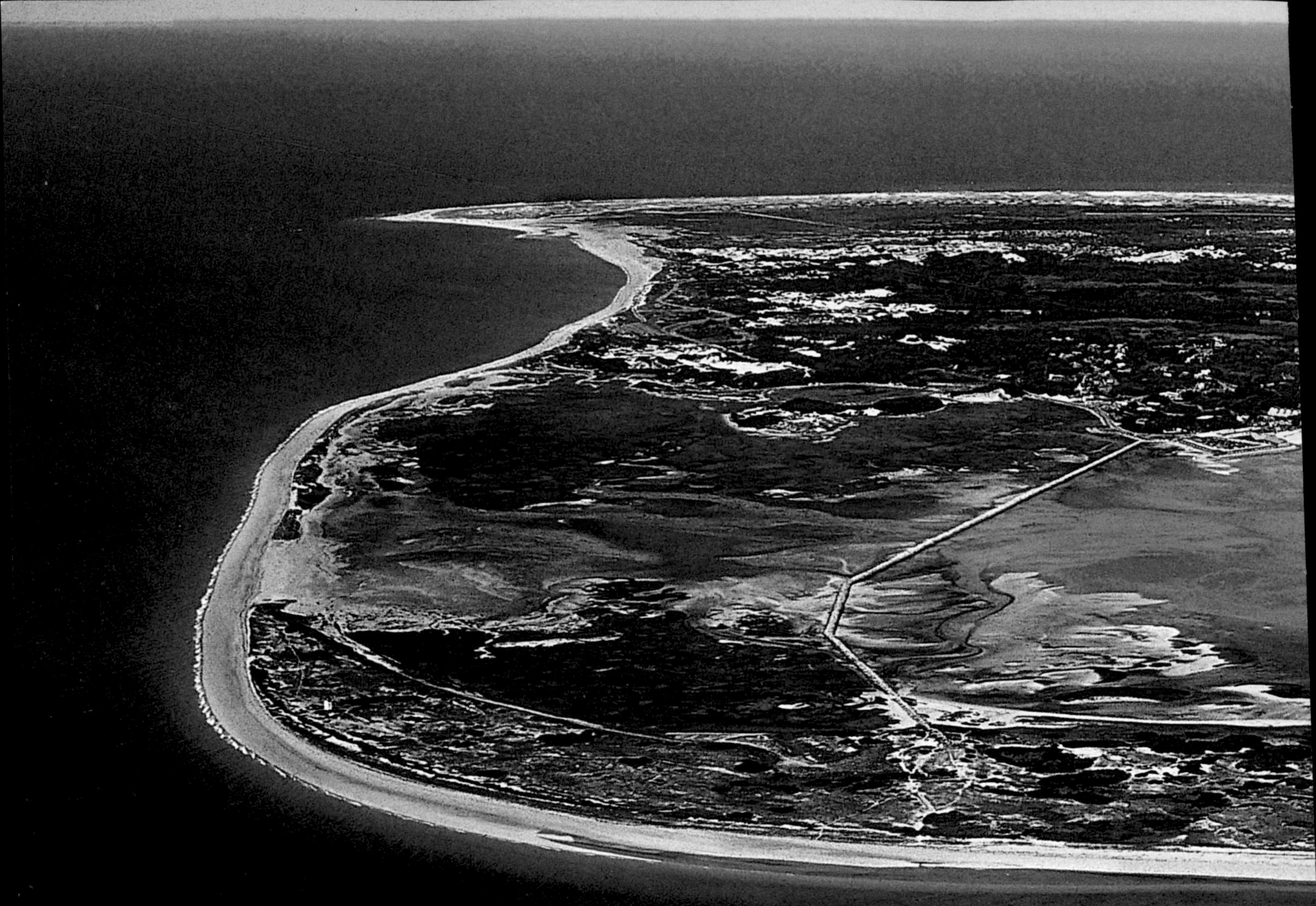

546
Point Judith and Point Judith Lighthouse at situated at the entrance to Narragansett Bay and Providence, Rhode Island. The present lighthouse was built in 1857. Like all U.S. lighthouses are is automated but the Point still has an active Coast Guard station.

547
Newport, Rhode Island, is populated by mansions built by America's industrial tycoons in the early 1900s.

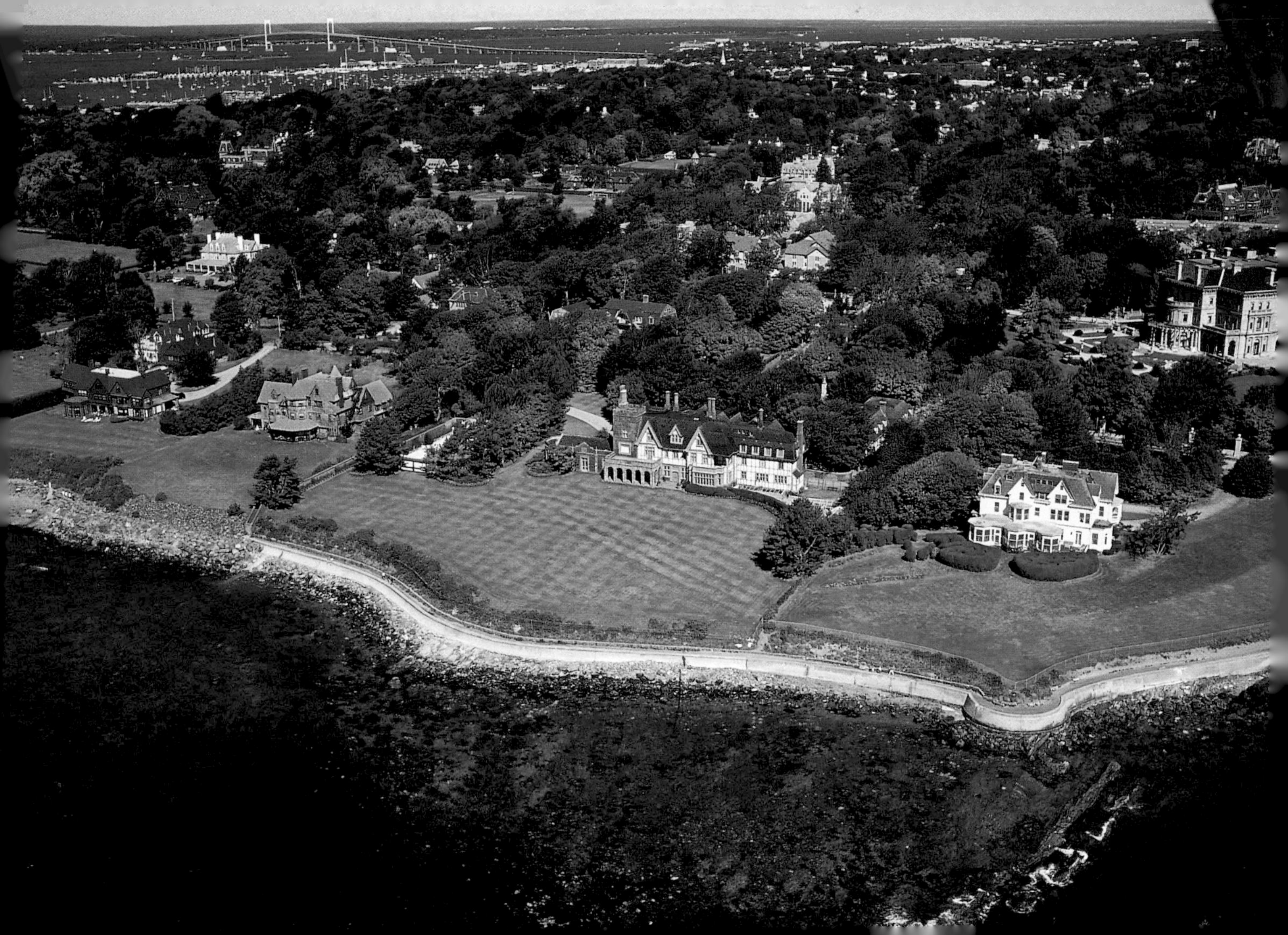

548

Sandy Hook, New Jersey, is a long narrow peninsula which reaches into lower New York Harbor. Fort Hancock defended the harbor until its closing in 1974.

549

Barnegat Light, Long Beach, New Jersey, is the second tallest lighthouse in the United States (165 feet). It was built in 1857 and dimmed in 1927. It is now part of Barnegat Lighthouse State Park.

550-551

The photo shows stately homes on East Hampton Beach, Long Island, New York.

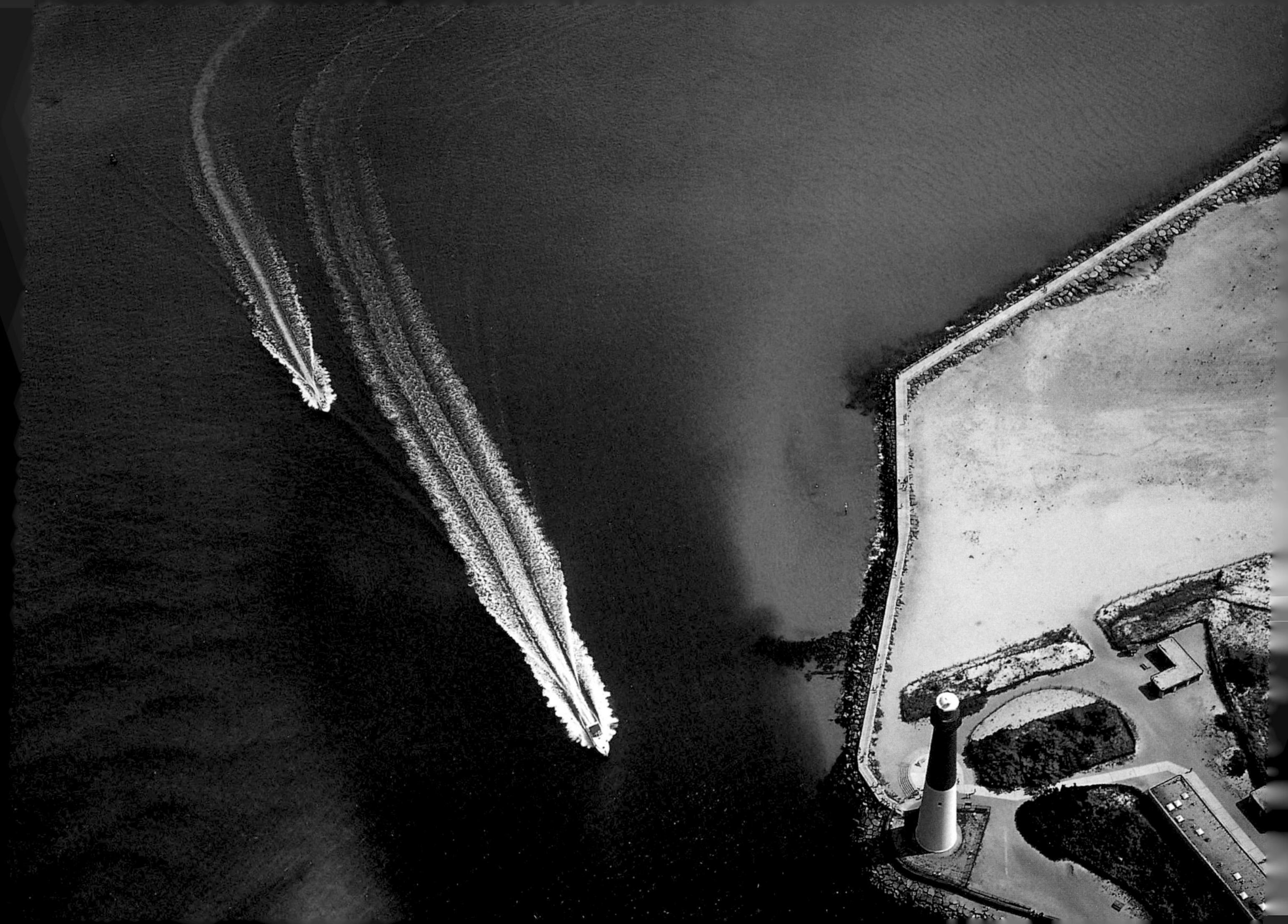

Blue boundaries

552
Tangier Island, in Chesapeake Bay, Accomack County, Virginia, was the first island visited by Europeans in 1605, the first settler arrived in 1686.

553
Chesapeake Bay Bridge goes over Fishermans Island (north end of bridge) looking southwest. This 18-mile bridge and tunnel which connects southeast Virginia with the Delmarva Peninsula is the world's longest such structure.

554
This fishing cabin is located on a small island in Chincoteague Bay, Virginia. Nearby Chincoteague Island is famous for its herd of wild ponies.

555
Assateague Island Lighthouse, south tip of Assateague Island, Virginia, the original light was erected in 1833 and was rebuilt a height of 145 in 1867.

Blue boundaries

556 and 557
These beach homes on Parramore Island, Virginia, are threatened by surf erosion.

558

Cape Hatteras, in North Carolina, is part of the North Carolina Outer Banks Islands.

559

Fishermen have been photographed at the tip of Cape Hatteras, North Carolina. A large campground is located about a mile north of this point.

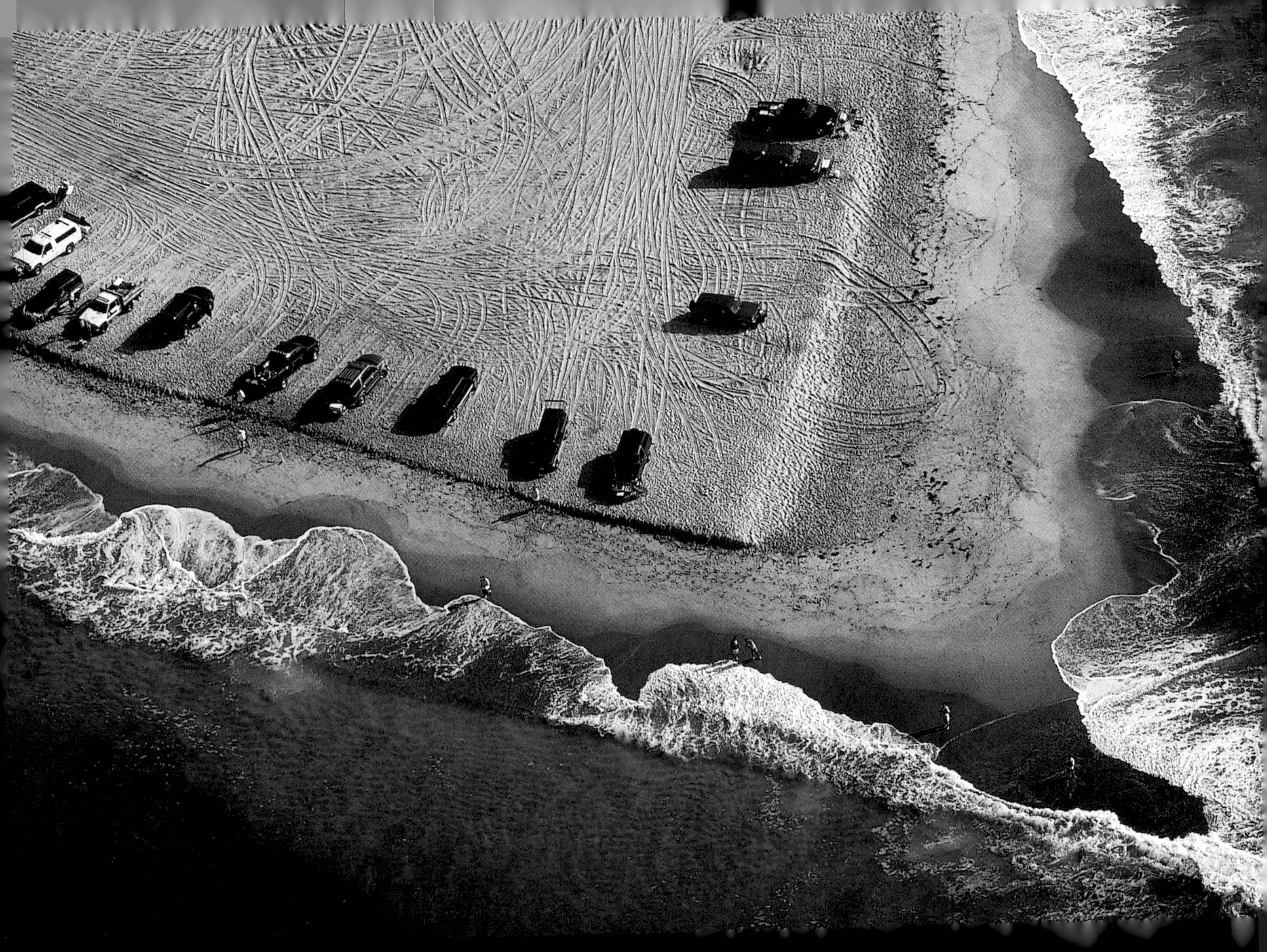

560-561
Nags Head, Bodie Island, North Carolina, is charcaterized by beach cottages.

564

Long Key Viaduct is situated between Conch Key and Long Key, Florida. The first Key highway was completed in 1938 and it was reconstructed in 1983.

565

In the photograph one can admire the famous Seven Mile Bridge, in the Florida Keys.

566
Another landmark of the Florida Keys is Channel Five Bridge.

567
This spectacular view shows Key West and the Gulf of Mexico.

568

These beach homes are situated on Dog Island, in Franklin County, Florida Panhandle. In recent years the gulf beach front has lost as much as 200 yards of beach to storm erosion.

569

Dog Island is located about 20 miles east of Apalachacola, Florida on the Gulf of Mexico Coast. This small island is totally private with no stores and one rooms-only inn. It can reached only by boat or small airplane. In World War II the island was used for amphibious assault training.

570-571

St. George Island, in Franklin County, Florida Panhandle, is 7 miles south of Apalachacola, Florida. It is connected to the mainland by a bridge and the island is heavily developed.

72

THE COLORS OF THE SEASONS

FLYING HIGH

FLYING HIGH AMERICA

573
Autumn in Maine's Hardwood Forest (left); winter in the Colorado mountains (right).

What is it about trees? Is it their shapes, their leaves, their colors, their cooling shade, the sounds they make in the wind, or is it just the fact that they can be so enormous and alive? Is there anyone who has not spent time in a tree house – at least in his or her mind? Who can resist the chance to take in the autumn colors of the New England hardwoods or the aspens of the Rocky Mountains? If there is one bit of verse that almost everyone knows, it is the beginning of Joyce Kilmer's poem, *"I think that I shall never see a poem lovely as a tree."* Another line that most of us are familiar with is about not being able to see the forest for the trees. With the aerial view we can clearly tell the forest from the trees. We can see how nature has shaped the forests and the meadows, interspersed evergreens with leafy trees, and splashed an astonishing palette of color over the autumn landscape. From the higher aerial view, that of the satellites, we can see and monitor timber cutting, wildfires, and the effects of drought, disease, and infestations. The aerial view in this book is the macro one, close-in, but not inside and lost in the trees. Seeing the trees from above provides a fresh appreciation of their beauty. Even dead trees have a beauty of form that can be seen in the Rivers and Lakes chapter of this book, in the photos of dead cottonwoods of Lake Pueblo, Colorado.

We all know of the consumptive uses for trees: timber for construction, wood for furniture, baseball bats and hockey sticks, pulp for making paper, and fuel for heating. Less frequently in mind are the non-consumptive roles of trees: wildlife habitat, recre-

574
These spruce trees show the effect of the first breath of winter on Colorado's Continental Divide Banded Peak, in Archuleta County.

The colors of the seasons

ational activity, windbreaks for prairie farms, shelter for livestock, soil stabilization in hills and mountains, and helping to maintain the air's carbon monoxide-oxygen balance. A home well-shaded by trees is cooled not only by the shade but also by evaporative cooling from their leaves. Such a home will not need mechanical air-conditioning. Last, but not least, trees provide a comfort to the human spirit that comes from just being amongst them.

Pre-European America with the exception of the prairie grasslands and the desert southwest was predominatly a forest. The first sawmill in America was at Jamestown, Virginia in 1622. While the effects of agriculture, timbering and urban habitation have taken a necessary toll, one-third of America remains classified as forest land. True, some forests, especially those in the west, are scarred with areas of timber clear-cutting. Some of it is ugly and harmful to the land. Prime old-growth areas enjoy some protection and commercial timber is too valuable to not be re-cultivated. If you took a small-plane flight over the heavily populated northeastern United States you might be astonished to see vast areas of heavy forestation where not a sign of human activity is visible.

The net consumption of America's western softwood forests was negative at the turn of the century but expected to reach equilibrium by 2040. A softwood tree takes about fifty years to reach harvest size. The net consumption of eastern hardwoods was positive and expected to remain so. Of greater threat to the forests than harvesting may be the forces of nature and of unintended industrial consequences. In the year 2000 an estimated 80,000 wildfires in America burned more than 10,000 square miles, an area which is larger than the individual areas of six of America's states. Lightning is the most common cause of wild fires, but human carelessness and arson also play significant roles. The United States government policy since 1910 of suppressing all wildfires has resulted in a dense load of underbrush in many forests that is capable of fuel-

The colors of the seasons

ing intense forest-destroying fires. This combined with recent intensifying drought conditions and an increase in mountain human habitation and recreation use has resulted in many disastrous fires in recent years. Some of these fires have heavily affected national parks and mountain communities. The Yellowstone National Park fire of 1988 consumed almost 1,200 square miles of forest. Many forests are also being severely damaged by insects and disease which nature normally cleanses by more frequent, less intense fires. The United States Forest Service estimates that one-third of the forests on federal land are under high fire risk. The remaining lands are under moderate risk. Similar numbers would apply to private forest lands. Prescribed burns or intentionally set fires are now being used to try to bring some forests back into a natural balance. After a major forest burn immediate steps should be taken to stabilize the soil. This usually consists of ditching to control runoff flows and mudslides, and then reseeding with hardy grasses. The soil after a wildfire is rich in nutrients from the ash and it easily supports rapid re-growth. If left to nature the pioneer growth in western forests is usually fireweed which will usually appear in the first year after a fire. This is a beautiful purple flowered, pulpy plant that grows up to seven feet tall. The plant is known to native peoples to have many therapeutic medicinal values. Acid rain also takes its toll, especially in the northeast, through processes that affect the soil of the forest by decalcification, nitrogen enrichment and increasing aluminum toxicity. Current federal policies are moving to change fire management procedures and mountain states are enacting laws to mitigate the human fire threat factor. Environmental laws are beginning to have a positive effect on air pollution issues.

The economic benefits of America's forests are many but the wildlife habitat, texture, color and solace that these forests provide to the American landscape are priceless. The citizens of the United States know this and the forests of America will survive.

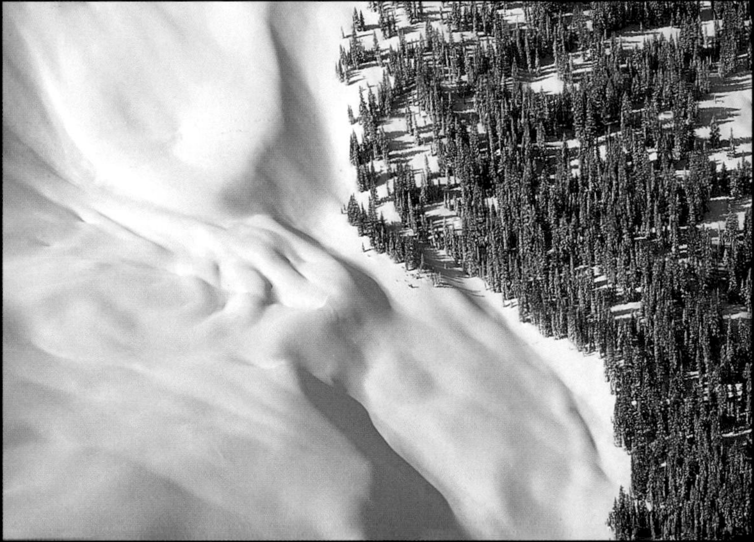

578

An aspen forest in New Mexico's Sangre de Cristo Mountains loses the last of its leaves to an October storm.

579

Heavy snow can be seen in the sub-alpine zone of the west Elk Mountains in Gunnison County, Colorado. Heavy snowpacks like this are needed as water reservoirs for the habitation and agriculture of Colorado's eastern plains.

580

Heavy snow packs in the foothills of the Sierra Nevada Mountains in Tulare County are a water reservoir for Southern California.

581

The slender shaps of these fir trees in Sequoia National Forest, Tulare County, California, enable them to shed heavy snow loads.

582
In the image is depicted the Presque Isle River, Wisconsin.

583
Along the Lewis and Clark Trail is the Lolo Pass, Spruce Creek, Idaho. The Lewis and Clark Expedition passed through here in September 1805 and June 1806.

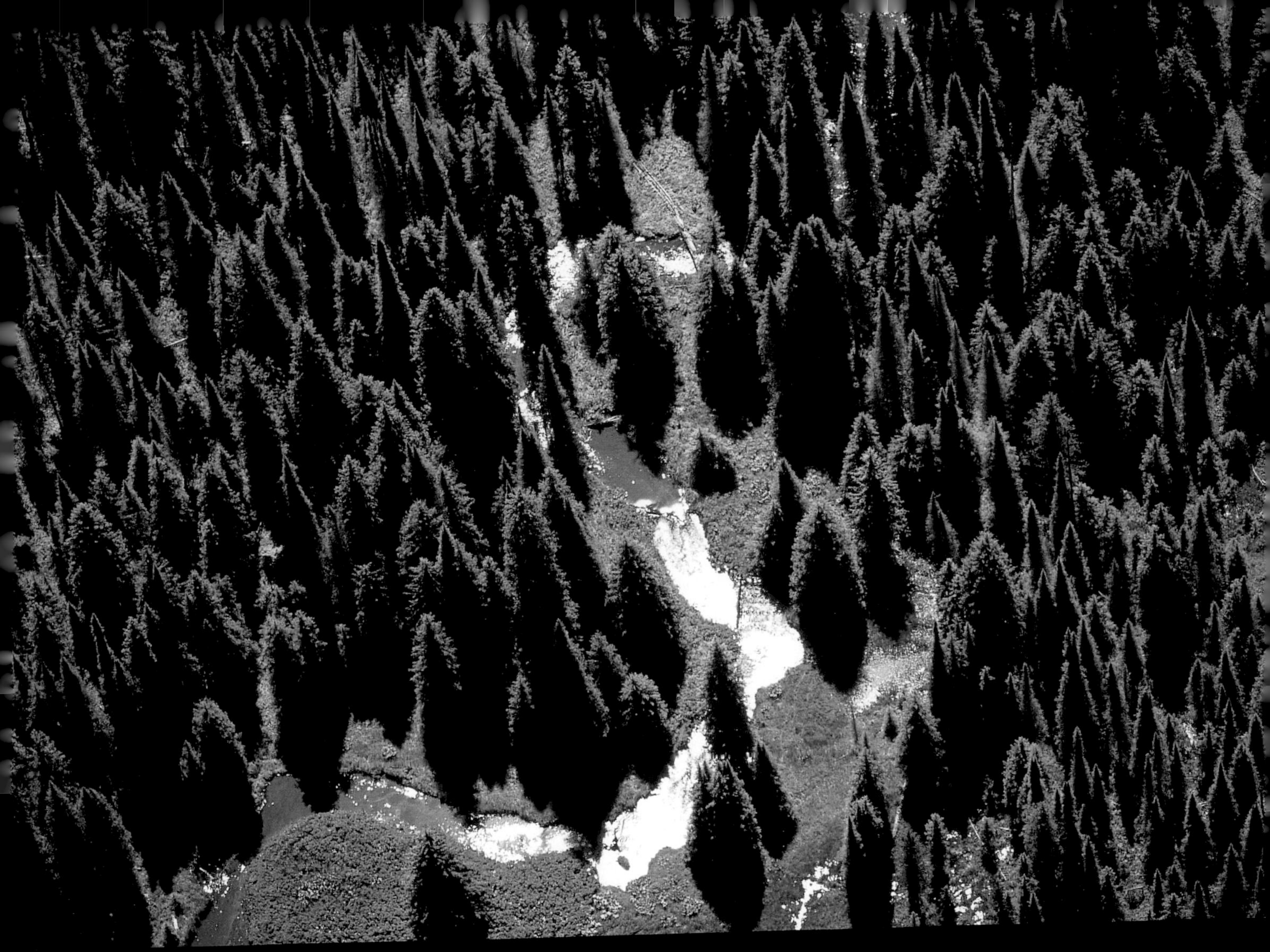

584
Early autumn colors embrace the White Mountains, New Hampshire. These mountains are part of the Appalachian Mountain Range.

585
Typical aspen forest characterizes the base of Marcellina Mountain, in the Ragged Wilderness Area, Gunnison County, Colorado.

586
Aspen groves are typical of Kebler Pass, in Gunnison County, Colorado.

587
Aspen trees surround an igneous dike in Cuchara Pass, Huerfano County, Colorado.

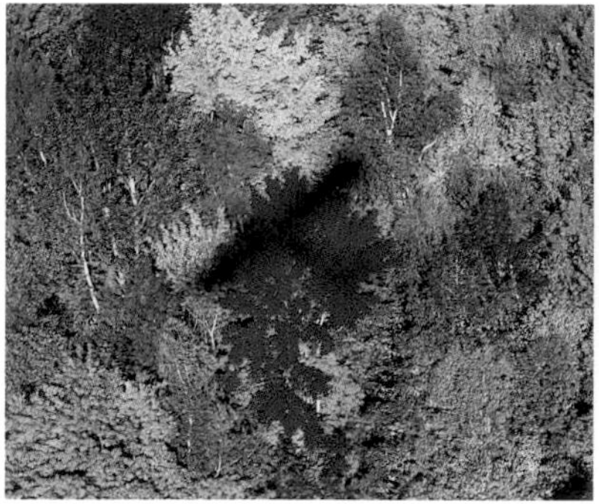

588 and 589
Beautiful fall colors, which go from emerald green to brilliant red passing through different hues of yellow and orange, characterize the forests of Penobscot County, Maine.

592
Baskahegan Lake in Aroostook County, Maine is bordered by a colorful forest.

593
Fall colors characterize Aroostook County, Maine.

594-595
Aspen communities, like this in Aquarius Plateau, Wayne County, Utah, are single organisms linked by underground root systems. Individual communities can be identified by the different autumn leaf colors.

596-597
This single community of aspens is situated near Taos, New Mexico, in the Sangre de Cristo Mountains.

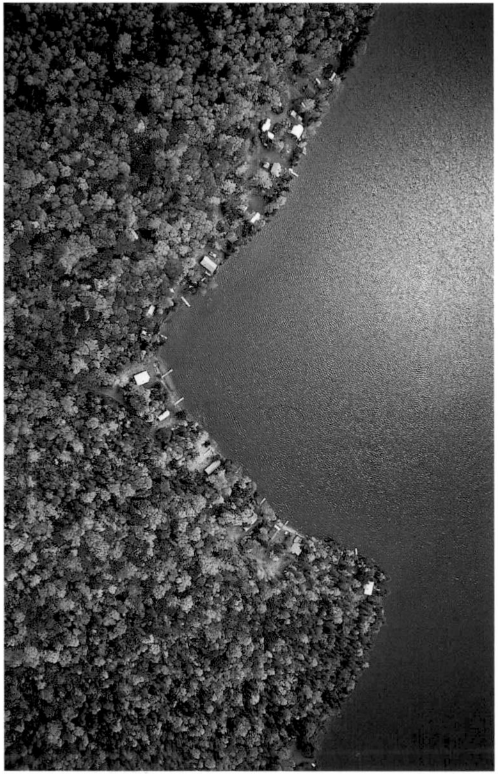

598-599

Cleared trees form a wall of autumn color at a farm in Orleans County, Vermont.

600-601

This farm situated in Rutland County, Vermont, has been built at the forest border.

602 and 603

This cimmaron wildfire in Colfax County, New Mexico. Wildfires or forest fires have become a plague in the western United States due to persistent drought years and decades of fire supression which has allowed the growth of scrub vegetation fuel.

604

Fireweed begins the forest rebirth two years after a devastating wildfire near Tok, Alaska.

605

Fireweed – growing near Tok, Alaska – is known among native peoples to have many medicinal properties.

THE DEPTHS OF THE EARTH

FLYING HIGH

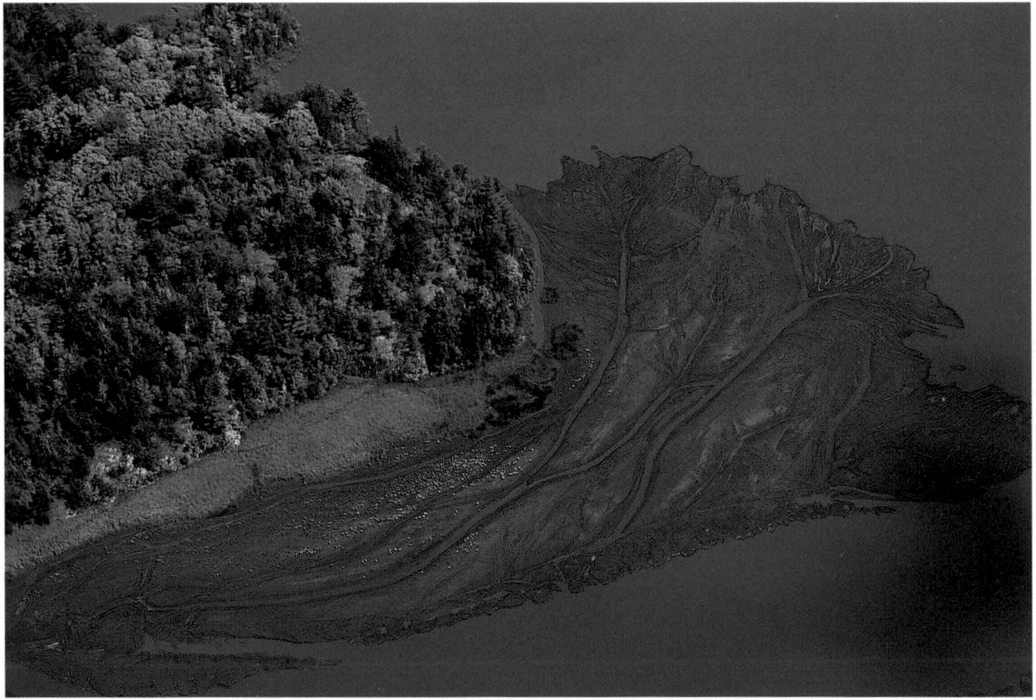

607
Mines offer grand shows at Copper Hill Tailings Pond, Dinam County, Arizona (left) and San Manuel Copper Pit. Pinal County, Southeast Arizona (right).

What images does the word 'mining' bring to mind? Regretfully, it is often one of greed, environmental harm and lasting scars on the landscape. There is some validity to this statement, but mining's real significance to society is much different. Mining has had a place in civilization since before recorded history. The first written reference to mining may be from the Bible, dating from about 1800 BC. Job 28:2 states, "Iron is taken out of the earth, and brass is molten out of stone." Aristotle spoke of mining in the fourth century BC. In 1556, Georgius Agricola wrote a 700-page textbook on mining methods, *Re De Metallica*, which is read today by students of mining engineering.

In truth, mining is the most essential of all human endeavors. It is the enabling source of every material possession and the requisite precursor of all modern human enterprise. Without mining, there would be no modern agriculture, no modern medicine, and no modern transportation, not even pencil and paper! Air is the only material thing in our lives not dependent on mining, but even air is often purified and conditioned with machinery made possible by mining.

Sixteenth-century Native Americans had little use for mining other than to provide them with pottery clay, pipestone and red hematite iron ore for war paint. However, much earlier Native American tribes (prior to 1000 BC) were mining copper from the Upper Peninsula of Michigan and from Lake Superior's Isle Royale. This copper, which did not need to be refined, has been found in Indian artifacts as far away as South America. The early American settlers were mining small deposits of copper, lead, iron and coal in the

608
Iron ore concentrator tailings turn bright red the waters of a pond, Ishpeming Marguette County, Michigan.

611
Potash Evaporation Ponds create unintentional surrealistic works of art near Moab, San Juan County, Utah.

1700s. Gold was discovered in California in 1848 and the mining boom was on. In 1849 the population of San Francisco grew from 800 to 50,000! By 1900, most of the major mining districts had been discovered. America had a unique plan for development of its frontier lands – the land would simply be given away to its citizens who met some minimum requirements. The Homestead Act of 1862, which gave land to farmers, was followed by the Mining Law of 1872, which gave land, called claims, to miners. It was only required that the miner show some evidence of minerals and do some physical work on the claim. This policy of free land to the people, which included free land to railroads, resulted in the settlement of the vast lands of the American West in less than half a century. Two centuries of mining in America has created some interesting artifacts. Consider the 'ghost town.' These settlements, some of which had populations of tens of thousands and sprang up almost overnight, were often abandoned just a few years later, because the mines were exhausted and closed. Most of these places still have a few crumbling structures, and some have been restored as tourist attractions. The most visible artifacts are the huge open-pit mines of the West with their collateral waste dumps and tailing ponds. Despite the negative images that the thought of such structures bring to mind, the truth is many are strikingly beautiful, especially from the air. Who can deny the sculptured beauty of the abandoned Casa Grande Copper Pit - an almost perfectly round downward spiral into a black hole with walls the color and texture of tapestry. The Bingham Copper Pit in Utah is the world's largest 'hole in the ground.' It is said that its benched slopes, which form a giant coliseum, could hold the entire population of New York City. These things if found in a natural state would be national treasures. Their beauty is best appreciated from the aerial view. The legacy of mining in America is a mixed one of prosperity and great social benefit along with some environmental problems, which are being mitigated, and some beauty, which will endure.

FLYING HIGH AMERICA

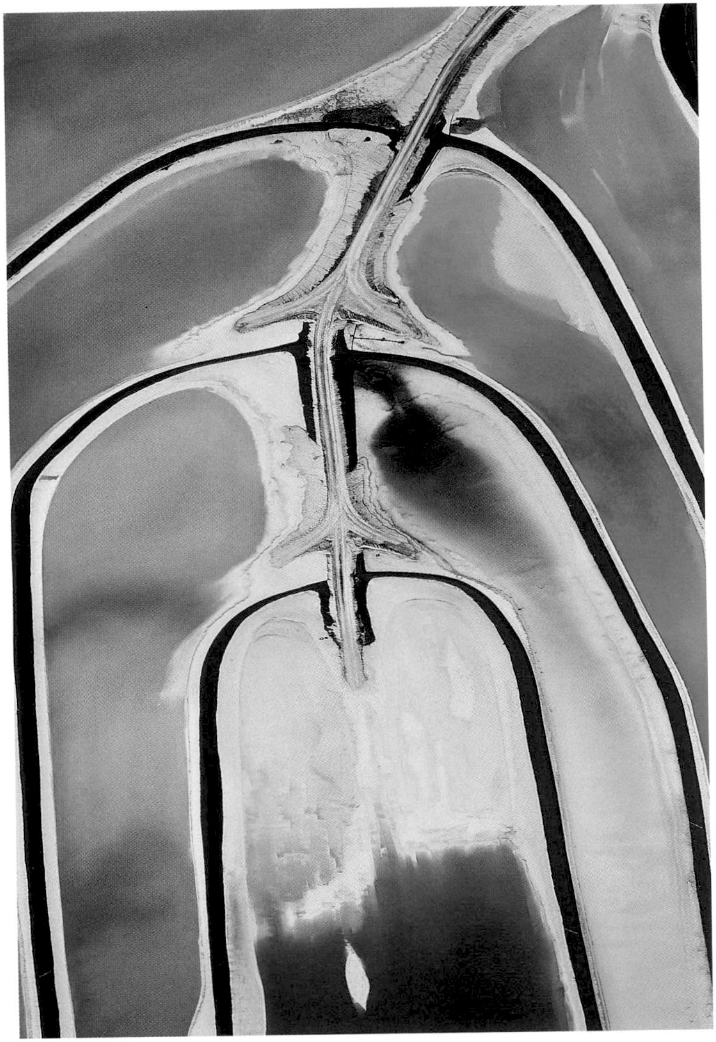

612 and 613

The red color of the water filling iron ore concentrator tailings and thickener ponds at Ishpeming, Marquette County, Michigan, is from the iron mineral hematite which is non-toxic. The open-pit iron mine and concentrator plant are in the middle distance.

614
Near Ishpeming, Upper Peninsula, Michigan, 95% of the water used in the concentration process is recycled.

615
Iron ore is concentrated by grinding the raw ore to a very fine powder and using a physical process which floats the iron to a surface where it is skimmed off. High Intensity magnetics are also used.

616

Set against the red sandstone of the Utah Canyonlands, potash evaporation ponds near Moab, Utah, would be a wonder of the world, and a National Monument if it were a feature of nature.

617

The potash here was initially intended to be mined as is done in an underground coal mine. It was soon realized that a method called solution mining would be safer and more efficient. In solution mining water is pumped into the potash formation, allowed to become brine, and then pumped to the surface and into these ponds.

618
The different colors of the brine signify different levels of evaporation. The initial brine is dark blue.

619
The primary use of commercial potash is as an agricultural fertilizer, with corn growing being the biggest consumer.

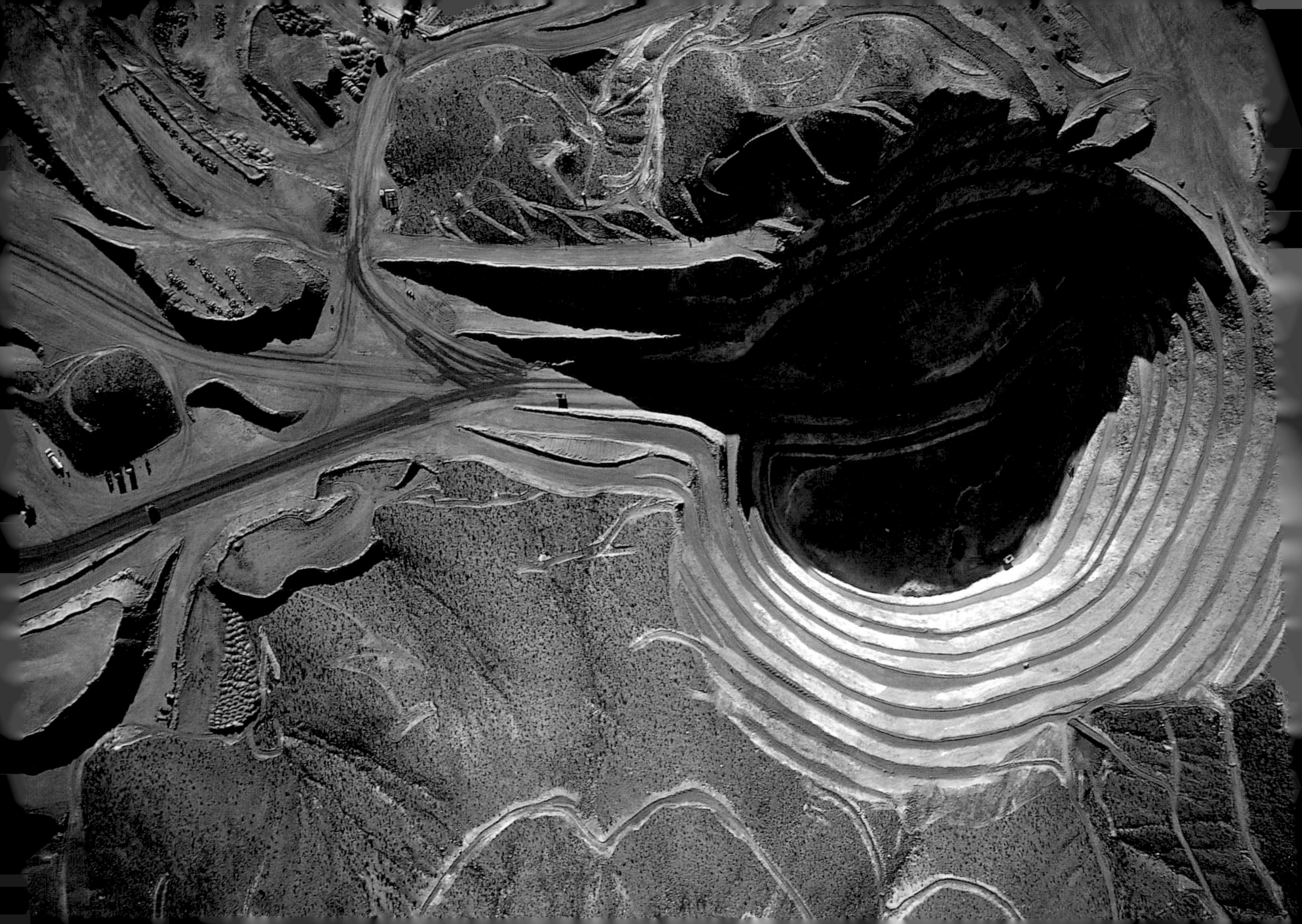

620 and 621
This open-pit gold mine is situated near Searchlight, Clark County, Nevada. Of the twenty-five largest mining operations in the U.S. in 2001, nine were copper mines and eight were gold mines.

The depths of the earth

622
The San Manuel Copper Mine, Pinal County, Arizona., was operated as both an open-pit and underground mine.

623
This small abandoned open-pit copper-mine near Casa Grande, Pinal County, Arizona, had a brief, prosperous life in the 1960s. The wide spiral leading to the pit bottom is the haulage road. The narrower ridges are artifacts of the benches by which the mine descended.

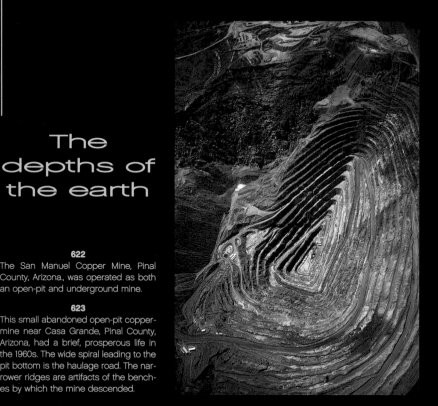

624
Laurie Tyler's Aviat Husky flies over the San Manuel Copper Pit. The diagonal line behind the airplane is the contact between copper ore (red) and waste rock.

625
This cliff-like escarpment is the face of a copper mine tailings dam near Superior, Pinal County, Arizona.

626 and 627
A narrow causeway lead to the center of the discharge point of copper mine tailings pond. South Bisbee, Cochise County, Arizona.

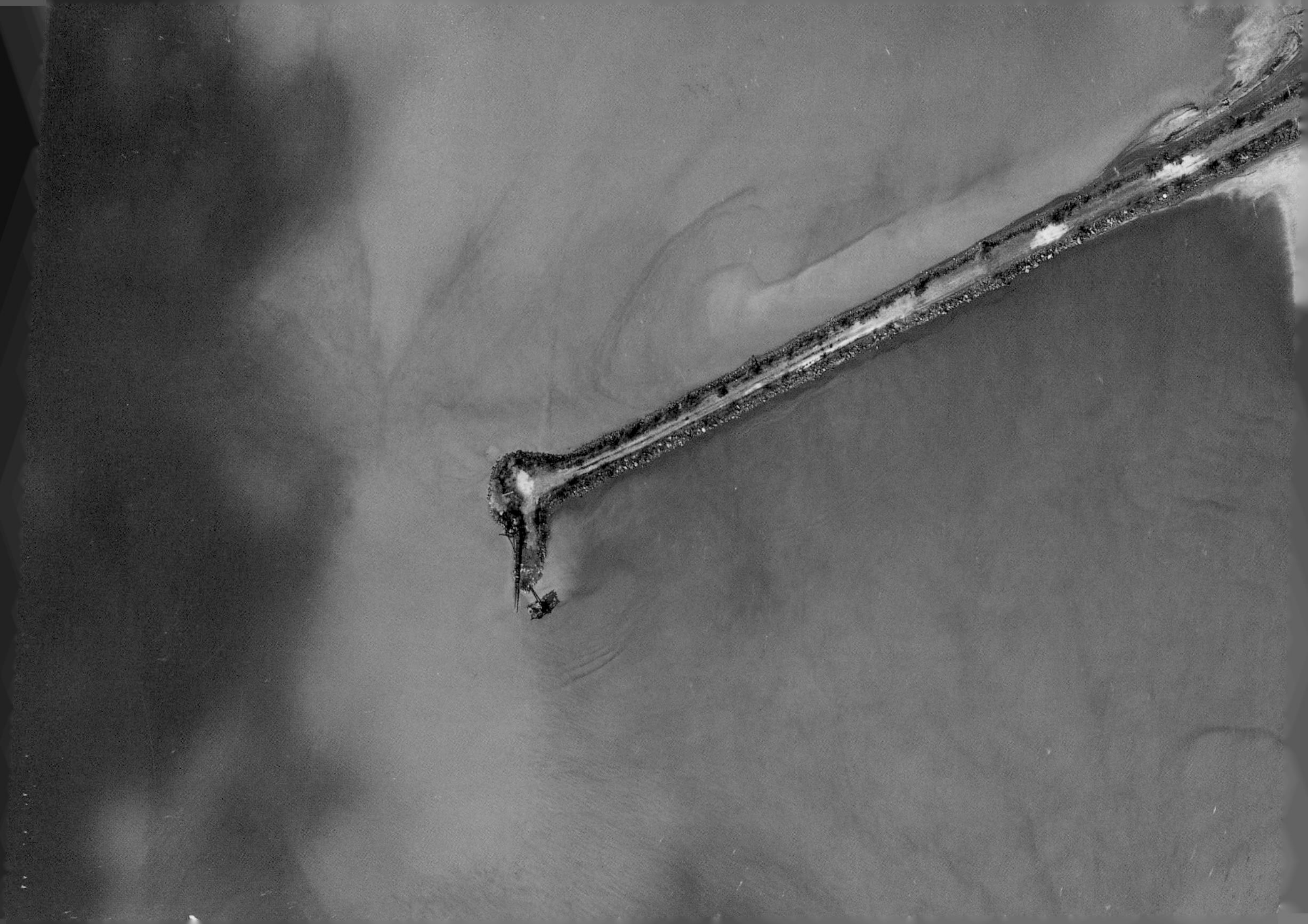

628

Contrasting, rather uninviting reflections come from this copper mine tailings pond near Superior, Pinal County, Arizona.

629

The complex of copper mine tailings structures of Morenci Mine stretches in Greenlee County, Arizona. A tailings pond is constructed by first building a starter dam using mine waste rock. The enclosure is then filled with a slurry of finely ground mill tailings and water.

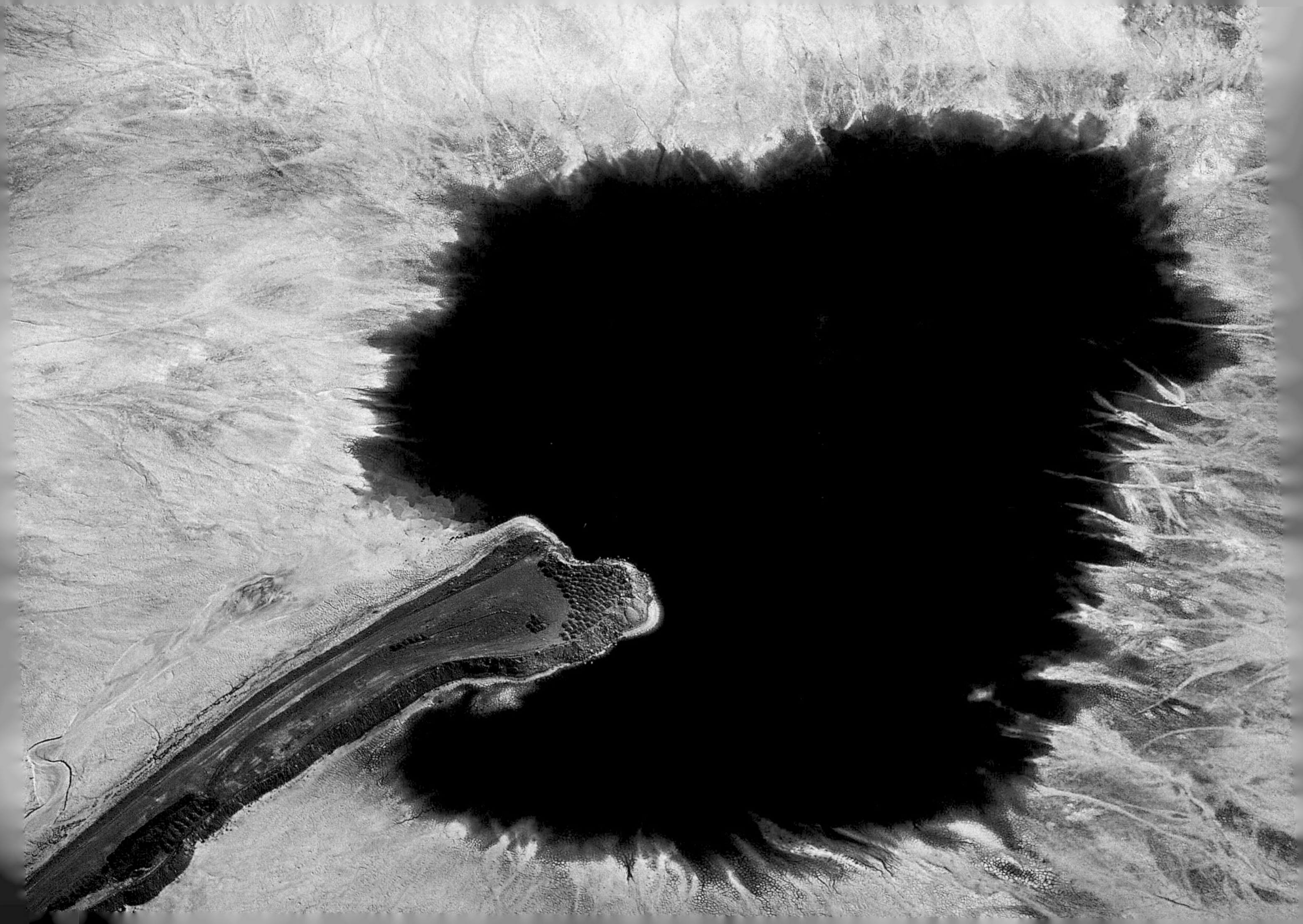

630 and 631
As the deep hue of this discharge point shows, copper ore is typically less than 1% copper, consequently at least 95% of the ore mined end up as talings sand. Terraced tailings pond, Morenci Mine, Arizona.

632

Coal strip-mining spoil piles eat into Farmland, Beulah, North Dakota.

633

Photographed near Sahuarita, Pima County, Arizona, this copper mine waste rock dump contains excavated material that does not hold minerals of sufficient value to warrant grinding and processing.

634-635
This very large tailings dam in Pinal County, Arizona isconstructed entirely of mine waste rock. The dam height is being raised by dumping new rock. Each time the dam is raised the pond's area becomes smaller.

Index

Index

Index

Cover
Colorado River, Canyonlands National Park, Utah.

Backcover
New York City, Lower Manhattan.

Acknowledgements

Gail Berthe; Mike Cafasso; Steve Durtschi; Randy Kilbourn; Mike Lauro; Brenda Marks; Valerie Mass; Tom Shappel; Laurie & Taz Tyler; John Wark
Dedicated to my wife Judy for her infinite patience and goodness.

Photo Credits

All photographs are by Jim Wark except the following:

Pages 4-5 Alamy Images
Pages 12-13, 34, 38, 40, 41 Antonio Attini/Archivio White Star
Page 42 Massimo Borchi/Archivio White Star
Page 43 Antonio Attini/Archivio White Star
Pages 44, 45 Jason Hawkes Aerial Photo Library
Page 46 Antonio Attini/Archivio White Star
Page 47 Royalty Free/Corbis/Contrasto
Page 48 Jason Hawkes Aerial Photo Library
Pages 49, 50-51, 54, 55, 56, 57, 58, 59, 60-61, 62, 63 Antonio Attini/Archivio White Star
Page 64 Alan Schein Photography/Corbis/Contrasto
Pages 66, 67, 68, 69 Antonio Attini/Archivio White Star
Pages 70, 71 Massimo Borchi/Archivio White Star
Pages 72, 73 Dennis Degnan/Corbis/Contrasto
Pages 78, 79, 80, 81, 82, 84, 85, 86 right, 86 left, 87, 88-89, 94, 95, 96, 97, 98, 99 Antonio Attini/Archivio White Star
Page 101 Alan Schein Photography/Corbis/Contrasto
Pages 102, 103 left, 103 right Antonio Attini/Archivio White Star
Page 104 Yann Arthus-Bertrand/Corbis/Contrasto
Page 105 Antonio Attini/Archivio White Star
Pages 106-107 Alan Schein Photography/Corbis/Contrasto
Pages 108, 109, 110, 111, 112, 113, 114, 115, 116, 117, 118, 119, 120, 121, 126 Antonio Attini/Archivio White Star
Page 127 Massimo Borchi/Archivio White Star
Pages 128, 129 David Butow/Corbis/Contrasto
Pages 130, 131 Antonio Attini/Archivio White Star
Page 132 Richard Cummins/Corbis/Contrasto
Pages 133, 134, 135, 136, 137 Antonio Attini/Archivio White Star
Pages 138-139 Paul A. Souders/Corbis/Contrasto
Pages 140-141 Alamy Images
Pages 142, 143, 146, 149, 150, 151 Antonio Attini/Archivio White Star
Pages 152-153 Craig Aurness/Corbis/Contrasto
Pages 154, 156, 157 Antonio Attini/Archivio White Star
Pages 158, 159, 160-161 Douglas Slone/Corbis/Contrasto
Pages 163, 164, 165 left, 165 right, 166 left, 166 right, 167, 176, 318-319, 528, 529 Antonio Attini/Archivio White Star
Page 565 SCPhotos/Alamy Images
Page 566 Alamy Images
Page 567 Royalty-Free/Corbis/Contrasto

Page 9 Courtesy of Cherry Crest Farm, Ronks, Pennsylvania (www.cherrycrestfarm.com)

640
Mural in Pueblo, Colorado.

5520 M